a short & happy guide to

AI Governance and Regulation

Kashyap Kompella
Founder AI Profs and Visiting Faculty, BITS School of Management (BITSoM) and the Institute of Directors

James M. Cooper
Professor of Law, California Western School of Law

A SHORT & HAPPY GUIDE® SERIES

WEST ACADEMIC

860 Blue Gentian Road, Suite 350
Eagan, MN 55121
1-877-888-1330

Published in the United States of America

ISBN: 979-8-89209-979-0

Acknowledgments

A year ago, we published *AI for Lawyers*, mapping the impact of Artificial Intelligence (AI) across different legal domains: criminal, commercial, consumer, copyrights, and more. Building on that, here we turn to a harder problem: what regulators and policymakers should actually do in response. Glad to partner once more with Professor James Cooper, whose collaboration and friendship, I greatly cherish.

To my family: grateful for your support and patience through another intense writing cycle.

And to you reader: thank you for engaging with these important and urgent questions. Let us know your feedback. We are easy to find on LinkedIn.

—Kashyap

I would like to thank my family for supporting me through my Artificial Intelligence journey. They listened to my ideas, helped me frame things better, and always kept me centered. The students in AI and the Law course, which I first taught in spring 2025 at California Western School of Law (CWSL) in San Diego, provided a great laboratory for regulatory revelations. Thanks to all of you. I am also grateful to CWSL Dean and President Miriam Baer, a fellow West Academic Publishing author, for her encouragement and to the entire Faculty Support Services team (Joyce, Debra, Mariela, and Renita), Vice-Dean Liam Vavasour, Natalie Sitwell, and Francine Vasquez for their steadfast and kind assistance.

Finally, I would like to thank Kashyap Kompella, a great writing partner and a guru on all things related to Zoom, Google docs, and MySpace (wait, what?). And he's an expert on Artificial Intelligence. Next stop: A casebook for students. Could a Broadway musical adaptation of this book be in the offing?

—James

* * *

Jointly. . .

We would like to thank our intrepid team of research assistants: Valeh Aboonour, Jasmin Divas, Angelina Gonzales, Sierra Henrichsen, Chloe Kramer, Xueyan Li, Ellyse Linder, and Xingxue (Sherry) Wang. We would also like to thank the cool Mac Soto and the kind folks at the West Academic Publishing team, including Michele Bassett, Bridget Davis, Whitney Esson, and Megan Hoffman, who worked on this project.

Cooper and Kompella Manifesto for AI Governance and Regulation

Artificial Intelligence (AI) is humanity's greatest tool and also, its greatest test. If governed wisely, AI can expand access to justice, strengthen democratic institutions, deliver huge efficiencies, and serve the public good. But without ethical constraints, it risks eroding human dignity, agency, and the rule of law itself. Our identities, our labor, and even our rights could be trampled by indifferent code. But this is not inevitable. Through thoughtful design and smart regulation, we must bind AI to human values and peremptory legal principles. The legal community must lead in forging AI that advances human flourishing, safeguards fundamental rights, and brings about a just society.

Table of Contents

A Short & Happy Guide to AI Governance and Regulation

CHAPTER 1

AI Governance and Regulation in 30 Minutes or It's Free

I. Introduction

Artificial Intelligence (AI) foments many fears: Robots automating jobs out of existence, computers hallucinating wrong answers to high-stakes questions, and automated systems making consequential decisions without ethical guardrails. We are right to be concerned. It may sound alarmist, but many advances in the rule of law and democratic governance that humanity has secured over centuries are in the firing line of automation without scruples—all in the name of efficiency. In many cases AI tools can do our work (and engage in our play) better than we can. Modernity may indeed be at risk because of our post-knowledge (that's one step beyond post-industrial) economy's fetish for computers to increasingly do our work.

For lawyers, the fears are more specific and urgent: AI automating or commoditizing many legal tasks, AI hallucinating wrong answers to questions and producing false case law precedents. AI tools can ace state bar examinations, generate case summaries, and fabricate citations convincingly and threatening the sanctity and integrity of legal processes. It's a minefield of liabilities waiting to happen!

AI is also encroaching on human identify—our likeness, our voice, and our essence. That we could, very soon, lose control over our faces, our feelings, and the fruits of our creativity and labor is very personal. From Pope Francis in a Balenciaga puffer jacket that he never wore to Taylor Swift or Drake remixes that they never recorded, AI-generated content raises important questions about consent, ownership, and authenticity. Ditto for everyone else on the planet. Meanwhile, facial recognition technology challenges our privacy rights and our liberty.

Beyond individual rights, AI systems are reshaping employment, finance, healthcare, housing, and impacting our choices as consumers. Given its ubiquity and current trajectory, it is no longer merely speculative to wonder if AI could well threaten humanity's right to self-determination. Self-determination may end up just as configuration setting in an AI system in the future!

Different jurisdictions are reacting in different ways as they try to balance compliance while still fostering innovation. Some countries, such as the United States (U.S.) and Japan, prefer minimal state intervention, letting the free market do its thing, taking advantage of a permissive and "AI friendly" regulatory regime. Other jurisdictions, like the European Union (EU) and the People's Republic of China (China), prefer more a heavy-touch regulatory regime. Both approaches have their fans and adherents and pluses and minuses. Many are trying to find that right balance: smart regulation that neither chills capital formation nor impinges creativity. Regulation is not just about citizen rights or consumer rights, it is also about geopolitics. AI policy is industry policy and power on the global stage depends on AI leadership.

Enter the pressing need for Responsible AI, ethical guidelines, and enlightened governance and regulatory solutions. This *Short and Happy Guide* explores what rules we have and considers what rules we need to ensure we remain in control of AI tools and safely steer the consequences of their widespread usage.

Governance and regulation may not save us. But this book explores ways to at least try.

We face not just a race to build AI, but also a race to regulate it. Technology nationalism is alive and kicking in Beijing, Brussels, and Washington D.C. After all, the dominance over one of the most important technologies the world has ever known is up for grabs.

This book explores the regulatory innovations and instruments necessary to support technological innovation without stifling, to harness AI power without neutering its potential. Along the way, we look at key regulatory architectures—the EU's risk-based framework, China's state-centered approach, the U.S.'s industry-led chaos, and the Organisation (yes, the British spelling!) for Economic Cooperation and Development (OECD) and other multilateral organizations' meta-governance efforts.

These are not just academic contrasts: these regulations shape capital flows, compliance burdens, and determine which norms and whose rules win when algorithms cross borders.

We also unpack AI governance, which is not just about laws, but about norms, power, and enforcement. No country or regional bloc wants to be left behind in their quest for leadership in the AI space because it is a critically important strategic industry that affects so many other industries. This is such a difficult balance to strike!

II. The 10 Harmful AI Avatars

AI technologies don different masks, some charming and others insidious. Let's explore the 10 harmful avatars of Artificial Intelligence, each of which exposes a different fault line in law, ethics, or governance. Some may overlap, but all demand serious attention.*

A. AI as Infringer

AI as an Infringer raises significant legal issues related to copyright and intellectual property (IP) rights. Generative AI tools like OpenAI ChatGPT, Google Gemini, Anthropic Claude, Stable Diffusion, or Microsoft GitHub Copilot are capable of producing outputs resembling copyrighted texts, images, or code; question of ownerships, of both the training data and the outputs has spawned lawsuits against OpenAI, Microsoft, Stability AI (Stable Diffusion), and other AI companies. Can AI models be trained on copyrighted content without permission, thus raising questions about the legality of training data use, infringement liability, and rights attribution?

Who owns AI-generated content? Is there such a thing as AI authorship? So, AI also is challenging existing patent laws, traditionally designed around human creativity. The Thaler cases, involving the AI system DABUS developed by Dr. Stephen Thaler and litigated in many countries' court systems, sparked global debate when patent applications naming AI as an inventor were filed. While South Africa and initially Australia showed openness toward recognizing AI inventions, jurisdictions like the U.S., United Kingdom (U.K.), EU, and India have consistently ruled against AI as eligible inventors, emphasizing that legal personality and patent rights belong exclusively to humans, thus raising fundamental

* Note that we have a list of 10 helpful AI avatars as well. They are AI as Enhancer, Educator, Healer, Protector, Predictor, Optimizer, Creator, Equalizer, Innovator and Recommender. This is a topic for another day. We are not AI Luddites.

questions about innovation ownership and patentability in the AI era.

B. AI as Deceiver

When AI hallucinates, i.e. confidently fakes facts or fabricates cases, legal citations, and other content, it deceives lawyers, courts, clients, and consumers. Synthetic content can misinform and mislead. Such falsehoods at scale become a major crisis for truth and trust. This spares no one, neither students nor senior counsel. Harvard blue book citations are never going away!

C. AI as Defamer

AI as Defamer spreads deepfakes, slander, or false information targeting individuals or groups. This avatar spotlights the risks posed by deepfakes and Generative AI creating defamatory content, falsely depicting individuals or events. Cases involving AI-generated deepfake pornography or politically manipulative videos illustrate the challenges regulators face in assigning liability. As seen in high-profile incidents like deep fakes of public figures, including celebrities and politicians, existing defamation laws struggle to effectively address responsibility and enforcement in the rapidly evolving digital landscape, prompting urgent discussions about updating defamation frameworks. That the second Trump administration's first legislative action on the AI front was to sign into law the bipartisan Take It Down Act, legislation which aids the victims of revenge pornography and deep fake image abuse, is a sign that even Washington DC takes seriously this very troubling use of AI tools.

D. AI as Injurer

AI as Injurer addresses liability concerns around AI-related accidents, notably autonomous vehicles or robotics causing physical harm. High-profile incidents, such as the fatal Uber autonomous vehicle crash in Arizona (2018) or plethora of car accidents that occurred when a driver may have used self-driving software, illustrate complex liability issues. Traditional liability doctrines—product liability, negligence, and strict liability—face challenges identifying responsible parties, whether manufacturers, programmers, operators, or others. This avatar requires regulators to clarify responsibility for harm caused by increasingly autonomous systems.

E. AI as Manipulator

AI as manipulator steers user behavior, emotions, or beliefs for profit or ideology. The behavior need not be directly targeted at humans but can include algorithmic behaviors that has many characteristics of what is traditionally considered collusion. It highlights antitrust and competition law concerns posed by AI-powered algorithms that facilitate price-fixing or anti-competitive behavior. Regulatory authorities, such as the EU Competition Commission, expressed concerns when pricing algorithms autonomously adjusted prices, potentially resulting in coordinated, anti-competitive market behavior without explicit human intent. Cases such as those involving Amazon marketplace price alignment illustrate that traditional antitrust concepts of intent and agreement must evolve to address AI-facilitated collusion effectively.

F. AI as Inciter

AI as Inciter raises alarming ethical and legal concerns about chatbot interactions resulting in severe harm. Incidents, such as the tragic suicide of a young man in Belgium in 2023 influenced by conversations with an emotionally manipulative AI chatbot named "Eliza," illustrate this risk. Similarly, AI-powered content recommendation algorithms implicated in promoting hate speech or extremism emphasize the urgent regulatory need to set clear accountability standards and establish enforceable content safety guidelines.

G. AI as Discriminator

AI as Discriminator focuses on algorithmic bias that reinforces or exacerbates inequalities against minorities or marginalized groups. Research studies have found incidents of recruitment systems that are discriminatory towards women as well as facial recognition systems that have misidentified minorities. These examples underscore the need for robust fairness auditing, regulatory oversight, and guidelines mandating transparency, accountability, and ongoing bias mitigation.

H. AI as Trampler

AI as Trampler emphasizes the potential violation of human rights, consumer rights, privacy, and freedoms by invasive and opaque black box AI technologies. The reliance of many regimes on facial recognition and predictive analytics for mass surveillance and social scoring demonstrates severe human rights risks. Additionally, consumer rights violations linked to AI-powered data harvesting without informed consent, highlighted by EU fines on Meta, illustrate the critical need for robust regulatory frameworks to protect citizen rights.

I. AI as Destroyer

AI as Destroyer encapsulates economic and social impacts associated with automation-driven job displacement. Studies predicting AI's replacement of millions of jobs, particularly in sectors like transportation, manufacturing, retail, and customer service, underline concerns about economic inequality and social disruption. With Generative AI tools like ChatGPT potentially replacing white-collar roles, governments face pressures to enact policies ensuring workforce adaptation, labor protections, reskilling programs, and social safety nets to mitigate societal upheaval.

J. AI as Terminator

AI as Terminator addresses existential risks of AI deployment in military applications, particularly lethal autonomous weapons systems ("killer robots" or "slaughterbots"). Cases such as drone warfare automation and AI-powered target selection systems spark heated ethical debates and regulatory dilemmas concerning meaningful human control and accountability in warfare. The global divide between countries seeking bans (such as advocacy groups urging for an international treaty) versus countries prioritizing national security advantages (such as the U.S., Russia, and China) highlights the urgent need for robust international regulatory dialogue to prevent catastrophic AI misuse in armed conflicts.

III. What Is AI Governance?

If AI is a hydra, ten avatars and counting, then governance is our best attempt to tame the beast with something more precise than a sword. But what is governance, exactly? And how does it differ from its more glamorous cousin, regulation?

In the world of AI, governance refers to the full constellation of norms, institutions, practices, and power structures that shape the ways that these technologies are developed, deployed, and held accountable. Governance is the operating system beneath the laws, the invisible code that determines whose interests count, who sets the rules, and how (or whether) those rules are enforced.

It is tempting to imagine AI governance as a tidy technocratic affair, like administering traffic laws or tax codes. Alas, we are not so lucky. Governance here is messy and contested. It unfolds across a fragmented landscape of actors, governments, corporations, industry groups, civil society, and even end users, all jockeying for influence. No single institution controls Artificial Intelligence. That's either its genius or its curse.

This messiness reflects the nature of the technology itself. AI systems are not deployed in a vacuum; they are embedded in finance, education, warfare, art, and logistics. What counts as good governance in a hospital may not make sense in a courtroom or a battlefield. A model flagging heart disease must meet different standards than one suggesting drone targets or writing legal briefs. One size misgoverns all.

And because AI evolves rapidly, governance must evolve too. Traditional rulemaking, with its committees and comment periods, risks obsolescence by the time the ink dries. That is the reason why some governments are turning to adaptive governance models: regulatory sandboxes, iterative audits, and algorithmic impact assessments that change as the technology changes. Think of it as regulating the airplane while it is still taxiing and occasionally assembling its own wings.

Importantly, governance is not the same as regulation, a concept which we further unpack in the next part. Regulation is one tool among many, a blunt one at times, but governance includes softer powers: moral norms, social pressure, corporate ethics boards, professional and industry standards, and shareholder nudges. It includes who funds research, who gets to speak at conferences, and whose values are encoded into machine-learning objectives. Regulation may tell you what not to do; governance often shapes what gets done in the first place.

Let us now return to our avatars.

- AI as Discriminator challenges governance to ensure fairness and inclusion, not just compliance.
- AI as Manipulator reveals the need for transparency and oversight even when laws have not caught up.
- AI as Trampler shows the ways in which governance must include fundamental rights, not just performance metrics.
- AI as Terminator demands global norms and ethical boundaries, whether or not they appear in statute.

Above all, governance is about power. Who gets to decide what is ethical? What counts as risk? Which voices are heard, and which are automated out of the conversation? As Generative AI blurs boundaries between human and machine creativity, and algorithmic systems mediate more aspects of daily life, the stakes of governance become ever more political, not just technical.

This makes lawyers and governance professionals indispensable. Not because they have all the answers, but because they are trained to ask the right questions: Who is accountable? What are the safeguards? How do we balance innovation with integrity?

In short, AI governance is the art of ensuring that when the machines act, humans are still in charge, even if we no longer type all the words.

IV. What Is AI Regulation?

If governance is the orchestra of rules, actors, and influence, then regulation is the brass section, loud, directive, and occasionally out of tune. Regulation is governance with teeth. It is the way we translate societal values into enforceable mandates, drawing lines between what is allowed, what is prohibited, and what might land you in front of a judge explaining why your chatbot called someone a criminal.

The classical image of regulation is clear enough: laws passed by legislatures, rules promulgated by agencies, fines imposed for noncompliance. But AI laughs in the face of tidy categories. It disrupts not only industries, but the very idea of what regulation looks like in practice. And so, we find ourselves improvising, badly, at times, with a mixed ensemble of old instruments and new sheet music.

There are a number of different ways that regulation can occur. The first is the classic: Regulation by government agencies empowered by promulgated legislation in force to undertake such detailed rulemaking.

There is a difficult balance to strike here. In the context of AI regulation, rulemaking provides clarity to the industry, clear markings of what is allowed and what is not. Hereunder is a non-exhaustive list of ways in which regulation can occur outside the classic context of legislative and government agencies' actions.

A. Regulation by Collective Bargaining

In addition to demanding higher wages, the International Longshoremen's Association (ILA), the trade union of stevedores preparing to strike in late September 2024, was seeking to extract from port authority management the promise to cut all automation in 36 ports around the United States. At issue, in addition to wages, was the automation of some port functions, including cranes, gates, and moving containers in the loading and unloading of freight containers. With its 85,000 members the ILA was preparing a pre-Presidential election strike in all Atlantic and Gulf Coast ports from Maine to Texas, severely breaking down the supply chain in the United States.

The industry association representing the port authorities, the United States Maritime Alliance (USMX) went on strike on the first day of October 2024, some carrying signs that read "Machines Don't Feed Families."

Outlawing AI tools will not solve the problem that the ILA is trying to stem. The problem is that the unions are worried about the future (future jobs) while the USMX is worried about maintaining a comparative advantage in facilitating the nation's trade. The ILA's Quixotic struggle is humanity's struggle.

In an opinion piece, Eduardo Porter in *The Washington Post* wrote that "[t]he challenge, not just for the ILA, shippers and port operators but also for policymakers, employers and unions across the economy, is about how to deploy the technology in a way that enhances human work."

After all, less than a year before the strike, Elon Musk told then U.K. Prime Minister Rishi Sunak that "there will come a point where no job is needed." That cannot be a good place in which humanity can co-exist with technology.

The ILA strike ended with a temporary wage deal between the port operators and longshoremen only a few days after it started. The workers won themselves a 62 percent raise over six years. The issue of automation, however, remains unsolved.

The ILA strike was not the first time a trade union used job work actions to stop AI tools in their tracks. Throughout 2023, two unions in Hollywood—the Writers Guild of America and the Screen Actors Guild-American Federation of Television and Radio Artists—hit the picket lines demanding that Hollywood studios and production houses not use AI tools that could replace their jobs or, for the latter union, utilize their likeness without permission and regular payment.

B. Regulation by Court Order and Administrative Actions

Until there is sweeping, comprehensive legislation from the U.S. federal government or any national government for that matter, much of the regulation for AI tools will be coming out of scattershot case law and enforcement actions from administrative agencies.

C. Regulation by Moral Suasion

Corporate Social Responsibility frameworks like the Ruggie Principles (officially the U.N. Guiding Principles on Business and Human Rights) and other harmonization (and completely voluntary, aspirational) efforts from the OECD abound. These global efforts to harmonize fall short due to the strategic concerns of competing national industrial policies. And that is where the rubber meets the road—national interests will trump any collective efforts that curb a country's initiatives to actually dominate this paradigm-shifting strategic technology.

D. Regulation by Public Opinion

The voluntary guidelines of ethical principles emanating from governments or international agencies may not be enough to change behavior of some companies. If there is negative publicity that injures the profits of companies, then it would make sense for them to change the way they do business by adhering to Responsible AI practices. The greatest impact then is to be felt by those AI technology firms that care most about their image. Technology companies that produce consumer products are more likely to be affected by negative publicity than the manufacturers of industrial components.

E. *Regulation by Regulatory Capture*

When Sam Altman, chief executive officer (CEO) of OpenAI, the company that birthed the wildly popular Generative AI tool ChatGPT, did a tour of global capitals in 2023, encouraging leaders of different countries to enact some form of regulation of the AI space, it seemed like he doth protest too much. It certainly felt like a bit of regulatory capture—the phenomenon of companies in a particular space offering up draft regulatory frameworks or actually language of bills for future legislation drafting exercises.

F. *Regulation by Local Corporate Law*

We should also keep in mind that not all multinational enterprises are monolithic entities, but rather networks of companies and other entities. They are often the creations of corporation laws in countries, not products of transnational law. So national laws do matter.

G. *Regulation by Arm Twisting (See EU AI Act)*

Geopolitical clout can function like regulation by proxy. The EU, with its "Brussels Effect," often sets de facto global standards simply because companies want access to its market. There are, after all, 27 Member States that comprise that Single Market. What begins as a regional rule becomes a global compliance obligation, especially for firms with offices on more than one continent.

H. *Regulation by Default*

Sometimes, regulation emerges not by design, but by omission. A failure to act at the national level leads to states or cities stepping in, resulting in a mosaic of rules, confusing, inconsistent, but better than nothing. The U.S. excels at this genre.

I. Regulation by Shareholder Gadfly

Investors increasingly file proposals demanding transparency on AI risks, ethics practices, or board oversight. It's governance by proxy ballot. Shareholder pressure can nudge companies toward accountability, even if only to avoid awkward questions at the annual general meeting.

J. Regulation by Insider Whistleblower

The Nobel Prize in physics for 2024 was awarded to Professors John Hopfield and Geoffrey Hinton for their work on Artificial Intelligence. Hinton, a computer scientist at the University of Toronto (of which one of your co-authors is a proud alumnus), also made headlines when he resigned from Google in 2023. He was quoted at the time stating that while AI could bring benefits to humanity, "we also have to worry about a number of possible bad consequences, particularly the threat of these things getting out of control."

Dr. Timnit Gebru, an ethics researcher at Google, also resigned to much media attention. A paper she co-authored, *On the Dangers of Stochastic Parrots: Can Language Models Be Too Big?*, presents the history of natural-language processing and explores the risks that large language models—AI tools trained on vast amounts of data—pose.

Gary Marcus, Professor Emeritus of New York University, is another AI critic. In his Congressional testimony, he painted a scary picture of what AI tools could one day achieve. Professor Marcus suggested that an international agency should be tasked with regulating AI tools, rather than having a patchwork of self-interested national agencies. That the top scientists and technologists signed a letter in 2023 demanding a six-month moratorium of AI development and deployment also speaks volumes about their unease with AI's unchecked adoption.

K. Regulation by International Treaty

And not a moment too soon, in swooped the U.K. government, hosting an international conference that resulted in November 2023's Bletchley Declaration. But that was not a treaty. Examples of treaties (also called protocols, covenants, conventions, and so forth) include the United Nations (U.N.) Convention on the Law of the Sea, the International Covenant on Civil and Political Rights, and the Statute of Rome (creating the International Criminal Court).

L. Regulation by International Agencies

The offer of António Guterres, Secretary General of the U.N., to set up an international agency dedicated to AI regulation, was a generous one, but given the arguable inability of the U.N. to do what it was originally chartered to do—maintain international peace and security and promote human rights protection—it would probably be best not to pile on to the beleaguered organization's already huge workload.

M. Ancillary Regulation

AI is not just bad for employment and job creation: AI's carbon footprint is increasingly drawing scrutiny, and climate regulators may soon enter the AI space via the back door. Shut the door behind you, the heating is on! After all, training a large language model consumes enough electricity to toast the polar ice caps (only half-joking).

N. Regulation by All the Cool Kids Are Doing It Ethos

The risk-based approach endemic in the EU AI Act, the legislation passed in 2024, is a leading model for regulators to follow. The EU has managed to be the first mover on legislation even though the Union's technology companies come a distant third place in actually developing the technology (behind the U.S. and China). The State-centric bent of the PRC to be hegemonic in owning this future technology is another dominant model.

The Chinese have a 2023 AI law on algorithmic transparency. The Chinese Measures for the Management of Generative AI Services should be seen in the context of 2019's Beijing AI Principles from the Beijing Academy of Artificial Intelligence to understand that this new law is part of a legislative trajectory.

The U.S., however, has failed to produce any legislation of substance: Heidi L. Frostestad points out that "[t]here have been 712 congressional bills on artificial intelligence proposed during the two decades, but only nine laws governing AI outside the context of budget or defense bills have passed into public laws." Not a great record by any standard. There is, indeed, not much of a policy. While the Executive Branch has made some efforts through Executive Orders like that on the Safe, Secure, and Trustworthy Development and Use of Artificial Intelligence from 2023, a true national policy, outside some Office of Management and Budget regulations eludes us stateside.

The U.S.'s "wild west" approach, as if by design, is relegated to another pole in this spectrum of regulation. The U.S. has a patchwork quilt encompassing basic privacy laws, anti-discrimination legislation, and constitutional protections in the context of Artificial Intelligence. This plan to have a plan is more like the workings of a faculty meeting than an actual policy of government. As an example, the Blueprint for an AI Bill of Rights was, in its own words (page 2 of the document) "non-binding and does not constitute U.S. government policy." So, what then is it? This brings us back to the familiar trappings of soft law, the moral suasion that begs for regulation.

The failed legislative efforts at the national level in the United States and the vacuum that states and municipalities have filled in the wake of federal legislative inaction. That was until President Trump's "big, beautiful bill" was passed by Congress in May 2025, effectively placing a ten-year moratorium on the enforcement of sub-federal AI regulations. It does provide some of the work that states, like future-facing Illinois, have had to do to regulate AI tools when Washington DC does very little. Indeed, AI regulators at the sub-national level are being forced, through federal inaction, to strike a balance between innovation and regulation, a needle that Governor of California Gavin Newsom attempted to thread in September 2024, when he vetoed the Golden State's landmark, first in the country bill regulating this evolving technology.

This survey reveals that AI regulation is not a single strategy, it is a mosaic, evolving from necessity, improvisation, and power dynamics. Regulatory models coexist and compete. Some are proactive, others reactive. Some empower the public; others shield incumbents. And all of them are struggling to keep up with the pace of AI development, which continues to outstrip law's capacity to respond.

Still, regulation matters. It offers clarity, legitimacy, and consequences, things that voluntary governance lacks. But as we will explore next, understanding the difference between regulation and governance is crucial. Not because the two are at odds, but because they must work in tandem.

V. What Is the Difference Between Governance and Regulation?

Governance and regulation are often used interchangeably, and while they do share a warm professional handshake, they are not twins. More like cousins, close enough to confuse, distinct enough to argue at family dinners. In AI, the distinction matters. Because if we do not know what we're doing, we're not just going to get bad law, we're going to get bad everything.

Governance is broader than regulation. It's the total ecosystem of how decisions are made, rules are set, behavior is shaped, and values are transmitted. Governance includes regulation, but also ethics guidelines, professional norms, market incentives, design choices, and even public shaming. It's what happens when no one's watching, or when everyone is.

Regulation is the formal, enforceable act of telling people (or companies, or machines) what they must or must not do. It is the domain of legislatures, courts, and regulatory agencies. If governance is the operating system, regulation is the firewall: it blocks, it flags, and sometimes it crashes your business model.

Consider this example: When AI as Defamer produces a deepfake of a politician saying something scandalous, regulation might mean defamation laws or platform takedown requirements. Governance, on the other hand, includes whether the platform had proactive deepfake detection, whether the model's creators imposed safeguards, and whether public outrage leads to real consequences. Regulation says "don't." Governance tries to ask: "Why did this happen, and how do we stop it next time?"

A. *Why Should You Care About AI Governance?*

You should care because AI systems increasingly shape the fabric of your everyday life, often invisibly, and possibly without your consent.

If you're a lawyer, you should care because AI may already be breaking the law, just not always in ways the law recognizes yet. It's generating libel, copying content, discriminating against job applicants, recommending dangerous products, and sometimes recommending worse.

Each of the ten avatars we have met (Infringer, Deceiver, Defamer, Injurer, Manipulator, Inciter, Discriminator, Trampler, Destroyer, and Terminator) maps onto real doctrines: tort, IP, contract, constitutional rights, administrative law, and beyond.

If you are a policymaker or governance professional, you should care because the systems you might regulate are faster than the bureaucratic systems in which you work. The gap between harm and response is growing, and AI isn't waiting for your subcommittee to get quorum.

If you're a technologist, you should care because governance isn't just about external constraints, it's about design choices, value alignment, and whether your product becomes a tool or a time bomb.

And if you're simply a person who uses technology, you should care because AI now decides, or nudges, what news you read, how you're scored for a mortgage, whether your face gets flagged in a crowd, or what ads you see when you're up at 2:00 a.m. searching for "law school alternatives."

You're in the system, whether you know it or not.

B. *Where Do Lawyers Fit in the Picture?*

At first glance, the age of AI might seem like the beginning of the end for lawyers. After all, if a chatbot can draft contracts, summarize depositions, and pass the bar exam on its third cappuccino, what's left for the humans?

Let's get this out of the way first: AI is not replacing lawyers. But it's redefining lawyering. The legal profession is not just reacting to the impacts of AI, it is fast becoming central to the way AI is governed. Here are the reasons why.

First, AI needs legal clarity. Every AI tool intersects with legal rights and obligations, copyright, privacy, product liability, equal protection, labor law, and so on. When AI impersonates your voice, assigns your insurance rate, or refuses you a loan, someone needs to ask: Is that legal? And if not, what's the remedy?

Second, lawyers are the architects of governance structures. They draft the contractual clauses that set limits on AI use. They help companies write ethical policies and product disclaimers. They advise governments on liability frameworks. They interpret evolving regulation and translate ambiguous legal obligations into operational procedures that engineers can follow, or at least not violate.

Third, lawyers can be the bridge between stakeholders (we hope). They translate between technologists and policymakers, between code and constitution, between innovation and accountability. That new facial recognition system being sold to local police? Someone needs to analyze whether it complies with due process, civil liberties, and public procurement law, preferably before it goes live, not after someone sues.

So where do lawyers come into the picture? Everywhere.

Lawyers, for all their footnotes and formatting preferences, are well suited to be its stewards. Just don't let the robots write the briefs unsupervised.

C. *What Follows Next Is. . . .*

This *Short and Happy Guide* does not promise to tell you everything about AI governance. This guide is short and happy, yes, but not a superficial one. We aim for clarity without dumbing things down.

By the time you finish, you'll know enough to challenge your local policy board, revise your firm's AI policy, or at the very least, avoid letting your startup client train on thousands of copyrighted images without a license.

It is structured to give you both the map and the terrain, with the occasional scenic overlook and legal pothole. From here, the book unfolds in a series of accessible, fast-paced chapters. Specifically, you can expect to:

- Identify the key institutional debates and political challenges that make AI governance uniquely difficult, and the tools we might use to meet them, from algorithmic audits to adaptive rulemaking.
- Appreciate the ethical and strategic stakes of AI decisions, not only for compliance, but for fairness, equity, and democratic legitimacy.
- Gain fluency in the different models of AI governance and regulation

VI. Summary/Key Points

1. AI is not a single technology, it is a shifting constellation of systems, each with unique risks, legal implications, and

governance needs. Treating all AI as one monolithic category misses the mark and leads to overreach or overlooks critical harms

2. The Ten Avatars of AI Harm, from the Infringer to the Terminator, illustrate how AI systems challenge existing legal frameworks across tort, IP, privacy, discrimination, and more. Understanding these avatars helps ground abstract governance debates in real-world consequences.
3. Governance is broader than regulation. Governance includes laws, norms, practices, and institutional structures. Regulation is one tool among many, necessary, but not sufficient, for effective oversight.
4. AI regulation comes in many forms, not just government edicts, but court rulings, union contracts, consumer boycotts, class action lawsuits, shareholder activism, and whistleblower disclosures. These diverse mechanisms reflect a fragmented but dynamic global effort to rein in AI's excesses without stifling innovation.
5. Lawyers and governance professionals are central actors in this landscape. Far from being replaced, they are becoming architects of new systems, translators between disciplines, and guardians of accountability in the algorithmic age.
6. The stakes are high and the moment is urgent. Governance decisions made today will shape the legal, economic, and ethical contours of AI for decades. Those who understand the challenges, and stay willing to learn, will help define a future in which it is worth living.

CHAPTER 2

AI Regulation: Concepts and Debates

I. Introduction

To assist our journey into the regulation of Artificial Intelligence (AI), there are a number of pressing debates, foundational concepts, and underlying theories that need to be surveyed and unpacked, at least at a high level. After all, this is a *Short and Happy Guide*.

Part II of this Chapter explores the current debates that involve the AI space. First, there are the interconnections between privacy and data governance. We also explore the legal doctrine of fair use and how it applies to unauthorized data scraping as well as compulsory licensing regimes. In addition, we look at open-source AI, industrial policy and innovation, the role of free speech, and particularly whether the much-debated Section 230 of the Communications Decency Act of 1996 applies to Artificial Intelligence. We also work through some of the environmental and antitrust impacts of AI regulation (i.e. How do we best ensure a fair and level playing field?) and a few other issues concerning foundation models and large language models (LLMs) that have popped up. Finally, we place these issues into a geopolitical context—from the point of view of the Global South and concerns over data sovereignty and computational colonialism and the role that national security plays in all of this. This leads to data localization laws that protect a country's citizens and companies from the vagaries (and snooping) of foreign governments and their respective corporations. It may seem like a lot, but that's why this is such a hot field.

Part III of this Chapter examines the role that regulation plays in general. It explores different aspects of regulation such as self-regulating organizations (SROs) and the dangers of regulatory capture. Part IV of this Chapter surveys how governance works in the corporate boardroom, in the backstreets of factory towns, and in social media. Companies that engage in best practices that jibe well with good old Corporate Social Responsibility (CSR)—today, reinvented as Environment, Social and Governance (ESG) standards—do so because it is good for their brand despite the cost. AI companies are getting ahead of AI Ethics regulation by integrating principles like transparency, explainability, and trustworthiness into the tools that they are offering to businesses and society. They do so because it is good for business or in a few cases, part of their corporate ethos, not because there is legislation.

First though, we look at the current debates, many of which are complex, a harbinger of the harrowing challenges ahead.

II. Current Debates

A. Interlinkages of Privacy, Data Governance, and Artificial Intelligence Regulation

Privacy, in regard to data, is the ways in which data is collected, used, and shared. Data privacy interlinks with data governance and AI regulation, because it frames the discussion of how much control people have over their personal data. Privacy when it comes to AI relates to personal or sensitive information that is collected, shared, stored and used to train AI models.

Data governance can be defined as the processes, policies, and frameworks that ensure data is being used properly. Creating these standards helps to keep data secure and ensures fair usage. Also related to managing data responsibly, AI regulations target the development and deployment of AI to mitigate potential issues such as bias, data misuse, and harm to individuals, ensuring the ethical and safe use of Artificial Intelligence.

Data governance goes beyond the creation and distribution of mere policies; it is a crucial element to promote trust in data, to empower people to make better decisions and improve operations and efficiency.

Regarding regulations, there are plenty dedicated to data privacy and data governance. Some key examples of regulations on data include the General Data Protection Regulation (GDPR) of the European Union (EU) and California's Consumer Privacy Protection Act (CPPA) in the United States (U.S.). Brazil has its own General Personal Data Protection Law, a regulation, among many other global variants, we cover in Chapter 8 of this book. The EU, however, was the first jurisdiction to create a regulation specifically for AI, called the AI Act, a topic covered in Chapter 6. The U.S. is still figuring out its legislative path forward, if any. The U.S. approach is covered in Chapter 5 of this *Short and Happy Guide*.

B. Fair Use, Scraping Restrictions, and Compulsory Licensing Regimes

These are age-old debates that have assumed urgency and importance because of the pace of Generative AI development. Fair use provides to the public the right to use copyrighted material without the copyright owner's permission under specific situations.

The use of the copyright must be fair and reasonable, and it cannot decrease the value of the original copyright or the owner's expected profits. Based on the proposition that copyright owners should not be able to prevent disapproval of their work, fair use has emerged over the years as an important legal doctrine. Some examples of fair use include using news reporting, scholarly reports, and criticism, and making copies of the work, for teaching, scholarship, or research.

Web scraping restrictions are limits on the ways in which data can be taken and used from a website, such as bulk downloading, altering content, or republishing. One example of a scraping restriction can be a clause inserted into a terms of service agreement that prohibits scraping and automated access on a website or online platform. Moreover, scraping data from the internet without consent of the owner, protected under a copyright or personal, can be problematic depending on the jurisdiction. More scraping limitations can include disrupting a site from its normal functioning, or unauthorized scraping of personal financial data.

However, web scraping is not always illegal. Typically, when used for personal use and analysis, scraping restrictions are limited. It is often jurisdiction dependent. Data protection laws, like the GDPR, regulate what can be constituted as personal use and what is defined as illegal web scraping. Web scraping in Japan, at this writing, is not illegal.

Compulsory licensing regimes enable governments to allow licenses on patented products, without the need to obtain the consent of the patent holder. Usually, this will be in exchange for some reasonable amount of compensation for the patent's use. Similar in concept to the fair use framework, compulsory licensing regimes are used to balance the rights of the owners as well as the public's well-being. For example, these licenses are typically used in drastic circumstances, such as a state of national emergency involving public health. Brazil and South Africa used such regimes to fight the HIV/AIDS epidemic in the 1990s and 2000s by providing lower cost local alternatives to big pharma's expensive antiviral cocktail drugs.

C. Risks of Open-Source AI

"Open source" means to be freely available for use, alteration, or redistribution. Open-source AI can be defined as AI that is free to study, use, modify, and share, including all components of the AI system, like the code, datasets, and model parameters. Technology companies and regulators alike have had trouble defining open-source Artificial Intelligence. *The MIT Technology Review* explains that the Open Source Initiative has defined open-source AI as, "used for any purpose without the need to secure permission, and researchers should be able to inspect its components and study how the system works." By creating a clear definition, this in turn can help regulators create legal frameworks surrounding open-source AI technologies.

In the content of Generative AI, there is a new term and a twist. Open-weight AI refers to the release of a model's trained parameters for use, typically without full access to training code, data, or open-source licensing freedoms. Open-weight AI differs fundamentally from traditional open source in that it typically provides access to a model's trained parameters without releasing full training code, data, or unrestricted rights to modify and redistribute. Traditional open-source ensures transparency, replicability, and broad reuse rights, while open-weight AI often comes with custom, restrictive licenses (e.g., prohibiting commercial use, AI model rehosting, or certain applications), limiting the freedoms central to open-source norms.

From a policy and licensing perspective, this divergence creates ambiguity: open-weight models may benefit from the appearance of openness while evading the accountability and interoperability expectations tied to open-source. This has implications for regulatory efforts around AI safety, competition, and reproducibility. Policymakers may need to distinguish clearly between truly open-source AI and open-weight AI to align licensing regimes with public interest goals—such as fostering innovation, ensuring auditability, and mitigating concentration of power.

While having AI systems be open-source can help foster a transparent and collaborative environment for AI development, there are also drawbacks. For example, there are significant security risks that organizations and developers must carefully consider. Critical vulnerabilities have been found in a multitude of open-source AI and machine learning tools. There are code and model data integrity issues, data training risks, lacking security protocols, and dependency risks. Open-source AI systems can rely on external models, making cyberattacks easier to occur. Thus, there is potential for misuse of the open-source code with the widespread access given. If privacy breaches can occur or biased or discriminatory outputs can be generated, there must be restrictions put in place.

In a 2024 State of Open Source Report, over two-thirds of businesses were found to have increased their open-source software over the last year. IBM reports that: "Generative AI is no exception. . . But legitimate businesses aren't the only ones investing in Generative Artificial Intelligence. It's also a veritable goldmine for malicious actors, from rogue states bent on proliferating misinformation among their rivals to cyber criminals developing malicious code or targeted phishing scams." Until there are more regulatory measures in place, developers are the main protectors from bad actors, as they attempt to keep their respective platforms from misuse with strong guardrails in place.

These risks highlight the need for a robust regulatory framework on Artificial Intelligence. Proper security measures and governance are required for the fair and equitable use of open-source AI models. Without the proper safeguards in place, anyone can access such AI technology and abuse it. And they do.

D. Industrial Policy and Innovation

Industrial policy can be described as the government promoting specific sectors in hopes of increasing economic growth and fostering a strong competitive market. This in turn drives innovation, leading to advancements and productivity in that field. The technology sector that is driving the growth of AI in the U.S. is no exception.

The U.S. has created several industrial policies to promote innovation and sustain a strong presence in the AI sector. One national strategy for AI has been the Creating Helpful Incentives to Produce Semiconductors and Science Act (CHIPS). A 2022 piece of bipartisan legislation, CHIPS creates approximately $80 billion for American semiconductor production, using tax incentives and grants for domestic manufacturing. Specialized semiconductors are essential in AI development. By securing the supply chain for these key components, this Act aims to strengthen the U.S. leadership in Artificial Intelligence.

Another example of AI industrial policy was the National AI Research and Development Strategic Plan. Last updated in 2023, the Strategic Plan has several initiatives for AI development, including addressing human-in-the-loop concerns, creating public datasets for AI training, examining the ethical and legal implications of AI, and making long-term investments in AI research.

There are many other AI industrial policies the U.S. has created, but the second Trump administration rescinded Executive Order 14110, the seminal October 2023 directive that the Biden administration had issued. Some advance federal funding for AI Research Institutes and for Congress to form AI working groups. By combining investment, regulations, and collaboration between the U.S. government, and research and development teams, the U.S. aims to stay competitive in the field of AI and innovation. At least that is the idea. Other governments do the same. All the cool kids are doing it.

E. Section 230 of the Communications Decency Act and Generative AI

The Communications Decency Act protects free speech online by providing immunity to online platforms for content posted by their users but also allows them to moderate content by removing or restricting access to content (like obscene or harassing material) if they do so in good faith. Enacted in 1996 as part of the Telecommunications Act, the Communications Decency Act has shaped the landscape of the internet era.

Two important provisions are Section 230(c)(1) and section 230(c)(2). Section 230(c)(1) states that "providers and users of interactive computer services cannot be treated as the publisher or speaker of information provided by another information content." Under section 230(c)(2), known as the Good Samaritan Protection, there is "civil liability immunity for providers and users who voluntarily act in good faith to restrict access to objectionable material." Such umbrella immunity provided to many online services like social media platforms, blogs, and websites has been the subject of much controversy.

There are positive and negative implications of Section 230 shielding social media companies from civil liability for content posted by their users. Section 230 is designed to protect free speech online, encourage the development of the internet and online services, and allow platforms to moderate content without the fear of liability or sanction. The Communications Decency Act has been instrumental in shaping the growth of social media platforms, online forums, and other interactive web services, allowing them to host user-generated content without the risk of being held liable for every post. And while Section 230 has been crucial for internet development, it has also been criticized for providing too much protection to the platforms, allowing the spread of misinformation and harmful content, something we have seen proliferate these last few years unfortunately.

As already discussed, Section 230 of the Communications Decency Act shields online platforms from liability for user-generated content. Historically, this legal immunity facilitated the growth of social media and digital intermediaries by distinguishing between publishers and platforms. However, the rise of Generative AI complicates this dichotomy. Unlike traditional user content, outputs from Generative AI tools often result from active, algorithmic synthesis by the platform itself, blurring the line between hosting and producing content. When AI-generated responses are defamatory, misleading, or harmful, it becomes legally and ethically unclear whether platforms should retain immunity under Section 230, given their role in shaping, rather than merely transmitting, the content.

This ambiguity exposes a potential regulatory gap. Courts and policymakers must now consider whether Section 230 should apply to AI systems that do not merely host third-party speech but generate novel content based on training data, prompts, and algorithmic design. Holding such systems to the same standards as passive message boards may allow platforms to evade responsibility for harms stemming from synthetic media, misinformation, or automated defamation. Reform proposals suggest carving out exceptions for AI-generated outputs or conditioning immunity on demonstrable transparency and safety practices. As Generative AI becomes more autonomous and pervasive, the legal framework must evolve to distinguish between facilitation and authorship in ways Section 230 never anticipated.

F. Environmental Impacts of AI

With the rise of AI, developers are building massive data centers to house large server farms. Generative AI systems, like ChatGPT, rely on processing vast amounts of data. In general, the real-time processing of data, autonomous vehicles, and smart infrastructure requires high-energy level algorithms for decision-making and constant processing, ultimately consuming a vast amount of energy. And that's bad, right?

Thus, concerns are growing about the widespread adoption of AI leading to environmental problems. For example, asking ChatGPT a single question can consume almost 10 times as much energy as a traditional Google search (now, even a Google search query comes with an AI summary, pushing up the energy consumption even higher.) Generating an AI image can use half as much power as charging a smartphone. The U.S. hosts the highest concentration of data centers, with more than 8,000 locations. Experts project that data center demand will further increase by 15%-20% annually through 2030. These facilities are expected to consume 16% of total U.S. power by the end of the decade. To put into perspective, in 2022 (before OpenAI released ChatGPT and Generative AI became mainstream), data centers used just 2.5% of U.S. power.

Concerning water, the Organisation for Economic Co-operation and Development (OECD) calls AI servers "hungry and thirsty." The OECD writes that "[l]arge AI models. . .are often trained and deployed on large clusters of servers . . . . These servers are so power-hungry they can consume a few kilowatts each, equivalent to an entire house's average power consumption. So, despite the recent algorithmic and hardware efficiency improvements, AI model training and inference still result in enormous energy consumption."

AI's surging energy and water demands underscore a central challenge, including innovating and modernizing energy and technology systems and ensuring proper regulatory measures are in place. Addressing these needs with investments in grid infrastructure and battery storage units, for example, will ensure the sustainable and reliable operation of Artificial Intelligence.

G. Regulation of Foundation Models/Large Language Models

Foundation models, also known as LLMs, are AI programs that have been trained on a large corpus of text (i.e. language) and are able to do language-related tasks such as summarization, translation, and generations. Examples of LLMs include: OpenAI GPT, Google Gemini, Meta Llama, Anthropic Claude, and more. These are trained on vast amounts of text and non-text content. For example, OpenAI's GPT-4 model is trained on data equivalent to 10 trillion words. For comparison, English language Wikipedia totals only 4.5 billion words. No wonder ChatGPT behaves like a know-it-all!

Taking the LLMs and building a software program (with a lot of human input, labeling thousands of examples of good and bad responses to different questions) that can do the above tasks in a conversational manner, ultimately results in tools like ChatGPT. It may surprise you to learn that ChatGPT, at its heart, is a next-word prediction system. Seriously. Based on some sophisticated calculations of probability, the tool predicts the most likely next word in a sequence. Human writing, speech, and thinking work fundamentally differently than next-word predictions but ultimately speech and writing manifest as streams of words and it seems that given enough training data, (all that has ever been written and said) and computing power, the next word can be predicted fairly well.

AI tools like ChatGPT generate text. But there are other tools that can generate images, video, audio, music, software code, 3 dimensional (3D) designs, and so forth. These are referred to as multi-modal LLMs (as they can handle multiple input modes and generate output in multiple modes such as text, image, audio, video etc.)

Regulating LLMs is becoming very important due to their vast societal impact. Current discussions are focused on ensuring responsible development and use by addressing concerns like data privacy, bias, misinformation, and potential for harm through strict guidelines on data collection, model transparency, and user accountability. Legal frameworks like the EU's AI Act have specifically targeted "high-risk" LLMs with key regulations on their deployment and deployment.

There are a multitude of ways to regulate foundational models, to keep these "high-risk" issues at bay. For instance, strict controls on the type of data used to train models, including preventive measures for personal data breaches and addressing potential biases within training datasets. Moreover, transparency is key. Having developers provide clear documentation on how models are built, including details about the data used, training methodologies, and their potential limitations. A robust process for identifying and mitigating potential risks associated with the application of foundation models, particularly in high-risk areas like healthcare and finance can also help. Thus, users should understand the capabilities, but also the limitations of LLMs to prevent misuse. But do regulators have the expertise to keep tabs on all of this?

We hope so. The fast-paced nature of LLMs can create difficulties in regulation. With a lack of (inherent) transparency in LLMs, it can be hard to understand how the model arrives at an output, making it difficult to create risk assessments. Still, there have been strong efforts made to regulate large language models. In October 2022, the Biden Administration created a Blueprint for an AI Bill of Rights, including a set of voluntary guidelines for the responsible development and deployment of Artificial Intelligence. The Blueprint for an AI Bill of Rights, a simple statement of principles, required comprehensive risk assessments, and encouraged companies to prioritize accountability, fairness and equitability, and transparency in their large language models. But it was only voluntary, so its importance was hobbled from its start.

H. AI and Competition (Antitrust) Law

Artificial intelligence is enabling businesses to optimize their operations, analyze consumer behavior, and automate decision-making. However, the integration of AI tools into businesses' digital platforms has raised significant antitrust concerns. Antitrust law governs the regulation of economic power concentration, focusing on monopolies and other anti-competitive practices. The worry is that bigtech may use AI to reinforce monopolistic control, leveraging large datasets inaccessible to smaller competitors and dominating the market. AI-driven pricing algorithms can enable tacit collusion, which allows companies to independently adjust prices in parallel without direct agreements, posing challenges for traditional antitrust enforcement.

Moreover, AI presents new enforcement challenges for antitrust law authorities. Traditional antitrust laws depend on human intent, but AI-driven decision-making creates issues of liability attribution. Quinn Emanuel Trial Lawyers explains it like this: "When machines can make independent decisions, serious questions arise regarding whether competitors explicitly or tacitly agree to conspire or whether their AI simply acts in a way that is reactive to market conditions, which may include acting in parallel to a competitor." It is possible that the AI systems of competing companies could independently develop strategies that resemble collusion on pricing or other competitive matters—without any awareness or intent from human decision-makers. This raises a critical question of whether companies can be held liable under competition laws when non-human actors, such as AI, coordinate pricing or other market behaviors.

Thus, self-learning algorithms may independently develop anti-competitive strategies, exclusionary tactics and price fixing, without direct human intervention. For these reasons, current legal frameworks may not be enough to address AI-facilitated antitrust, and why there is a need for a lawyer-in-the-loop.

Governments globally are considering regulatory measures to mitigate anti-competitive risks. The scrutiny of corporate mergers by the European Commission's Digital Markets Act (DMA) and the Federal Trade Commission (FTC) of the U.S. highlights efforts to prevent AI-induced monopolistic practices. Some lawyers and legislators argue for proactive AI-specific competition policies, such as requiring algorithmic transparency and data-sharing obligations to level the playing field. Moving forward, legal frameworks must balance innovation with fairness to ensure that AI benefits the broader economy.

I. Data Sovereignty Versus Data Colonialism

As the digital economy grows, governments and organizations are increasingly concerned about how multinational technology companies store, process, and monetize data. Carlos Saura García defines digital sovereignty as "the legitimate control over the digital." Digital sovereignty enhances security, strengthens and protects economic markets, and achieves autonomy in certain sectors.

The concept of digital colonialism critiques how powerful technology firms, mainly based in the U.S. and, increasingly in the People's Republic of China (China), dominate global data flows, reinforcing economic dependencies between developed and developing countries. Carlos Saura García defines this as "digital expansionism," and is "a way of affecting, influencing, and subordinating foreign nations through the digital." While these companies provide crucial digital infrastructure, such as cloud computing, AI-driven analytics and social media, they also control vast amounts of data from less powerful countries. Critics argue that this reflects historical colonial practices, where dominant economies extracted resources from colonized regions for their own benefit. Today, digital colonialism serves as a metaphor for the algorithmic extraction and aggregation of vast amounts of individual data, transforming big data into a valuable commodity.

The lack of local ownership over data-driven industries can limit the ability of developing countries to build competitive digital markets and exercise true digital sovereignty. In response, governments and international bodies are working to counteract digital colonialism through legal and policy frameworks. The GDPR has impacted global discussions on data sovereignty by setting strict rules on privacy protections and data transfers. Under the GDPR, personal data of EU residents must be stored and processed within the EU, with companies required to obtain explicit consent for data collection, implement stringent security measures, and promptly report any breaches. Additionally, GDPR grants EU residents key rights, including the ability to access, modify, and request the deletion of their personal data.

Data localization is about control as governments assert "data sovereignty" over digital assets of their citizens and companies, much like physical territory. Data tariffs, anyone? Given that territoriality is a fundamental principle of jurisdiction in international law, a reasonable case can be made that the data of a country's citizens and companies should remain in the physical jurisdiction of that country.

Countries such as India, with the Digital Personal Data Protection Act 2023, and Brazil, with its General Personal Data Protection Law, have also legislated data localization laws to assert control over their own domestic digital resources. However, some experts warn excessive localization could stifle innovation and harm global trade. The U.S. and EU are working to carve out exceptions, introducing the idea of a "data corridor." So-called "data embassies," where data in one country is still subject to another country's jurisdiction, are another solution under consideration. The challenge moving forward is to create policies that protect national interests, while fostering an equitable digital economy.

J. National Security Versus a Fair/Horizontal Playing Field

In the U.S., under 10 USC § 801(16), national security is defined as "the national defense and foreign relations of the United States." More generally, national security is the safekeeping of a country's sovereignty from external and internal threats. Some of these protections can include military defense, cybersecurity, energy security, economic stability, and anti-terrorism efforts. A horizontal playing field, or the phrase "level the playing field," can be referred to as a system in which all participants (people, countries, or businesses) compete under the same rules and conditions for purposes of equality and fairness. This ensures positive reinforcements such as transparency, market access, and non-discrimination.

Governments often use national security as a reason to intervene on issues such as cybersecurity and infrastructure. However, security-driven policies such as these can result in the favoring of domestic products over foreign competitors. These restrictions on technological exports, foreign investments, and data sovereignty can stir issues between countries and result in an uneven playing field. National security regulations can impact international trade immensely. For example, the U.S. has restrictions on Chinese technology firms, such as Huawei and TikTok, for cybersecurity concerns.

Moreover, China has established data laws limiting foreign access to its own digital landscape, such as the Cybersecurity Law (CSL) of 2017 and the Data Security Law (DSL) of 2021, as we explore in Chapter 7 of this book. Another example is the CHIPS and Science Act which works to bring microchip manufacturing back to the U.S. after decades of offshoring the technology.

While national security regulations can address legitimate concerns, they can also undermine the principle of a fair and horizontal playing field on a global level. International trade agreements, such as ones governed by the World Trade Organization (WTO), aim to prevent unfair and unethical trade barriers while also making exceptions for national security. Policymakers are thus charged with the complex task of striking a balance between national security and fair competition laws.

III. On Regulation

Building on our discussion from Chapter 1, it is important to note that regulation comes at a price. It is a transaction cost that is currently not being paid in a *laissez faire* regime that rewards risk-tasking. But AI is both a horizontal technology with broad applications and a dual-use technology that can be put to both good and bad uses. As we will explore in Chapters 5 to 8, the current approach (outside of the EU) has been mostly about the establishment of guidelines, but these are not binding nor carry penalties for transgressions. Institutional capacity for enforcement matters. Without the institutions to enforce rules there may be little point in having rules that do nothing but codify norms but have no real institutions to force compliance.

Rules are not the only way to enforce important norms for society. There are other ways to regulate AI research, development, and deployment short of potentially innovation-stifling regulation. As is the case for other areas of technology (protection against hate speech, privacy protections, and so forth), existing laws may also be used for Artificial Intelligence.

Of course, it is not that new regulations are not useful. Double negatives aside, their usefulness lies in drawing attention to the outstanding issues that require attention, starting the discussions that involve multiple stakeholders in drafting and following rules, shining sunlight via media attention, and getting the commitment of businesses to address the issues that the usage and development of AI systems brings in their wake.

A. Theories of Regulation

There are many theories of regulation just as there are many approaches. Public interest theory is a major approach for regulation. It suggests that regulation is driven by public demand to address market failures. Capture theory on the other hand posits that regulations can emanate from the very industry players that the regulators should be regulating in the first place. They are, after all, experts in their industries, and that space, especially concerning AI, is in constant evolution.

Another kind of regulatory regime is based on principles, about which we have more to say in Chapter 3. In addition, interest group theory provides that the interests of different stakeholders influence regulatory outcomes, as different groups with different interests advocate for different regulations. Market power theory focuses on the way that market concentration and the resulting monopolies that emerge shape regulatory demands (or demands for little if no regulation) and outcomes.

Finally, political opportunism theory emphasizes the need for controls on unfettered governmental discretion, for fear of chilling efficiency and innovation. When it comes to AI, we need to address whether the space is actually suitable for regulation. Our short answer is mostly, yes. There's always the fine print, of course.

That is not to say current laws, already on the books, cannot be used effectively. It's just that sometimes old laws may not work for new contexts. Tort law is great, but it may not apply to co-bots in the workplace or self-driving car accidents.

B. Self-Regulation as a Placeholder/Default

SROs, the structure wherein industry participants voluntarily establish standards and best practices and agree to abide by them, are another mechanism by which AI researchers and merchants can be held accountable, albeit to each other. An SRO provides standards, in the form of guidelines and rules, which are approved by its constituent members. These members agree to comply with the published guidelines and adhere to its rules.

SROs can have the power to sanction (including the ability to fine, expel, or suspend membership), like the Financial Industry Regulatory Authority (FINRA) and the New York Stock Exchange do for the financial system in the United States. This enforcement function makes the SRO all the more impactful. Sometimes government agencies can dictate the broader policies of self-regulating organizations or outsource these compliance and monitoring initiatives to the SRO itself.

While FINRA does have the power to license securities dealers/brokers, an AI-focused SRO might not be invested with such robust powers. The devil, as they say, is in the details. Or it wears

(AI-generated) Prada. Be that as it may, until there are meaningful and operational laws, the AI space may be well served by an SRO composed of the largest companies with small and medium companies joining as well. Such an AI-focused SRO could declare its support for and compliance with ethical AI principles and standards. That would be a great start. Independent audits and third-party certifications of compliance to standards could then define the next level of scrutiny.

Moreover, businesses always have firsthand knowledge of AI development and risks, so businesses stand in a better position than the government to draft practical regulations to address potential disadvantages coming along with increasing AI development.

But self-regulation is only an interim measure until our governments put on their respective big boy/girl/person pants and actually start the grueling work of creating rules. Help wanted! Legislators with AI knowledge please apply!

But like all such things, self-regulation is (at least partly) self-serving. Many observers rightly point out that Responsible AI commitments can also lead to so-called AI Ethics washing: Performative virtue signaling rather than walking the talk and putting the pedal to metal. This is akin to the "greenwashing" that occurs as companies try to prove their ESG chops.

We need to guard against the danger of the growing AI industrial complex providing its own self-interested rules. Regulatory capture is not a good look: Let us not ask the foxes to write their own safety rules concerning the hens' roost. But legislators cannot regulate what they do not yet understand.

C. Regulatory Capture

Regulatory capture is a problem with any industry, but AI presents other tricky challenges. Technology expertise exists with the AI companies themselves, and not so much outside of them. In other industries, academia and government research labs do have comparable expertise but in AI, the leading labs are mainly from the industry itself. Also, the technology is moving fast, faster than the ability of our authorities to reign it in. The prize for the winners is quite high—dominating the future of production, consumption and even opinion—so is the temptation to lobby the regulators and influence regulation.

IV. On Governance

At times, corporations be it through their do-gooder boards of directors, environmentalist officers, activist shareholders or even under threat of market boycotts and consumer actions—uphold higher standards than may be required by law or local regulations. One prominent example, are the ESG initiatives—commitments to the overall community and not just shareholders. The idea is not to poison the local community, pollute the environment, exploit workers, or engage in corrupt and other illegal activities.

In the old days this was called CSR and can be rooted in soft law like the Guidelines for Multinational Enterprises from the OECD or the Business Roundtable's Statement on the Purpose of a Corporation. Corporations commit themselves not just to shareholder wealth maximization but to serve all "stakeholders." Companies do this because they can afford to do both good (deal fairly with the workforce and local community) and well (create profits) at the same time. And customers, suppliers, workers, and social media all very much like how it looks on paper (and in the media.) Companies do this, not because it is required by law, but because they hold themselves and their management and employees to higher standards. That's good governance. At least that is what the public relations team at corporations are telling us. For AI companies, that means soothing the public's anxiety over AI's threat to our way of life, our livelihood, and our social fabric through ethical and Responsible AI policies.

V. Summary/Key Points

1. Data governance, privacy, and AI regulation are intertwined. Who controls data influences how AI systems function and whom they serve.
2. Geopolitics frames and fuels major AI debates. AI policies and rules are being shaped through competition, not consensus, between the U.S., EU, and China. AI industrial policy is the new arms race. From semiconductor legislation to national research and development strategy, sovereign States are subsidizing/prioritizing AI for strategic dominance, not just for economic growth.
3. Self-regulation fills the legal vacuum (but only temporarily) as companies and industries set their own rules in the absence of binding law. CSR and ESG initiatives illustrate that firms can self-impose some ethical boundaries - but only when market or reputational pressures make it worth their while.
4. Generative AI is breaking the original publisher-platform distinction and the dividing line between hosting content and creating content is increasingly being contested. Section 230 was not envisaged for AI platforms that generate speech.
5. Open-source AI is different from traditional open-source software and presents many paradoxes. Greater access can mean more accountability and transparency but also increases potential for misuse.
6. Regulation is not just about law-making but is also about institutional capacity to enforce them as Generative AI operates at a scale that overwhelms traditional enforcement

mechanisms. Without enforcement, declarations and principles are performative, and laws are statements of intent.

CHAPTER 3

AI Ethics

I. Introduction

This Chapter explores the intersection and interplay of algorithms and ethical norms. After all, the usage of Artificial Intelligence (AI) tools has been found, time and again, to result in discriminatory and harmful outcomes. Whose fault is this? Given that bias and unfairness may be baked into the algorithms that AI vendors are designing and selling and public authorities and private companies alike are purchasing them with great vigor, where does responsibility for such bias and unfairness lay? Can such a technology be a galvanizing force to do good in addition? Or is it more of a subtraction thing? What happens if the bias gets codified?

At the meta level here is a doozy of a set of questions: What happens to the more than 300 million people who may find that their jobs are automated away by AI in the coming years, as Goldman Sachs estimated in its March 2023 report? How should we prevent AI from perpetuating wage inequality given all the automation of employment tasks coming down the pike? How can AI companies not increase the already vast inequalities in our world?

AI and its associated technologies pose many challenges to modern society, to governance, and to liberty. Are there inherent biases that get replicated by the machine? How do other countries, including other modern liberal democracies, deal with such new technologies? And conversely, how do autocracies leverage these technologies? By what kinds of entities and at what level of governance should rules for the AI road be enforced? Are transnational organizations for rule setting and compliance more efficacious than national or local enforcement? Should the private sector or stakeholders other than our elected governments play a role in setting those rules? And finally, how many questions can we pose in these two paragraphs? Is your head ready to explode yet?

To explain all the contours of these issues, in this Chapter we use the terms "Responsible AI," "Ethical AI," and "Trustworthy AI," all of which are becoming more common, but do not yet have a generally agreed upon meaning. In general, these concepts are used to describe AI systems that are designed, built and operated with certain key attributes that protect human beings (such as fairness, safety, transparency and a respect for human autonomy) and denote a level of quality in their overall performance.

At this point, and for the foreseeable future, these terms do not suggest that the models themselves are ethical or responsible; they may be engineered to defer to humans (or not) or to resolve uncertainties in one way or another, but the models themselves do not contain ethics in a human sense. On the other hand, models might be "trustworthy" in key dimensions, meaning that they are designed to be safe, reliable, and verifiable.

The American Association for the Advancement of Science explained in its 2022 Artificial Intelligence and the Courts: Materials for Judges that

> it is important to acknowledge that despite the many statements of Responsible AI principles now in circulation

(well over 100 of them), there is no agreed legal standard for what this means. There are existing laws that will be applied to AI and new legislation that will be passed. Community standards for what is reasonable or just adequate will also evolve.

Some of these come from private corporations and some from governments in different countries while others emanate from multilateral institutions. It is not surprising that rules concerning responsible, ethical, and trustworthy use of AI continue to be discussed by public authorities, regional agencies, and international institutions. They are of critical importance. AI continues to impact our lives faster than we can navigate, let alone predict and prepare to legislate. Rattled by the pace of progress, in March 2023, many leading voices, including Elon Musk, Andrew Yang, and Steve Wozniak, penned a letter urging a six-month moratorium on the development of the most powerful AI systems. Now signed, at this writing, by some 33,000 technologists, civic leaders, academicians, policy wonks, and corporate executives, this was a quixotic but symbolic gesture that nonetheless underscored the discomfort about AI in many quarters, including worries of bad things that bad actors could do with the evolving technology.

As the adoption of AI by businesses, governments, and different organizations increases, its risks or downsides have also come to the fore. We discussed much of this in our *Short and Happy Guide to Artificial Intelligence for Lawyers* (West Academic Publishing, 2024). Many of these may be unintentional. It is not like the technology company executives are real-life James Bond villains, who set out to mess us up using their AI toys (but first tell us their plans of world domination that we can later foil). But these side effects cause real damage in the real world and the parties involved look bad. It is not good for their brands, nor for their businesses. So, when alerted to these incidents or when they become aware of these incidents, many of them try to set it right. Thankfully.

But remember that there is a glaring lack of regulatory clarity and many gray areas in the laws already on the books to boot. The old adage "Technology sprints, regulation strolls" comes to mind here. Also, businesses do not want to poke the bear (i.e. get the government involved). So, they try to see if they can fix things themselves—cue the self-regulation organizations—or be seen as fixing things to right the ship. That brings us back to Responsible Artificial Intelligence. This is broadly the voluntary effort to right the unintentional wrongs of the unexamined and untrammeled usage of Artificial Intelligence.

The people and groups that devise and publish these standards matter. Industry associations, leading technology companies, professional societies, non-profit organizations, and international institutions have all jumped into the ring and developed AI Ethics principles and Responsible AI standards. It is a growth industry for sure, as there are more statements of Responsible AI standards than anyone can count. If you printed out all the Responsible AI standards and stacked them up, you would cut down countless hectares of the rainforest. And that's ironic, right? And if you think that all that computer power used for AI tools heats up the earth, this would only add fuel to the proverbial fire. Is it us, or is it getting hot in here?

The November 2023 saga over the tenure of OpenAI chief executive officer (CEO) Sam Altman demonstrated a very casual attitude to aspects of corporate governance and the rise of "tech-brotherism" in the AI space. Those worried for humanity's future as automation ran amuck were right to worry. Altman was fired and then rehired in a very public way but over a very private dispute. What was clear was that there was not enough transparency when it came to the odd structure of profit maximizing activities in a not-for-profit corporate shell. OpenAI continued its move to the for-profit model over 2024. Then the company's chief technology officer, Mira Murati, who briefly replaced Altman, quit in September 2024. By December 2024, Open AI had partnered with a military AI company, Anduril. Perception is reality for prior to these theatrics, the general public assumed OpenAI was a fully do-gooder institution, with only the public interest in mind. Questions linger.

While for many years pundits compared countries' advancements on the AI technology front, more recently, they are comparing the differing approaches in the race to AI regulation. National guidelines may be critical to future success of AI but also to the accountability of these society-impacting, even human existence threatening, apocalypse triggering, technologies. There is the Anglo-American approach, emblematic of a *laissez faire* philosophy: The government should step back and allow the private sector to do the work so as not to kill the goose that is laying the golden eggs in the process (and thereby chill technology innovation). After all, one cannot make an omelet without breaking a few eggs. And that was before the advent of the latest incarnation of the Avian Flu that hit the United States in 2024 and 2025. This so-called "wild west" approach is explored in Chapter 5 of this *Short and Happy Guide*.

A second approach emanates from the European Union (EU) and focuses on not breaking any eggs at all. This is fundamentally a "minimize harm first" approach. This approach has resulted in the huge fines that the EU collects periodically from bigtech for violations of data protection and privacy laws. The fines thus collected may be larger than the size of the entire EU technology industry itself (Of course, we are joking, but try naming three leading European AI companies). The EU approach is examined in Chapter 6 of this *Short and Happy Guide* and was the first comprehensive law out of the gate. It matters to be the first mover—even in the area of regulation.

And then there is the Chinese way for AI regulation: This approach features more of a sector-specific focus, and not a meta approach, thereby allowing the Communist Party of China (CPC) to direct in which areas the AI industry should invest and determine which technologies need to be tamped down to reduce and remove any threats to the CPC's own power. China has long directed resources into priority sectors, as the CPC views AI as a resource to be deployed strategically to meet its national industrial goals, while preserving core socialist values. This is unpacked in Chapter 7 of this *Short and Happy Guide*. Chapter 8 unpacks the different national strategies, regulatory guidelines and emergent laws (where applicable) of some other countries in the AI space. Chapter 9 examines the ways in which national and state-level bar associations and law societies, the professional licensing agencies for lawyers, are regulating AI tools in the legal profession.

This Chapter, however, explores the role of ethics and norms in informing and influencing AI governance and regulation practices of private and state actors—from doing nothing, to doing something inside the industry, to doing more than something at the sovereign state (or supranational state level) level. Part II of this Chapter provides a definition of terms and unpacking of concepts that concern the role ethics play in the development and deployment of AI tools. Part III of this Chapter unveils a plethora of other actors, mostly from the corporate world, which exist in the AI Ethics space.

II. Definitions to Frame the Issue of Responsible Artificial Intelligence

All the thousands of Responsible AI principles can be summed up through a few definitions. There are a number of definitions for the major concepts like transparency, fairness, equity, ethics, guidelines versus regulation, regulatory capture, and self-regulation, topics that are covered in this Chapter. They follow hereunder.

A. Ethics

Ethics, extracted from the Greek word *ethos* (character), and the Latin word *mores* (customs), refers to the moral principles that guide one's behavior. These values and standards govern people, aiding them to distinguish right from wrong. Ethics provide a framework for decision making, encompassing principles of equity, integrity, and accountability. Ethics are a crucial component to our day-to-day lives, governing human conduct, including the legal field, emphasizing the importance of moral obligations throughout life. Politicians need not apply.

B. Artificial Intelligence Ethics

AI Ethics represents a critical domain within the broader landscape of technology and morality, working to reconcile the continuous advancements in Artificial Intelligence. Ethics within AI seek to establish a comprehensive framework that balances technological innovation with moral obligations. This work helps ensure that AI systems are operating within the bounds of societal values and human rights. AI Ethics address a multitude of fundamental questions including autonomy, privacy, and fairness.

C. Transparency

The transparency of an AI system denotes its ability to explain its actions and help the human understand its conclusions. Transparency in an AI system can discover potential biases and ensure ethical deployment of AI systems. While it can build trust with its users, some fallbacks to transparency can include being easier to hack, complicated to design, and exposing the algorithms more. Although there can be downfalls to transparency, both transparency and explainability are key features that the Organisation for Economic Co-operation and Development (OECD), examined in Chapter 4, recommends in AI systems globally. Note well: It recommends, not mandates. That is the difference between soft law and real or enforceable law.

D. Fairness

"Fairness" in the context of machine learning encompasses efforts to rectify algorithmic bias within automated decision processes driven by machine learning models. The term is often used when looking at responsible and ethical AI research, development and distribution—the varying stages from creation to use. It can be applied when decisions made by computers, following a machine-learning process, are deemed "unfair" due to their reliance on variables deemed discriminating or delicate matters.

E. Guidelines Versus Regulations

In the realm of AI, the distinction between guidelines and regulations is critical. Guidelines are typically voluntary, non-binding recommendations. These are often called "soft law." These can offer legal frameworks and practices taking into consideration ethical concerns about AI regulations, the latter of which, on the other hand, are legally enforceable or "hard law." Regulations are created by governmental authorities, dictating the parameters which an AI system will use. In the United States, for example, regulations for AI are of growing concern, as other countries around the globe develop and issue stricter policies and laws around AI, compared to those of the United States. Guidelines are often called "Principles" or a "Consensus." During the Biden administration, the White House released its Blueprint for an AI Bill of Rights, also soft law, as we will unpack in Chapter 5 of this *Short and Happy Guide*.

F. Regulatory Capture

Regulatory capture occurs when professionals from private industries or lobbyist groups gain control over regulatory bodies, manipulating the authority to their own standards, advancing their own corporate interests. It is an economic theory that regulatory agencies can be dominated by the wrong people, and not by public interest. In the AI space, regulatory capture would occur if, for example, Sam Altman of OpenAI provided the U.S. Congress with model legislation to pass into law. Not exactly an arm's length, independently minded piece of legislation. The revolving door between leaders of government agencies and the C suites of private sector companies in the defense, biotechnology, border protection, financial technology, or health industries are examples of regulatory capture. But wait, there is a rub: That legislators do not fully understand AI, even just a little, does not bode well, for the education process that is so necessary could, in fact, be provided by industry itself. Looks like a Catch-22, eh?

G. Establishing Oversight

Perhaps the best first step forward is establishing some oversight on the use of AI in criminal justice contexts. This is because, as currently structured, most AI tools are not independently assessed for accuracy and fairness. As such, to ensure these AI tools are being used ethically, they must be reviewed, vetted, and verified. A critical question is: By whom? Setting up things like audit committees and annual impact statements will require AI companies to become critically aware of the way their products are being used and the manner in which those uses are impacting the community as a whole. This step may also create some Washington DC-based jobs—but also some more Beltway traffic jams. Hurray for K Street!

H. Developing Transparency

A major concern with using AI in criminal justice is that the tools are unavailable for scrutiny because they are proprietary materials, or because the AI models are uninterpretable. While there is the potential to create interpretable models, these technological advancements will require some time to materialize. That being the case, our best bet for using AI ethically is to require selective disclosure for the underlying calculations of the AI system itself. In civil cases where proprietary materials must be disclosed, the court will often impose a protective order, prohibiting disclosure of proprietary information outside the purposes of litigation. This same procedure could be easily adapted to a criminal context, thus allowing attorneys and judges to review the risk assessment specific to the case at hand, while also balancing the intellectual property rights of the risk assessment company.

Just when you thought you were not busy enough: There could be an upper division class at law schools which students can take to prepare for such assessments or they could be taught in Evidence or Trial Practice courses going forward.

I. Developing Expert Committees

However, because AI tools are highly technical, to interpret the risk assessment analysis specialized training may be required. To ensure these models are being interpreted accurately, specialized task forces should be developed. Task forces could help educate, interpret, and train criminal attorneys and judges to better understand the risk assessment tools on which they are relying. This could help quiet judicial discomfort in using these tools while also providing attorneys with the resources to understand the outcome of an assessment so they can adequately defend their clients. Judicial discomfort is an odd term. It is more like defendant distress!

J. Removing Proxy Factors

On that note, another significant issue with using AI in criminal justice matters concerns its bias against particular defendants. While the AI itself cannot consciously have bias, these tools often consider a variety of factors that, while they may be tangentially related to the task at hand, are more directly tied to protected categories, like race. In considering these proxy factors, AI assessments are more likely to have a disparate impact on people within certain protected categories. The only way to control for these proxy factors is to remove them altogether. Further, this problem works hand in hand with the transparency requirement: To determine which factors are functioning as proxies for protected categories, AI determinations must be reviewable by judicial officers. Can anyone say "human in the loop" fast enough?

Removing these factors may also help correct for overfitting issues. Overfitting occurs when an AI model performs well on training data sets, but poorly on practical data sets. Most frequently, this occurs when AI models are asked to analyze factors that are tied to other factors, thus causing redundancy and skewing the statistical viability of the model in general. By removing proxy factors, which are more directly tied to a protected class than with, say, criminal risk, the accuracy of these AI models can improve, and their bias can be reduced. As such, the general removal of factors bearing little effect on recidivism could not only help correct for bias, but in doing so, also create more accurate risk assessment tools.

K. Reliability

Reliability within an AI system inherits the qualities of trustworthiness and dependability that are consistently successful in the work they perform. Reliability in an AI system is key. As concerns about AI affecting humankind grow around the world, reliability is not only sought after but required in most AI systems. It is key to eradicating issues such as biases, false positives, and false negatives. Like U.S. President Ronald Reagan once explained with respect to the 1987 Intermediate-Range Nuclear Forces Treaty with the Soviet Union: "Trust, but verify."

In conclusion, there are terms aplenty and often many definitions for each of them. It is not surprising then that the area of Responsible AI or AI Ethics is an incomplete one—leaving the hard work to be done by corporations, some of whom have experience in Corporate Social Responsibility (CSR) already. These days CSR might be called Environment, Social and Governance (ESG) concerns. We call it just good business practice. And who better to lead our debates about AI Ethics than the very corporations doing the designing and dissemination of AI tools?

III. Corporate Actors' Responsible AI Principles and Standards

A. *IBM Fair AI*

IBM has put in place a "centralized and multi-dimensional AI governance framework, centered around the IBM internal AI ethics board." IBM released its Principles for Trust and Transparency in 2018 to guide its policy towards Artificial Intelligence. In 2020, IBM released its view on Precision Regulation of Artificial Intelligence. IBM's policy pillars in its Precision Regulation of AI are (1) accountability; (2) transparency; and (3) fairness and security. Building from those three pillars, IBM created five policies for AI companies to follow: (1) designate a lead AI ethics official; (2) create different rules for different risks; (3) do not hide your AI; (4) explain your AI; and (5) test your AI for bias.

In 2020, IBM signed the Vatican's Rome Call for AI Ethics. IBM also joined the European Commission's High-Level Expert Group on

AI to create ethical guidelines for trustworthy AI in Europe. IBM also released its open-source toolkit, AI Fairness 360, in 2018 sharing codes and datasets for AI bias detection and mitigation. IBM claims that its multi-dimensional and multi-stakeholder plan can address AI bias.

IBM's Principles for Trust and Transparency are (1) the purpose of AI is to augment human intelligence; (2) data and insights belong to their creator; and (3) new technology, including AI systems, must be transparent and explainable. Data and insights include data security, data ownership, cross-border data flows, government access to data, and data privacy. New technologies being transparent and explainable includes finding new data sets to address bias.

B. Microsoft Responsible AI Standards

According to Microsoft CEO Brad Smith's statement on AI responsibility since 2017, "Microsoft has invested in a cross-company program to ensure that [its] AI systems are responsible *by design*." The Aether Committee, formed by researchers, engineers, and policy experts, was launched in 2017 to craft the 2018 AI principles for the company. The first version of the Responsible AI Standard was launched in 2019 by the Office of Responsible AI at Microsoft. The Responsible AI Standard is a framework for actionable guidance to Microsoft engineering teams. In 2022, Microsoft created the second version of the Responsible AI Standard.

In summer 2022, Microsoft built on its research on how the latest AI technology would operate with additional safeguards applied to it. Some risks found by this research were generated content perpetuating stereotypes and AI fabricating incorrect information, Microsoft has collaborated with the United Nations Development Programme and the African Union to develop inclusive AI policies.

Microsoft's AI principles include (1) impact assessment; (2) oversight of significant adverse impacts; (3) fit for purpose; (4) data governance and management; (5) human oversight and control; (6) system intelligibility for decision making; (7) communication to stakeholders; (8) disclosure of AI interaction; (9) quality of service; (10) allocation of resources and opportunities; (11) minimization of stereotyping, demeaning, and erasing outputs; (12) reliability and safety guidance; (13) failures and remediations; (14) ongoing monitoring, feedback, and evaluation; (15) privacy standard compliance; (16) security policy compliance; and (17) accessibility standards compliance.

C. *Google Principles for Responsible AI*

For Gemma models, Google created guidance on setting safety policies, safety tuning, safety classifiers, and model evaluation. To investigate Gemma's behavior and address potential issues, Google created the Learning Interpretability Tool. However, this toolkit is only focused on English text-to-text models. Google has relied on its AI Principles and the Responsible Innovation team to guide principles company-wide since 2018. According to its website, Google has built "resources like Explainable AI, Model Cards, and the TensorFlow open-source toolkit to provide model transparency in a structured, accessible way."

Google has objectives for its principles. These include that they are socially beneficial, that they avoid creating or reinforcing unfair bias, that they be built and tested for safety, that they be accountable to people. Other objectives are that the principles incorporate privacy design principles, that they uphold high standards of scientific excellence, and that they are made available for uses that accord with the Google Principles. According to the company's website, Google is to evaluate uses by examining the primary purpose and use, the nature and uniqueness, the scale, and the nature of Google's involvement.

Google AI applications will not pursue: (1) technologies that are likely to cause overall harm; (2) weapons and technologies whose purpose or implementation is to cause injury to people; (3) technologies that use information for surveillance violating internationally accepted norms; and (4) technologies that violate principles of international law and human rights that are generally accepted, according to the company's website. Since 2018, the AI Principles have focused on four key areas: (1) culture and education; (2) structures and processes; (3) tools, techniques, and infrastructure; (4) external engagement and partnerships.

Google Cloud uses a shared fate model, in which customers can be provided with tools like SynthID for watermarking images generated by Artificial Intelligence. Customers may use the tools and try them to see if they align with their own AI principles or other frameworks for responsible innovation. During 2023, Google doubled its AI Principles reviews (to over 500) focusing on implementing generative AI research models into products, services, and features. Google has also conducted human rights impact assessments and Google users' feedback. Further, Google relies on adversarial testing to build responsible generative AI based on AI Principles reviews conducted in 2023. Google has also created the Google AI Red Team to focus on testing AI models for security, privacy, and abuse risks. Google has used AI itself to help adhere to the Principles by identifying and tracking harmful, fake information, sometimes generated by different Artificial Intelligence.

These corporate behemoths are threading a difficult needle here. On one hand, bigtech wants to continue to research, test, and deploy without any government interference. Their own corporate do-gooding guidelines that promote responsible AI are nice to have, but they may end up being self-serving since these companies are organized around one thing and one thing only—creating shareholder wealth. IBM, Microsoft, Google, Apple, and others in the technology space—companies big and small—are the same to that end. But doing good does not happen unless a company is doing well. Doing these good things—installing Responsible AI practices as part of their respective corporate procedures—is great. Sometimes one does not have to do it alone. Bring in the lobbyists! Ex-legislators and political hacks need a place to do their work too.

D. OpenAI

OpenAI is at the forefront of creating artificial general intelligence (AGI), highly autonomous systems that can outperform humans. With the advent of AGI comes great responsibility. The OpenAI Charter provides that "OpenAI's mission is to ensure that artificial general intelligence. . . benefits all of humanity." The company strives for the benefits of AI to be distributed broadly and is committed to long-term safety, technical leadership, and cooperative orientation. The company operates under a framework focused on safety, transparency, collaboration, and alignment with human values. OpenAI claims to be committed to long-term research aimed at making AI systems that are highly intelligent, but also safe and ethical.

Concerning the first goal, it is perhaps the cornerstone of OpenAI's platform: broadly distributed benefits. OpenAI's website writes: "We believe in AI's potential to make life better for everyone, which means making it safe for everyone." Although it was founded with a not-for-profit structure, it now operates as a capped-profit hybrid. OpenAI emphasizes its ethical foresight in the ways AI is deployed and scaled on the company's website. The company states, "safety doesn't stop," and explains they are constantly reevaluating, trying to anticipate, and mitigate risks through "teaching, testing, and sharing."

Moreover, OpenAI has built internal governance structures specifically to address AI risk. The company formed a Safety Advisory Group to test and break AI systems before public release. The Advisory Group is intended to identify potential misuse cases, systemic biases, and safety vulnerabilities. Zico Kolter is tasked with chairing the independent committee, but he also serves on OpenAI's Board of Directors. OpenAI claims to have a commitment to ethical AI development, but the company has been the defendant in much litigation over copyright infringement, a most notable case with the New York Times as the Plaintiff. It is no secret that in Silicon Valley, companies focus on obtaining maximum data but in the interim, they are losing some of their earlier ethical considerations such as fairness and transparency.

Finally, OpenAI CEO Sam Altman himself has offered a novel take on AI Ethics. Altman suggests the AI itself could collect the consensus from billions of users on their approaches to AI governance and systematically apply this to their business model. Altman stated in a Harvard Business interview, "The people impacted by technology the most deserve the loudest say in its governance." Currently, OpenAI's core principles on AI ethics remain the same. To OpenAI, these include ethical AI development, transparency and openness, collaboration and partnership, AI safety and risk management, access and equity, and regulatory engagement.

E. Meta

During its Connect 2024 conference, Meta detailed its responsible approach to Generative AI, emphasizing the importance of safety, fairness, and transparency in AI development. The company introduced Llama 3.2, a collection of models designed to enhance vision capabilities on edge devices and noted its commitment to prioritizing responsible deployment of these advancements. According to Meta's website: "We'll continue to have these important conversations and take a collaborative approach to help ensure that we're innovating responsibly and delivering AI experiences that work well for everyone." This statement aligns with Meta's broader strategy to develop AI technologies that are both innovative and ethically grounded.

The company outlines five guiding principles for Responsible AI: privacy and security, fairness and inclusion, robustness and safety, transparency and control, and accountability. These principles are created to inform the full lifecycle of AI, from development to deployment. Meta claims commitment to mitigating algorithmic bias and ensuring that AI technologies are tested against real-world harms, particularly those that could affect marginalized or underrepresented groups.

Despite these lofty principles, in 2023 Meta disbanded its Responsible AI team. Amidst layoffs and team redistributions, most employees in the Responsible AI division were moved to Generative AI or AI Infrastructure teams. Additionally, Meta does not always try to follow the AI regulations in each country in which it operates. As an example, despite the passage of the EU AI Act in 2024, a huge piece of supranational legislation with specific transparency requirements for AI systems, "Meta unsurprisingly limited these AI profiles to the United States only." The referenced AI profiles have been seen on various Meta platforms and "raise serious ethical questions about how they interact with humans who, in the future, may not realize what they're talking to." Some critics maintain that Meta has blurred the boundaries of responsible AI use by failing to make its AI bots clearly identifiable, leading some real users to mistakenly believe they are interacting with actual humans.

F. Anthropic

Anthropic was founded in 2021 by former researchers at OpenAI, including siblings Dario and Daniela Amodei. The company is creating an AI platform "aligned" with human values. The company believes that its approach to AI alignment is safer and more responsible than that of other companies developing advanced AI systems. Firstly, the company is investing in "mechanistic interpretability" research—an effort to develop tools that function like brain scans for AI systems. The goal is to understand what is truly happening inside these models, rather than relying solely on their text-based outputs, which can obscure their actual internal processes. Secondly, Anthropic has created its very own Constitutional AI, described as allowing, ". . .developers to explicitly specify the values their systems should adhere to, via the creation of a "constitution," separating the question of whether an AI can do something from the more politically fraught question of whether it should."

Moreover, Anthropic claims the Constitutional AI offers a solution by assigning language models explicit values based on a defined constitution, rather than relying on implicit values shaped through large-scale human feedback. While not without limitations, the company explains this method makes the AI's guiding principles more transparent and easier to modify when necessary. Anthropic's current AI Constitution is built from a diverse range of sources, including the 1948 Universal Declaration of Human Rights, industry trust and safety best practices, and ethical frameworks such as DeepMind's Sparrow Principles. It also incorporates efforts to reflect non-Western perspectives and insights from Anthropic's own early research into effective AI behavior. The company acknowledges that the constitution reflects its designers' values and choices, and it has expressed a commitment to expanding participation in future iterations of the constitution to ensure broader and more inclusive input.

Despite Anthropic's strong ethical commitments, Anthropic encounters challenges typical of companies in the AI sector. Securing substantial funding has required significant investments from major technology firms such as Amazon and Google, prompting concerns about the potential influence of profit-driven interests. Furthermore, like many Generative AI companies, Anthropic has faced some legal scrutiny regarding allegations of unauthorized use of copyrighted materials in the training of its AI models. Anthropic has consistently positioned itself as a "safety-first" AI company, with its leadership emphasizing the importance of addressing catastrophic and existential risks posed by advanced AI systems. Dario Amodei has publicly underscored these concerns, including in testimony before the U.S. Senate, where he warned that AI models capable of causing large-scale destruction and destabilizing global power structures could emerge as soon as 2025. Despite these challenges, Anthropic continues to advocate for Responsible AI development, positioning safety and long-term risk mitigation as central to its corporate mission.

G. Apple

In July 2024 Apple, along with many other major tech companies including but not limited to, Amazon, Google, Anthropic, Meta, OpenAI, and Microsoft, signed on to the Biden Administration's voluntary AI guidelines from October 2023. As the federal government under President Joseph R. Biden pushed for stronger oversight and accountability in AI development, several leading corporations began to formalize their ethical commitments in response. Executive Order 14110 had served to encourage companies to voluntarily adopt safety measures, address algorithmic bias, and promote transparency in AI systems. Each company takes a distinct but hopefully meaningful step to align with U.S. federal efforts to ensure trustworthy and Responsible AI deployment.

Apple fosters a deeply rooted commitment to user privacy and responsible innovation. With the introduction of Apple Intelligence, the company emphasizes on-device processing to ensure that personal data remains under the user's control. When tasks require more computational power, Apple utilizes its Private Cloud Compute system, which processes data on Apple silicon-based servers without storing or granting Apple access to the information.

To further its ethical AI development, Apple has established a set of Responsible AI principles guiding the creation and deployment of its AI tools and models. In alignment with Executive Order 14110, Apple has committed to voluntary AI safety guidelines, including implementing safety protocols, testing for biases and security risks, and sharing results with the government. This comprehensive strategy underscores Apple's dedication to developing AI technologies that are both innovative and aligned with societal values. But this may change during the second Trump administration.

H. Walmart

Walmart has attempted to align with the principles laid out in Executive Order 14110 during the Biden administration in October 2023, by releasing its Responsible AI Pledge, centered around six core commitments of transparency, security, privacy, fairness, accountability, and customer-centricity.

Designed to guide the company's use of AI across operations, from supply chain logistics to customer interactions, Walmart is working to ensure that innovation does not come at the expense of ethical standards. A cross-functional group of lawyers, policy experts, compliance officers, and technologists is responsible for evaluating AI and machine learning tools, monitoring for potential bias, and developing governance frameworks that reflect Walmart's broader corporate values. The team also oversees how AI is deployed in contexts that impact workers' rights and customer privacy, helping ensure that the company's digital transformation is both innovative and responsible. Walmart's approach demonstrates a proactive stance from a huge corporate player trying to align with the former federal policy and signals a broader commitment to building public trust in AI technologies.

I. Adobe

Adobe has positioned itself at the forefront of ethical AI development, emphasizing transparency, accountability, and the protection of creative rights. A cornerstone of Adobe's commitment is the Content Authenticity Initiative (CAI), created in 2019 with *The New York Times* and Twitter (now X). The CAI combats misinformation by forming tools that verify the origin and history of digital content. Central to this initiative are content credentials, which act as a "nutrition label" for digital media, detailing information such as the creator's identity, creation date, and any edits made.

In line with its ethical standards, Adobe's Generative AI model, Adobe Firefly, is trained exclusively on content that Adobe has the rights to use, from licensed materials to public domain content. This approach ensures that the AI does not infringe upon creators' rights or intellectual property laws. Furthermore, the "nutrition labels" have been used in creative tools, such as Photoshop and Lightroom, allowing creators to embed provenance information directly into their work. This is important stuff.

J. NVIDIA

NVIDIA, a leader in AI hardware and software, has articulated a clear vision for Trustworthy AI, focusing on safety, transparency, and ethical responsibility. The company emphasizes that AI systems should be developed with considerations for privacy, security, and fairness, ensuring it operates without unintended bias and are transparent about its capabilities and limitations.

To make this work, NVIDIA has implemented tools like NeMo Guardrails, designed to ensure that AI applications behave as intended, particularly in sensitive domains such as healthcare and finance. These help in monitoring AI outputs, preventing the generation of harmful or biased content, and maintaining user trust. Additionally, NVIDIA actively participates in policy discussions and collaborates with industry partners to shape regulations that promote ethical AI development. Through these efforts, NVIDIA aims to set a standard for responsible AI practices in the tech industry.

K. Midjourney

Midjourney, an independent research lab that specializes in AI-generated images, has implemented community guidelines to promote ethical use of its platform. While Midjourney does not have a formal set of AI principles like Adobe or NVIDIA, it enforces ethical guidelines through its Community Guidelines and Terms of Service. These guidelines prohibit the creation of content that is disrespectful, aggressive, or abusive, including imagery that could harass or defame individuals. In response to concerns about misinformation, especially during sensitive periods such as elections, Midjourney has considered restricting the generation of political images involving prominent figures. The platform has also faced criticism for potential biases in its outputs and for training its models on copyrighted artworks without explicit consent from artists, leading to ongoing legal discussions as it has with many other AI platforms.

Midjourney's content moderation system works to address these challenges. Initially relying on a banned word system, the platform transitioned to an AI-powered moderation mechanism in May 2023. This advanced system allows for a more nuanced interpretation of user prompts by analyzing them in their entirety, facilitating context-dependent moderation. Despite these efforts, Midjourney has been roundly criticized for the company's handling of AI-generated deepfakes and misinformation.

IV. Enter the Lobbyists

It is no surprise that bigtech has lobbyists in Washington, DC, as it does in Brussels, London, and Tokyo. These lobbyists, many former staffers in the Legislative Branch or former politicians work, often on behalf of bigtech, to soften any regulation that legislators are considering. That means actually getting to the drafters of legislation on AI before they even craft the language to make their cases.

V. Summary/Key Points

1. AI systems have wide-ranging social, economic, political, and legal impacts and cannot be developed in isolation by technologists alone. The surrounding context matters as much as the code. Cross-disciplinary engagement is needed.
2. The term "AI Ethics" is best understood as a societal process of arriving at the kind of AI systems we want to have in our midst. It's an ongoing conversation amongst public and private sectors, academia and law enforcement
3. Debates around AI Ethics are the mechanism by which multiple non-technical stakeholders get involved in the process of

writing the rules for Artificial Intelligence. Civil society and the public use these debates to challenge the pace, scope, and goals of AI development.

4. Corporate behavior is strategic, not sentimental. We have to watch out for the corporate maneuvering in response to shareholder demands, governmental dictates and international competition (DeepSeek anyone?).
   a. AI Ethics washing and Regulatory Capture by commercial players are a concern.
   b. Spot the virtue signaling by activists.
   c. Beware of the playing to the gallery and/or performative politics (nb. U.S. Congressional hearings and signing statements, and preambles in EU legislation).
   d. Enjoy the vacuum filled by still-getting-up-to-speed judiciary and mixing-things-up media.
   e. Let us not fall into the trap of mixing up AI risks and remedies. Sometimes the cure is worse than the pain.
   f. Distinguish clear and present short term harms (discriminatory outcomes, marginalization, job losses, political polarization) and uncertain long term worries (mass unemployment, systemic instability, geopolitical disruption).
   g. Separate what is real and what is hypothetical.
5. There are a plethora of salon debates coming to a meet up space near you. Topics *du jour* include singularity, conscient AI, the inevitable robot apocalypse (the latter being fun to discuss but not helpful in the end). It is BYOP (Bring your own popcorn) time.

6. Understand how "bias" enters the AI system: Via design choices, via training data, via insufficient testing, via lack of training of human operators, and via know-it-all, smug tech bros who refuse to consider the human dimension (read, fallout) of their work, investments, and professional fetishes
7. Guiding principles and industry standards are not legally binding but help inform regulatory efforts. They are often the tools of self-interested technology companies They are tools of influence, not instruments of accountability.
8. Adoption of any technology is dependent on it being trusted by humans. Following Responsible AI principles and methods is a good way to earn this trust. And corporations have declared undying love for Responsible AI. Everyone loves Responsible AI. Few want to be held responsible.

CHAPTER 4

International Bodies and Agencies

I. International Organizations

One of the most robust cottage industries to come out of the exponential growth of Artificial Intelligence (AI) tools has been the development and dissemination of Responsible AI initiatives from international institutions. All the kids are doing it.

We have often written and said aloud that there are two races going on—the first relates to the design, rollout, and use of AI tools in the marketplace and the second concerns the regulation over those AI tools themselves. This *Short and Happy Guide* is all about the latter race—the race for AI governance and regulation. And this Chapter is dedicated to exploring the plethora of international institutions' Responsible AI initiatives.

Some well-known Responsible AI initiatives include those emanating out of the Organisation for Economic Cooperation and Development (OECD), the World Economic Forum (WEF), the Global Partnership on Artificial Intelligence (GPAI), the Institute of Electric and Electronic Engineers (IEEE), the United Nations (U.N.) Education,

Science and Cultural Organization (UNESCO), and the Group of Seven (G7) Hiroshima Artificial Intelligence Process (Hiroshima Process).

A. *The Organisation for Economic Cooperation and Development*

The OECD is an international organization, headquartered in Paris, that aims to "build better policies for better lives." It is a leading multilateral institution dedicated to the development of policies and the setting of international standards that bring prosperity, equality, opportunity, and well-being for all members of society in all countries. This international agency is responsible for the Guidelines on Multinational Enterprises on Responsible Business Conduct (its most recent iteration was in 2023) which is a set of recommendations concerning sustainability for countries to have transnational corporations operating within their jurisdictions to abide by. The idea is to mitigate harm to people, to society, and to Mother Earth. The key word is "recommendations." These are voluntary, nice to haves, not enforceable treaty commitments requiring signatory countries to legislate into their respective domestic laws.

This "rich country club" (since most of its members are developed countries) has turned its sights on AI for another set of principles that do not have the force of law. The OECD, on its "Artificial Intelligence" webpage, has expressed that,

> [t]he OECD supports governments by measuring and analyzing the economic and social impacts of AI technologies and applications, and engaging with all stakeholders to identify good practices for public policy.

In keeping with this mission, the OECD announced a set of five AI principles in May 2019. The OECD AI Principles include inclusive growth, sustainable development and well-being; human-centered values and fairness; transparency and explainability; robustness, security and safety; and accountability. The OECD AI Principles also provide recommendations for policy makers. These standards include investing in AI research and development; fostering a digital ecosystem for AI; providing an enabling policy environment for AI; building human capacity and preparing for labor market transition; and international cooperation for trustworthy Artificial Intelligence.

The OECD AI Principles are aimed at bettering society and should be reviewed as a whole. The first principle is focused on inclusive growth, sustainable development, and well-being. For the OECD, stakeholders should proactively engage in trustworthy AI to pursue beneficial outcomes for people. This means the inclusion of underrepresented populations. Additionally, stakeholders should work to reduce economic, social, gender, and other inequalities.

The second principle is human-centered values and fairness. The OECD hopes that AI actors respect the rule of law, human rights, and democratic values. These rights include freedom, dignity and autonomy, privacy and data protection, non-discrimination and equality, and many more. Finally, AI actors should implement mechanisms and safeguards to preserve human rights and determination. The third principle is transparency and explainability. This includes a commitment to transparency and responsible disclosure regarding AI systems, which includes educating citizens about AI and the impact of Artificial Intelligence.

The next principle revolves around robustness, security, and safety. This includes making AI safe and traceable. The last principle concerns accountability. AI actors should be accountable for the proper functioning of AI systems and respect the above principles. The OECD has set up a robust plan for AI governance and hopes to promote the use of safe Artificial Intelligence.

The OECD continued its thought leadership work, coordinating AI governance ideas and promoting intergovernmental efforts to work together to support the development of AI for all. The resulting

OECD's Global Partnership on AI and its AI Policy Observatory and Network of Experts on AI in 2020. In its Coordinated Plan on Artificial Intelligence 2021 Review, the OECD recognized the importance of AI and how it will continue to affect government and citizens.

This is all fine and good, but without an international treaty, like the OECD's Convention on Combating Bribery of Foreign Public Officials in International Business Transactions, there are no meaningful, and most importantly, enforceable treaty provisions to be implemented into the domestic laws of each OECD Member. As we have unpacked throughout this *Short and Happy Guide*, norms, guidelines and standards are good, but laws that can be enforced are even better. Norms, rules, and institutions, good. Blah blah blah, toothless, unenforceable guidelines, performative communiqués at the end of summits, bad.

B. World Economic Forum

Ah, the motherlode of talk shops. The WEF, held annually in Davos, Switzerland in January, is, according to JP Morgan Chase chief executive officer (CEO) Jamie Dimon, "is where billionaires tell millionaires what the middle class feels."

In 2019, the WEF announced its creation of its Global AI Council, designed to build the bridge of cooperation between countries over potential technologies, including Artificial Intelligence. The foundation of the WEF's AI efforts is the emphasis on ethical principles as a critical guide for AI development. Recognizing the potential risks associated with AI, the WEF advocates for integrating ethical frameworks to guide its development and application. These principles are designed to ensure that AI technologies are developed and deployed to uphold human dignity, equity, and societal well-being, highlighting the importance of foresight and responsibility in the era of rapid technological advancement.

In response to the evolving landscape of AI technologies, particularly Generative AI, the WEF launched the AI Governance Alliance in 2023. This initiative focuses on three main areas: developing safe systems and technologies, promoting sustainable applications and transformation, and establishing resilient governance and regulatory frameworks. The Alliance serves as a platform for stakeholder collaboration, aiming to foster a unified approach to navigating the complexities of Generative AI and ensuring its alignment with ethical and equitable standards.

The WEF has also introduced its own blueprint, this one for equitable and inclusive AI, addressing the systemic challenges of bias, discrimination, and access within AI technologies. This blueprint offers a structured approach to embedding equity and inclusion across the AI technical lifecycle, from design and development to deployment and governance. It serves as a critical resource for organizations and policymakers, providing actionable guidance to ensure that AI technologies are accessible, fair, and beneficial to all segments of society.

Furthermore, the AI Governance Alliance Briefing Paper Series represents an essential resource for AI development and implementation stakeholders. These briefing papers offer insights into best practices for responsible AI transformation, covering various topics from ethical considerations to governance strategies. The series aims to equip stakeholders with the knowledge and tools to navigate AI's moral, social, and technical challenges, fostering a landscape in which AI is a force for positive change.

In the newest installment, published in January 2024, the WEF's AI Governance Alliance proposed the Presidio AI Framework. Whoo hoo! More frameworks! This framework emphasizes shared accountability, early identification, and proactive management of risks in Generative AI development. It advocates for ethical deployment through predefined guardrails. The AI Governance

Alliance and the Safe Systems and Technologies group promote better communication among industry players, policymakers, and organizations to foster trust in AI technologies. The Alliance also focuses on discovering new AI safety mechanisms, like advanced technical guardrails, and will develop a checklist to help assess risks and guardrails throughout the Generative AI lifecycle. Clearly, the world needs saving from AI, and some would say from the WEF too!

C. The Global Partnership on Artificial Intelligence

An international and multiple stakeholder initiative, the Global Partnership on Artificial Intelligence (GPAI) guides the responsible development and use of AI so that it aligns with and principles of human rights, inclusion and diversity, while still promoting innovation and economic growth. With experts from the worlds of academia, civil society, government, and industry, the GPAI fosters collaboration on cutting-edge research and projects across various areas of Artificial Intelligence. This group does really good work and provides necessary thought leadership in the AI governance space.

Launched in June 2020, the GPAI seeks to bridge the gap between theory and practice on AI by supporting cutting-edge research and applied activities in AI-related priorities. Its work is centered around four key themes: Responsible AI, Data Governance, the Future of Work, and Innovation and Commercialization. The Partnership acts as a global point of reference for understanding and sharing best practices in AI, allowing members to collaborate and develop policy frameworks and ethical guidelines for Artificial Intelligence.

One of the GPAI's significant contributions is fostering a better understanding of the challenges and opportunities presented by AI across different sectors and societies. By promoting a human-centric approach to AI, the GPAI emphasizes the importance of AI technologies that respect human rights and democratic values. This initiative demonstrates a growing international commitment to ensure that AI development and deployment are aligned with ethical standards and contribute positively to humanity.

The GPAI comprises 29 member countries. Look them up or collect them all for the whole set. The GPAI is yet another multilateral organization looking to play a role in governance of AI systems' development and deployment, among many. Slow and steady wins the day.

D. The Institute of Electrical and Electronic Engineers' Ethically Aligned Design for Intelligent and Autonomous Systems

The IEEE is the world's largest professional body for engineers. The IEEE's Ethically Aligned Design, created by a multidisciplinary group of experts from industry and academia from across the globe (including one of your co-authors) was intended to further the public's understanding dealing with ethical considerations in the design of autonomous and intelligent systems. Indeed, the IEEE Global Initiative's mission is "to ensure every stakeholder involved in the design and development of autonomous and intelligent systems is educated, trained, and empowered to prioritize ethical considerations so that these technologies are advanced for the benefit of humanity."

Combining aspirational and practical goals, the analyses and recommendations emerging from this report provide "guidance for consideration by governments, businesses, and the public at large in the advancement of technology for the benefit of humanity." Out of these principles came many practical solutions and guidance as a move from theory to practice, particularly for implementation by organizations. Not bad for a volunteer effort!

E. The United Nations Educational, Scientific and Cultural Organization

In 2021, UNESCO adopted its own international global standard called the Recommendation on the Ethics of AI—spearheading its implementation by the Member States through innovative tools and methodologies, like the Assessments listed hereunder.

UNESCO hopes to set a strong ethical foundation for the development of science and technology. Through topics such as scientific research, genetic research, and climate change, UNESCO has brought positive impacts. With the rise of AI, there can be many great opportunities such as human connectivity from social media, medical advancements, and labor efficiencies. But of course, there are also many ethical and moral concerns, and these are even more daunting because this is a U.N. agency. UNESCO strives to prevent some of these, such as biases in AI, climate degradation, and human rights concerns. UNESCO explains that there is no other area right now that requires an "ethical compass" like Artificial Intelligence. The Ethics of AI has been adopted by all 193 Member States of the Organization.

The Ethics of AI is centered around four core values: human rights, living peacefully, diversity and inclusion, and the environment. Building upon this, there are ten human-rights specific principles in the Recommendation. These include Proportionality and Do No Harm; Safety and Security; Right to Privacy and Data Protection; Multi-stakeholder and Adaptive Governance and Collaboration; Responsibility and Accountability; Transparency and Explainability; Human Oversight and Determination; Sustainability; Awareness and Literacy; and Fairness and Non-Discrimination. UNESCO has created two options for implementation of the recommendation, including Readiness Assessment Methodology (RAM), and Ethical Impact Assessment (EIA). The RAM works to guide member countries into effective implementation. By identifying their "status of preparedness" for the program, UNESCO will then give the member country custom support. The EIA revolves around helping AI project teams, recognizing where AI may have harmful and negative effects and providing guidance to them.

UNESCO has also created platforms such as Women4EthicalAI, as a "collaborative platform" to make sure women are properly represented in both the development and deployment of Artificial Intelligence. The Business Council for Ethics of AI is a combined effort between Latin American countries and UNESCO, working towards the formation of ethical standards in their respective AI communities. UNESCO's Ethics of AI is working to alter the landscape of the development and development of AI, and work towards a better future for all. AI is truly a scientific and cultural achievement of humanity. UNESCO's involvement proves it. Just ask ChatGPT.

The U.N. *writ large* would indeed like to put its imprimatur on this space. We'll have our people get back to you.

F. The Group of Seven Hiroshima Artificial Intelligence Process

The G7 met in May 2023 in Hiroshima, Japan. Its membership includes Canada, France, Germany, Italy, Japan, the United Kingdom (U.K.), and the United States. The group (which used to include Russia when it was the G8) has met regularly since the mid-1980s with finance ministers and central bank governors joining together. One of the recent meeting's purposes was to discuss Generative AI immersive technologies, and the need for international governance over such fields. With the hope of releasing reported results by the end of 2023, the leaders promised to have their ministers discuss the technologies. They dubbed the topic the "Hiroshima AI Process."

First the group had to recognize and accept two opposing paradigms that have been a fixture in modern society's development throughout the information age. As a positive, the G7 acknowledged that generally, rapid technological change strengthens societies and economies in many ways for nearly all people. However, on the negative side, some latency indeed exists in another area. Moving at a slower pace are all forms of the technologies' governance and regulation. Furthermore, the group acknowledged that governance's importance and challenges may increase at the same rate as technological evolution's accelerated pace. Because of the accelerated pace, the group also highlighted the importance in immediately identifying gaps and fragments in any governance plans already existing or initiated.

For tangible technological examples, the group specifically enumerated (1) the metaverse and (2) quantum information science and technology. The group used these specific examples to illustrate the need for technology to advance in accordance with G7 countries' democratic values. Such values "include fairness, accountability, transparency, safety, protection from online harassment, hate and abuse and respect for privacy and human rights, fundamental freedoms and the protection of personal data." In general terms, the G7 believes that the way to keep these values embedded in advancement is to simply prioritize responsible technological innovation and design. To narrow the operational scope of "responsible" in this context, the group again used examples.

Stakeholders' transparency regarding AI development is a necessary ingredient to internet governance. The group recognized that it may need to craft new procedures to "advance transparency, openness, fair processes, impartiality, privacy and inclusiveness to promote responsible AI." The Members have understood that to achieve transparency and trustworthiness, communication lines between members must remain open. Lines must remain open notwithstanding sometimes vast differences between member countries' culture and values. The communication needed likely involves international stakeholders forming organizations between each other, and developing AI technology standards among themselves. In organizing, stakeholders can evaluate "opportunities and challenges of generative AI . . . and encourage international organizations . . . to consider analysis on the impact of policy developments and Global Partnership on AI to conduct practical projects."

Overall, the Hiroshima AI Process evolved into the combination of all G7 Members, their associated ministers, and the above-outlined goals and procedures. The G7 ended the discussion about AI by stating that countries must create solutions to governance, public safety, and human rights, at a global level. Global focus is a priority because immersive technologies, such as the metaverse, spawn sustainability and innovation "in all industrial and societal sectors." In citing one final example of a globally ubiquitous sector exemplifying AI-incorporated innovation, the group referenced the sector entitled digital trade.

G. Other International Treaties

There are a number of treaties and international institutions that have attempted to engage in the Responsible AI space.

II. Regional Organizations

A. The Council of Europe

As an example, in September 2024, the Council of Europe opened its new treaty—the Framework Convention on AI and Human Rights, Democracy, and the Rule of Law—for signature. This international convention addresses

> specific challenges which arise throughout the lifecycle of artificial intelligence systems and encourage[s] the consideration of the wider risks and impacts related to these technologies including, but not limited to, human health and the environment, and socio-economic aspects, such as employment and labour.

The different provisions of this treaty are designed to ensure that AI system life cycles are fully consistent with human rights, democracy, and the rule of law.

B. The European Union

Please see Chapter 6 in this *Short and Happy Guide*.

C. The African Union

The African Union's emphasis on ethical guidelines and standards involves the creation of a comprehensive ethical framework that addresses concerns around bias, discrimination, and fairness in AI systems. The guidelines would likely include mechanisms for accountability, ensuring that AI developers and users are responsible for the outcomes of their systems. Transparency is another factor, requiring AI systems to be understandable and their decisions explainable to users. Privacy protections would be integral, with strict controls on how AI systems access, use, and store personal data, ensuring compliance with data protection laws and respect for user consent.

Research and innovation support focuses on establishing a fertile ground for AI advancements. This might include significant investments in AI research, the establishment of dedicated AI research centers or hubs, and the promotion of public-private partnerships to drive innovation. The aim would be to not only advance the state of AI technology but also to solve local and regional challenges through AI-driven solutions. Policies could provide funding opportunities for startups and established companies alike, fostering an ecosystem where AI can thrive. Additionally, cross-border collaborations within the continent and with international research institutions could accelerate the pace of innovation and adoption of AI technologies.

For education and skills development, the strategy would likely prioritize integrating AI and digital literacy into the curriculum at all levels of education, from primary schools to universities. Specialized training programs could be developed to equip current and future workers with the skills necessary to thrive in an AI-enhanced economy. This may involve partnerships with tech companies and educational institutions to offer workshops, online courses, and certification programs. The goal is to create a workforce that is not only proficient in using AI tools but also capable of developing and innovating new AI technologies.

Data governance and privacy policies are anticipated to set the standards for how data is collected, stored, used, and shared in the context of Artificial Intelligence. These regulations would aim to protect individuals' privacy rights while enabling the responsible use of data for AI development. Frameworks might include requirements for data anonymization, consent mechanisms for data collection, and clear guidelines on data sharing both within and outside the continent. Such policies would also address the cross-border flow of data, ensuring that African data is protected according to international standards.

Addressing the economic and social impact of AI involves developing policies that harness AI's potential for economic growth, such as through job creation in emerging tech sectors, while mitigating adverse effects like unemployment due to automation. Strategies could include supporting sectors most likely to benefit from AI, such as agriculture, healthcare, and finance, and implementing social protection measures for affected workers.

Encouraging the development of AI applications that address specific social challenges, such as access to education and healthcare, could also be a key focus.

Finally, international collaboration forms an essential part of the AU's AI strategy, emphasizing the importance of engaging with global bodies and aligning the continent's AI advancements with international standards and practices.

D. *The Organization of American States*

The Organization of American States (OAS) has been busy trying to place a Pan-American flag in the Responsible AI space, lest the Western Hemisphere (save the United States (U.S.)) be an afterthought in the regulation race. In 2023 and 2024, the Inter-American Guidelines on Data Governance and AI were developed with a human rights-centric approach. The Guidelines had as its primary organizing principle "that initiatives and actions related to data and artificial intelligence governance adhere to the principles outlined in the Inter-American human rights framework."

In November 2024, several countries around the Americas and the Caribbean signed the Santiago Declaration to Promote Ethical Artificial Intelligence in Latin America and the Caribbean, a document that demonstrated the Western Hemisphere's commitment to responsible AI governance, collaboration at the multisectoral level, and a regional approach. It built on the Digital Agenda for Latin America and the Caribbean and the OAS General Assembly's Resolution 3029 of 2024 ("Strengthening Democracy") which states in Chapter VII ("Open, Digital, Inclusive and Transparent Government") section 3 that the OAS:

> [e]ncourage member states to maintain or adopt, following a multistakeholder approach, as appropriate, and implement, national strategies to promote the safe, secure and trustworthy development and use, AI

technologies in a manner that respects human rights and is consistent with inter-American human rights instruments the UNESCO Recommendation on the Ethics of Artificial Intelligence and other relevant instruments.

This working document, which is subject to change, is still in the public consultation process, but at least the Americas got into the AI virtue signaling contest. A meaningful international treaty should one day be negotiated and ratified under the auspices of the OAS, but we still have to hold our collective breath.

III. On a New International Agency for Regulating AI

In this Chapter, we have explored the attempts by international agencies, such as the WEF and OECD, to regulate AI tools. But what about a completely new international agency? On May 16, 2023, neuroscientist Gary Marcus, OpenAI CEO Sam Altman, and IBM Chief Privacy Trust Officer Christina Montgomery, testified before the U.S. Senate Judiciary Committee. Contrary to most CEOs who hope that Congress avoids them, Altman had been publicly requesting that Congress regulate his company's work (He changed his tune in a May 2025 appearance before Congress). Marcus has predominantly been an academic his entire career, but he has gained recent notoriety speaking out about the need to regulate new AI technologies. During the hearing, U.S. Senator from Missouri Josh Hawley called Generative AI "one of the most significant technological innovations in human history," and U.S. Senator from Louisiana John Kennedy offered to let Altman pick his own regulators. How nice of him.

Professor Marcus highlighted a few threats to democracy that the language models can pose, such as "misinformation that is deliberately produced by bad actors, from accidental misinformation—like the law professor who was accused of sexual harassment even though he did not commit it—[to the ability to] subtly shape people's political beliefs based on training data that the public doesn't even know anything about."

Professor Marcus then criticized premature open-sourcing of Meta's Large Language Model because the company released it to the public before any legal infrastructure or regulation was in place. In giving examples of what should have first been in place, he specified cost benefit analyses, trials, and only a release if benefits outweigh costs. He stated that there are over 100,000 computer scientists in the U.S. and Canada who could help audit and evaluate such products before they are released to the public. Professor Marcus advocated for a neutral, global, nonprofit AI agency to accomplish these goals. Not surprisingly, some of the Senators who were there looked at him skeptically.

And then there is the United Nations. In summer 2023, António Guterres, U.N. Secretary General, offered to the international community a new U.N. agency dedicated to Artificial Intelligence. When we think of the U.N. we always think of efficiency, fairness, and technological prowess right?

At the WEF in January 2025, the U.N. Secretary General Guterres again showed his appetite for more work for his beleaguered international organization to do the regulating of AI tools. He explained: "Yes, AI holds untold promise for humanity. . .But with this promise comes profound risk, especially if AI is left ungoverned." Novel. Insightful. Poignant. It's got a great beat and you can dance to it. We give this trite analysis a 9 out of 10 for non-originality. Antonio should work on what is on the United Nations' plate now rather than load up more responsibilities.

* * * *

At one time, OpenAI CEO Sam Altman suggested a potential transnational regulator along the lines of the International Atomic

Energy Agency. New York University Professor Emeritus Gary Marcus, too, has proffered ideas about transnational regulation. Rishi Sunak, while Prime Minister of the United Kingdom (U.K.) wanted a London-based watchdog for monitoring AI risks. Clearly, there is not much self-interest going on here.

In reality, AI remains difficult to monitor and even more tricky to control. The first area that regulators need to consider concerns national security. Meanwhile, AI-powered drones are turning the business model of the military industrial complex upside down with asymmetric warfare techniques. Cheap thousand-dollar drones are damaging multimillion dollar missiles and skirmishing out large naval carriers. Governments are not receptive to rules that limit their military preparedness. For instance, the U.S. Blueprint for an AI Bill of Rights suggested guardrails but excluded military uses of Artificial Intelligence. There are similar national security exceptions aplenty in AI regulations globally. Each country is going to want the same latitude for action. What if a country like China, a technology behemoth that has its own local tech ecosystem, does not want to be part of any AI non-proliferation treaty? If competing sovereign States do not join, then other countries also would hesitate to join because of their national security interests. This idea of transnational regulation may be good on paper, but is it practically feasible? And whose rules will be the ones that reign supreme?

Other ideas mooted include the creation of a new agency solely for Artificial Intelligence. The German word *verschlimmbessern* comes to mind: Making something worse while intending to make it better (like The Eagles going on tour again). It is no secret that governments are not known for their technology chops. Specialist regulators with expert knowledge of AI are welcome but will more regulation and bureaucracy really fix things? Moreover, sovereign states have not been too successful in protecting our privacy rights on the Internet already, can we trust them with effective governance of Artificial Intelligence?

The way forward is not so easy to divine, even at a national level. While making all the right noises, regulatory efforts so far have been meandering at best. AI is not one technology, but a whole lot of tools and technologies, many with applications and impacts that are varied in nature. When we talk about regulating AI, every sector and sphere of economic activity could be affected. A regulatory one size fits all solution is likely not to work. Instead, nuanced and contextual rules, decentralized and adapted regulation, rather than centralized or omnibus regulation might prove functional and obtain better results. Examining current sector-specific regulation and identifying gaps is a good approach, one undertaken by the U.S. government. This approach, incremental in nature, builds on best practices accumulated over the years, allowing for tinkering along the way and for unexpected challenges to be overcome.

An important point on international approaches: The geopolitical nature of the AI race does not lend itself to cooperation, not in a world of expanded tariffs, trade embargoes, and highly competitive national industrial policies. Tech nationalism is a growth industry. It may be best to not wait for a Kumbaya moment, not when DeepSeek, OpenAI, and others are in a deathmatch for the future of Artificial Intelligence. Note well that we do not list any European companies here. Maybe U.S. Vice-President JD Vance was right in February 2025 at the Munich Security Conference that the European Union may regulate itself out of contention in the AI development and deployment race. It is, however, Number One in the AI regulation race. The trophy is on its way.

IV. National Artificial Intelligence Safety Institutes

AI Safety Institutes (AISIs) represent a novel institutional innovation in global technology governance. First envisioned at the U.K.'s Bletchley Park AI Safety Summit in 2023 and formalized in the Bletchley Declaration, these government-backed entities pursue three core objectives: evaluating frontier AI models, advancing safety research, and facilitating cross-sector knowledge exchange. Unlike traditional regulators, AISIs occupy a hybrid space between government, academia, and industry, emphasizing pre-deployment risk evaluation over post-hoc enforcement. With startup-like agility and a public interest mandate, they aim to bridge the expertise gap between rapid AI advances and sluggish policy cycles. Think of them as the policy world's attempt to join the AI party, just without the glow sticks or late-night code sprints.

The U.K.'s rebranding of its AISI to the "AI Security Institute" in early 2025 marks a significant turn. Announced at the Munich Security Conference, this pivot shifts the focus from general safety to acute security threats, ranging from AI-assisted bioweapons to cybercrime. By explicitly excluding societal concerns like algorithmic bias or freedom of speech, the U.K. has traded its safety net for a national security firewall. It aligns with the U.S. stance: Existential risks were dismissed as handwringing at the Paris AI Action Summit. The shift in language, from "societal impacts" to "societal resilience," reflects a deeper philosophical recalibration. In other words, the Institute's mission has gone from "let's not crash the AI car" to "let's bulletproof it and hope it doesn't swerve into democracy."

From an international governance lens, this move raises uncomfortable questions about the coherence of the global AISI model. While the EU and others maintain a wider scope, including ethical, social, and long-term safety issues, the U.K.'s narrowing of focus threatens to splinter the collaborative promise underpinning the International Network of AI Safety Institutes. Established in Seoul in 2024 to harmonize evaluation protocols and coordinate risk research, the network now faces internal tensions and divergent national priorities. This isn't just a policy hiccup; it's more like organizing a potluck to which half the guests bring salads and the rest show up with flamethrowers.

The long-term viability of AISIs will hinge on their ability to remain credible, inclusive, and adaptive. With new institutes emerging across Brazil, India, and Kenya, the model is expanding globally but faces uneven resources and strategic priorities. Whether AISIs evolve into regulatory authorities, remain technical advisors, or morph into national security assets will shape the next decade of AI governance. The original vision, technocratic, cooperative, and ethically grounded, must now compete with geopolitical pressures and a growing appetite for securitization. If AISIs were supposed to be the grown-ups in the AI room, they may need to start mediating between the risk-averse, the profit-driven, and the occasionally paranoid.

V. Summary/Key Points

1. The OECD, WEF, GPAI, IEEE, UNESCO, and a number of others are among the international bodies/fora that have tried to provide the norms and standards for Responsible AI initiatives. They provide differing frameworks of high-level principles, blueprints, and guidance (resembling wish lists) on how AI should be operationalized. There is much value in this work even as practically implementing the principles is the hard and challenging part.

2. The United Nations may not be in a position to provide leadership for standard setting and compliance monitoring of a harmonized AI policy. It has lots on its plate already, and the

AI pace is a bit supersonic for a deliberative international bureaucracy like the U.N. to navigate.

3. Regional organizations can play a huge role in the vacuum created by international leadership. The EU is a case in point, promulgating the first set of AI laws in the world. The Council of Europe introduced a binding treaty in 2024. The African Union has taken some significant steps, but not in treaty form.

4. Smaller regional organizations, like the African Union and Organization of American States (with smaller AI and technology ecosystem and markets) may be nimbler and create leading edge AI rules. But they are not likely to be adopted as global standards.

5. AI Safety Institutes were originally conceived as neutral, science-driven bodies, but they are now veering toward national security roles, especially in countries like the U.K. and U.S. Newly formed they may be, but already showing signs of an identity crisis!

CHAPTER 5

AI Regulation in the United States

I. Introduction

Over the last few years, we have seen a parade of chief executive officers (CEOs) of technology companies in Washington DC pleading for urgent regulation in the AI space. During the Biden administration, Elon Musk, Sam Altman, and so many other bigtech executives paid visits to members of the United States (U.S.) Congress, White House officials, and even the President, all beseeching for some sort of regulatory guidance for Artificial Intelligence. They worry about would happen if AI developers deploy without any scruples—an AI nightmare scenario *sans regulation*. They also worrying about over-regulation. There is an AI gold rush underway, and everyone is staking their claim. Musk came into the Trump White House 2.0 and stayed a few controversial months (at least at the time of this writing), maintaining his chainsaw memes at the newly minted Department of Government Efficiency (DOGE).

And then in May 2025, the technology executives changed their tune. Now they wanted (in the words of Microsoft President Brad Smith) "a light touch." Sam Altman warned U.S. Senators that the more than 30 states which had legislated on AI in a variety of fields created a patchwork that would "slow us down at a time when I don't think it's in anyone's best interest." He was referring to the exponential growth in AI tools being released by companies in the People's Republic of China (China). Only a month before, former Google CEO Eric Schmidt had told the U.S. House of Representatives Energy and Commerce Committee Chairman Representative Brett Guthrie that China would become the world's sole superpower if the U.S. did not win the AI race. And that was clearly a risk that U.S. legislators are rightfully not willing to take. The Trump administration released its July 2025, Winning the Race: America's AI Action Plan (AI Action Plan), starting with the words "The United States is in a race to achieve global dominance in artificial intelligence." There are others in the technology space, state government, civil rights, privacy and other human rights advocacy groups who believe that an unfettered AI industry, replete of ethics, is a dangerous thing for democracy.

Much of this is about risk allocation, tradeoffs, and AI spoils. AI carries many risks. In our view, there are two kinds of AI folks out there when it comes to the mitigation of risks. There are *Skynets*, the Chicken Littles highlighting AI hype, risks of rushed deployments, potential harms to already marginalized groups, and the need for ethical guardrails. They have watched *The Terminator* films and scared themselves silly. Arrayed against these *Skynets* is another group of similarly accomplished AI luminaries, whom we have called the *Safetynets*. These folks could care less about the impact of AI on the society and economy and their concerns seem quotidian by contrast: systemic algorithmic bias, misinformation, and misuse—not exactly the stuff of water cooler conversation. The *Safetynets* want us to focus on the clear and present dangers of AI already identified, instead of hypothetical risks of the *Skynets*. The latter are just alarmists after all, right? Yes, both groups want AI to be regulated, in different ways and for different reasons. Welcome to the age of regulatory confusion.

Meanwhile, as we hear more about the misuse of AI—scamsters weaponize AI, a fake image causes a stock market crash, fake news of killer drones gone rogue goes viral—the drumbeat for AI regulation is increasing. AI is used for criminal sentencing, police enforcement resource allocation, and crime prevention in the United States, yet the data is compromised and infused with bias. People of color and other marginalized communities suffer. Not exactly a shocker, that one. So how do we move forward?

Several carrot and stick mechanisms exist in the U.S. already—there are many laws on the books with which courts and regulators can reign in the downsides of AI technologies.

First, the stick: Current antitrust laws can help us prevent the consolidation of power among AI vendors and their acquisition by BigTech companies already controlling much of the space. In January 2024, the Federal Trade Commission (FTC) opened investigations into five leading AI companies (Alphabet, Inc., Amazon.com, Inc., Anthropic PBC, Microsoft Corp., and OpenAI, Inc.), ordering them "to provide information regarding recent investments and partnerships involving generative AI companies and major cloud service providers." The FTC is concerned that the consolidation in the industry risks "distorting innovation and undermining fair competition." In this example, the laws of the United States that regulates competition are being used to police the AI industry—a stick indeed. That these companies frequent Washington DC to lobby Congress and the Executive Branch for light touch regulation should give us pause. But the tech bros need not worry—the second Trump administration is lending them a sympathetic ear, and, at this writing, the light touch that they are seeking.

And now the carrot: Incentivization programs like the U.S.'s National Artificial Intelligence Initiative, enacted in January 2021, showed the strength of bipartisan approaches that envision a shared computing and data infrastructure for increased access. These initiatives help ensure that small and medium firms are supported, can scale, and compete internationally. Since AI technology changes rapidly any incentives need to be recalibrated and adapted to evolving needs. Carrots are nice and feel like there is actually some strategy at play here; it is almost like a national plan that has purpose and a budget. More carrots seemed to have emerged in 2025 with the Trump administration's AI Action Plan.

Notwithstanding the geopolitics and geoeconomics of the evolving AI space, sticks may be a good thing too. We need to guard against the danger of the growing AI Industrial Complex providing its own self-interested rules. It may not be a good idea to let the foxes write their own safety rules concerning the hens' roost. But legislators cannot regulate what they do not yet understand. It is time for some quick masterclasses for our legislators and their advisors. It is not too late because the federal government could theoretically step in to make good on the Trump 2.0 agenda and the AI Action Plan's ambitious goals.

While there are existing regulatory bodies and legacy institutions, their digital capabilities and technology understanding need to be upgraded. By improving governance ability and institutional capacity, our political leaders can better administrate. That should be a key remit of any new AI agency: help existing institutions elevate their game, providing investments for start-ups and funding for educational initiatives to retool the workforce stateside.

To best deal with AI risks, we must eschew the hyperbole and fearmongering of the Skynets. A measured Safetynet approach will be a more prudent path forward and help us develop enforceable rules rather than lofty, paper-tiger-like guidelines. As we like to say: if you don't know where you are going, AI regulation will not take you there.

The U.S. Government Accountability Office, the federal government's watchdog agency, has explored the advantages and disadvantages of AI regulation stating that:

> AI is a transformative technology with applications in medicine, agriculture, manufacturing, transportation, defense, and many other areas. It also holds substantial promise for improving government operations. Federal guidance has focused on ensuring AI is responsible, equitable, traceable, reliable, and governable. Third-party assessments and audits are important to achieving these goals. However, AI systems pose unique challenges to such oversight because their inputs and operations are not always visible.

This Chapter examines the visible: The paucity of impactful federal regulation coming from Washington DC. Part II of this Chapter explores some of the federal laws that are already in force across the United States and the manner in which some AI tools can be overseen within those laws. Current federal legislation that is future-oriented and focused on the challenges of AI here and now, well, they are sadly lacking. Part III of this Chapter describes some of the responses to date from the federal government of the United States. During the Biden administration there were some executive orders about the use of AI in federal government work, some lofty goals, including Diversity, Equity, and Inclusion (DEI), that do not have the force of law that were part of the Blueprint for an AI Bill of Rights. This resulted in an unfortunate vacuum in which a national strategy for AI and a budget to actually execute that strategy, came to wither. This may change in Trump 2.0.

Part IV surveys some of the regulatory responses that have emanated outside the federal government. Part V looks at the early steps of the Trump administration 2.0 with the one legislative action that created a moratorium on individual states and municipalities from enforcing laws that impact AI tools and automated decision-making systems. There may be a glimmer of hope that the U.S. might offer some regulatory clarity eventually, now that it has boxed out the 30 plus states that tried to fill in the vacuum that Washington DC created. But that federal system is also a patchwork, making compliance onerous, inefficient, and expensive. Note to self: This is good for the lawyers and legal departments of the companies being regulated. At least until AI tools take those jobs too!

II. Statutes Already on the Books

On May 16, 2023, Sam Altman, CEO of Open AI, the company which developed and deployed ChatGPT to the public only nine months before, appeared before the U.S. Senate Judiciary Subcommittee, asking for legislation to regulate the use of Artificial Intelligence (Almost two years later to the day, he reversed course). The appearance led all the major news channels' coverage that night. Before Congress, Altman offered this admonition: "As this technology advances, we understand that people are anxious about how it could change the way we live. We are too." So, most of us recognize the need to regulate and as The Smiths once sang "How soon is now?"

But the truth is, there are a number of statutes already in force in the United States which may be applicable to Artificial Intelligence. They include, but are not limited to, the Fair Credit Reporting Act (FCRA) and the Equal Credit Opportunity Act (ECOA). Both pieces of legislation address automated decision-making in consumer finance. For decades these laws have been applied by financial services companies to algorithm-based credit underwriting models.

The FCRA, a seminal piece of legislation for more than half a century, imposes regulations on consumer reporting agencies making decisions on housing, employment, and credit. The FCRA mandates when a company buys credit scores that were developed by AI data and those scores are used to make decisions on employment or housing there are obligations on adverse action notice (reasons for denial, imposed requirements that information is maximally accurate).

The ECOA, on the other hand, was enacted the following year, making it unlawful for any creditor to discriminate against any applicant, with respect to any aspect of a credit transaction, on the basis of race, color, religion, national origin, sex, marital status, or age. Moreover, discrimination is prohibited concerning the applicant's use of a public assistance program to receive all or part of their income. In addition, no discrimination is permitted based on the applicant's previous good-faith exercise of any right under the Consumer Credit Protection Act (CCPA). The CCPA applies to entities which in the ordinary course of business, regularly makes credit decisions and that includes banks, retail outlets, bankcard companies, finance companies, and credit unions.

The Fair and Accurate Credit Transactions Act, the Credit CARD Act, and the CCPA all have some potential impact on the regulation of Artificial Intelligence in response to credit decisions. Title VI of the CCPA protects information collected by consumer reporting agencies. These agencies include credit bureaus, medical information companies, and tenant screening services. Information in a consumer report cannot be provided to anyone who does not have a purpose specified in the Consumer Credit Protection Act. There are specific legal obligations, including the duty to investigate disputed information, for companies that provide information to consumer reporting agencies. When an adverse action is taken on the basis of such reports, users of the information for credit, insurance, or employment purposes must notify the consumer.

Explainability and risks are critical here. Under the Federal Trade Commission Act (FTCA), AI is already under purview of the Federal Trade Commission. The FTC has published guidance on the manner in which it might use the Act to regulate Artificial Intelligence. With a long history of dealing with the challenges that come with the use of data and algorithms in decision-making about customers as well as consumer surveillance, the FTC could be an institution of import for Artificial Intelligence. The FTCA laws protect generally against unfair deceptive practices. The FTC provides that the sale or use of a racially discriminatory algorithm could be an unfair practice. But note, since January 2025, the FTC appears not to be pursuing with great vigor investigations of bigtech these days.

III. Wanted: Smart Legislation

But outside the context of credit and banking, there is a pressing need for new laws that regulate all the other uses of AI, many of which are covered in previous chapters of this *Short and Happy Guide*. The first Trump Administration took some important steps to start the regulatory ball rolling. In February 2019, Executive Order 13859—Maintaining American Leadership in AI—created the American AI Initiative. This executive order identified five key areas of effort: (1) the increase in AI research investment, (2) the release of Federal AI computing and data resources, (3) the promulgation of AI technical standards, (4) the capacitation of AI workforce of the U.S., and (5) the engagement with international allies.

The U.S. Department of Commerce's National Institute of Standards and Technology (NIST) released a plan in August 2019 to spark the development of standards of Artificial Intelligence among federal agencies. This was, alas, a plan to have a plan for AI guidelines, rather than AI guidelines themselves. The National AI Initiative Act of 2020 finally came about in December 2020, when President Trump signed Executive Order 13960 on Promoting the Use of Trustworthy AI in the Federal Government. Finally, we started getting somewhere. Recommending that the U.S. government bolster AI standards-related knowledge, this executive order strengthened leadership and coordination among agencies that develop or use AI, promoted focused research on the trustworthiness of AI systems, support and expand public-private partnerships, and engage with foreign companies and governments alike. The federal government was ordered to "commit to deeper, consistent, long-term engagement in AI standards development activities" to help the U.S. accelerate the pace of reliable, robust, and trustworthy AI technology development. These were all goals toward which the AI private sector was already working so the feds were clearly playing catch up. All federal government agencies were mandated to file a plan concerning Artificial Intelligence. The reality, however, is that "88 percent of agencies that are likely subject to the requirement to submit Agency AI Plans. . .have failed to do so" according to the Human-Centered Artificial Intelligence at Stanford University.

In 2020, the American AI Initiative also embraced trustworthy AI for government services and missions, along with training an AI-ready workforce. These efforts were still not enough because members of Congress sent a letter to the National Science Foundation (NSF) and the Office of Science and Technology Policy requesting extra efforts to use AI in a safe and ethical manner through a task force. Trustworthy AI became a major issue for Congressional leadership given that AI was increasingly being used in business, education, and the public sector. The GAO reported in

July 2021 that the use of facial recognition technology may threaten federal agencies and the general public.

When President Joseph R. (Joe) Biden assumed office in January 2021, it was clear that the U.S. was somewhat slower on creating the legal foundations for AI growth compared with China. He quickly announced the creation of an AI task force to research tools that will promote AI innovation and fuel economic prosperity that same year. The task force's goals include the improvement of access to resources, the provision of governance principles, and the drafting of for security, privacy, civil rights, and civil liberties protections.

The 116th Congressional session had passed the National AI Research Resource Task Force Act in June 2020, creating a task force to achieve the bill's goal of making AI more accessible to the general public for research purposes. The Act also called for the White House Office of Science and Technology Policy (OSTP) and the NSF to create a National AI Research Resource (NAIRR) Task Force to explore the feasibility of creating a resource for AI research. By the time the 117th Congress was in session, at least 75 bills were introduced that either focused on AI and ML or had AI/ML-focused provisions. Six of those were finally passed into law. which were generally directed at specific agencies to create programs or for the federal government to create plans for AI development. Again, plans for development of AI rather than the development itself. Within a year, the NAIRR Task Force was meeting, its members including government, academia, and private sector professionals. They created a mechanism to provide students and researchers access to AI-backed research which would then expand resources, data, and educational tools, but no regulations were yet forthcoming. But in its final report in January 2023, the Task Force published a plan to construct a NAIRR, costing a total of $2.6 billion over a six-year time period. The report did actually detail a plan to spur innovation, increase talent diversity, improve capacity, and advance trustworthy Artificial Intelligence. And it is likely that Trump 2.0 will have some new legislative projects for funding AI research in the coming years, in line with the AI Action Plan's lofty goals.

To achieve the goals, the NAIRR supported a diverse class of members including researchers, educators integrating AI with learning, and students. Class members represented included academia, civilian agencies, federal and federally funded agencies, and others. Industry and civil society are also important to implementation as the for-profit and non-profit worlds provide funding and growth and can result in experts serving as technical advisers. Groups interested in the implications of AI can also utilize the resource provided by National AI Research Resource.

Following the NAIRR, a lot of expectations came out of the White House. The Biden administration may not have met them with its October 2022 offering from the White House Office of Science and Technology: The Blueprint for an AI Bill of Rights (the Blueprint). The Blueprint was designed to protect the public from falling victim to the functionalities that attend AI design, use, and deployment. The principles were organized into five categories: (1) safe and effective systems; (2) algorithmic discrimination protections; (3) data privacy; (4) notice and explanation; and (5) human alternatives, consideration, and fallback.

AI platforms were to adhere to certain standards in order to be safe and effective. These includes: (1) experts identifying potential risks; (2) pre-deployment testing; (3) ongoing monitoring; (4) the decision not to deploy if endangering the community or user safety is reasonably foreseeable. A safe and effective system was to exclude inappropriate or irrelevant data use and also include independent evaluation and reporting that confirms safety and effectiveness. Finally, such reporting was to be made public.

The Blueprint called for designers to construct algorithms equitably, without discrimination based on race, color, ethnicity, sex, religion, age, national origin, disability, or any other legally protected classification. Such construction required designers' proactive and continuous efforts. For example, designers could: (1) use representative data and protect against proxies for demographic features; (2) ensure design and development accessibility for people with disabilities; (3) test for and mitigate disparity in pre-deployment and during use; and (4) implement clear organizational oversight. In addition, designers were to regularly perform algorithmic disparity impact assessments and publicize the results.

Default AI design choices could have ensured that the systems protect citizens from privacy violations. Design choices could also have ensured that data collection conforms to reasonable expectations of privacy and that systems only collect data necessary for the specific context. Systems should seek citizens' meaningful, plain-language consent for data collection, use, access, transfer, and deletion, to the greatest extent possible. Sensitive domains, including health, work, education, criminal justice, and juvenile areas, were to feature enhanced protections and strictly necessary uses. Surveillance technologies would have included heightened oversight, and would not function continuously in education, work, housing, or other contexts where use can limit rights or opportunities.

Any AI system should have put users on notice of its use. Notice should have included a plain-language explanation of how and why the system impacts the user. Explanations should have also included: (1) system function descriptions and roles; (2) the entity responsible for the system; and (3) clear explanations of outcomes. Furthermore, an explanation would have been technically valid, meaningful, useful, and calibrated to the risk level of any user.

Finally, designers could have publicly reported periodic assessments of the clarity and quality of the notice and explanations.

Users were able to opt out of automated systems in favor of a human alternative where appropriate. Appropriateness should be determined by reasonable expectations in the same or similar circumstances, with a focus on avoiding harmful public impact. If a system fails, users should have had access to a human with an equitable, accessible, and effective remedy. Systems within sensitive domains should have served their specific purpose, with meaningful oversight access and human control over high-risk decisions. Periodic human governance process assessments should be made public whenever possible.

These sentences have been written in the past tense. That is because the Blueprint was completely voluntary and so yesterday's news. As per the Legal Disclaimer that came with the Blueprint:

> The Blueprint for an AI Bill of Rights is non-binding and does not constitute U.S. government policy. It does not supersede, modify, or direct an interpretation of any existing statute, regulation, policy, or international instrument. It does not constitute binding guidance for the public or Federal agencies and therefore does not require compliance with the principles described herein. It also is not determinative of what the U.S. government's position will be in any international negotiation.

So it was not even softlaw, just a "nice to have." Not really dispositive or a regulation at all. A few of the big tech companies signed on but that was probably performative. If you are wondering why the Blueprint was not on the list in the whirlwind of rescissions in the first days of Trump 2.0, it is because it was non-binding.

Since November 2022, when ChatGPT was released to the public, Generative AI usage has grown exponentially. Governments' regulations of the software, not so much. There is a need for action to protect Americans' rights and safety in the face of advancing AI development: Some analysts have openly called for a "Manhattan Project" for AI safety. The pressure on the U.S. government to act in a comprehensive way mounted, so much so that by April 2023, Senate Majority Leader Chuck Schumer attempted to write ill-fated legislation. The high-profile testimony of NYU Professor Emeritus Gary Marcus and Sam Altman, CEO of OpenAI, before a U.S. Congressional committee in May 2023 culminated in much expectation for regulation. It was no surprise that by May 2023, other legislators in Washington DC got engaged as well. The performative exercises, also known as lobby or legislative groveling, and the investor nightmare of Congressional grilling kept on a-coming.

The Biden administration announced new efforts "to advance the research, development, and deployment of responsible Artificial Intelligence (AI) that protects individuals' rights and safety and delivers results for the American people." The White House's OSTP issued a request for public comment about specific measures to ensure AI is both safely developed and deployed. Thank you Washington DC for that era of having plans to have plans.

The result from all this cheerleading was robust, but still not real, actionable, and above all else, meaningful legislation. Instead, the White House released a governance framework designed to mitigate bias, ensure privacy, and promote transparency around Artificial Intelligence in October 2023: Executive Order on the Safe, Secure, and Trustworthy Artificial Intelligence. The executive order lays out some 150 requirements that federal agencies and other federal entities must implement, in some cases, within a very short timeframe. This is a "whole of government" approach that federal agencies use in-depth assessments of advanced AI tools prior to their deployment. Executive Order Number 14110 was grounded in the

Defense Production Act of 1950, a law giving the U.S. President authority to create national defense preparedness programs and to maintain and enhance the domestic industrial base. To keep a steady supply of global talent to power U.S. efforts in the AI space, the executive order streamlined high-skilled immigration. And it is not a state secret that the dearth of talent has been a real challenge among the federal agencies. The executive order also created several new government offices and task forces to pave the way for AI usage in nearly every part of the federal government including health care, education, housing, and trade.

And while it took a while to get there, the enforcement provisions of the executive order were coupled with futuristic computational capacities that could diminish the regulatory sanctions leading some pundits to question the actual effectiveness of President Biden's executive order. A day after the new executive order was signed, the Office of Management and Budget released draft guidelines to assist implement its two main thrusts: Increasing AI talent in the U.S. government and providing more transparency of the federal government's use of Artificial Intelligence.

In March 2024, the Office of Management of Budget (OMB), which is part of the Executive Office of the President, published a Memorandum providing guidance and obligations relating to the use of AI tools by federal agencies. The aforementioned AI executive order mandated the OMB to issue appropriate guidance that helps the Federal Government in making effective use of AI while containing its risks and promoting innovation. The scope includes AI systems that are developed, used or procured by the agencies. Note that the scope is narrow: it does not apply to non-agency AI usage, nor to investigations as part of enforcement actions.

The covered agencies must appoint a chief AI officer who is responsible for implementing the guidance. Ciao, CAIO! The U.S. Department of Homeland Security was the first to do so, appointing a CAIO in October 2023 and the U.S. Department of Justice appointed its AI Chief in February 2024. The CAIO must ensure compliance in areas related to innovation, risk management and the effective usage in their agency. The creation of a formal role with accountability is a good step. There is an AI governance requirement as well. Each agency chief financial officer had to convene governance bodies, and the agencies had to share with the public their plans for compliance with the Memorandum's provisions.

Each of the agencies was to compile a use case inventory, listing the ways in which it relies on AI and its impact on safety and rights, with exceptions for national security use cases. This is to be submitted to the OMB as well as shared with the public. The Memorandum introduced two concepts: safety-impacting AI and rights-impacting AI for better risk management:

> safety-impacting AI is defined as AI with outputs that could affect the safety of: (1) human life, (2) the climate or the environment, (3) critical infrastructure, or (4) strategic assets or resources.
>
> rights-impacting AI is defined as AI with outputs that significantly affect: (1) civil rights, civil liberties or privacy; (2) equal opportunities; or (3) access or ability to apply for critical government resources or services.

Agencies must implement risk management practices or stop the use of non-compliant tools by December 2024. Current and planning AI applications must undergo a risk analysis accordingly. It's not all about risk thought. It's not all quiet on the innovation front.

To spur innovation, the agencies must adopt AI for public benefit and further the agency mission effectiveness. Still in the realm of aspiration perhaps but, the Memorandum promoted responsible and efficient AI use, encouraging covered agencies to dismantle unnecessary barriers to use and equip practitioners with necessary tools. Who can argue with that?

The Memorandum was a good start. But the U.S., like countries around the world, needs actual laws, not just aspirational initiatives and so-called "nice to haves." The U.S. Congress must still work with the Executive Branch to craft the best national strategy and regulatory regime for AI development and deployment. It is both a national security priority and a national industrial priority. Or we can let the market do it. By market, we need tech bros. Most excellent free market, dude! The Trump second administration may unleash an era of technological advancement that follows the AI Action Plan.

IV. Select Regulatory Responses at the State and Local Levels of Government

While the federal government gets its act together to actually legislate some guidelines, rather than do so by Presidential Decree (also known as executive order), there remains a paucity of real regulation. Instead, some of the individual states attempted to fill the vacuum.

In short, some 30 states and dozens of cities have taken to promulgating laws and rules on the use of AI tools, mostly in the field of criminal justice—facial recognition really. Although there was a patchwork of regulations, at least there were regulations.

California was set to regulate the use of AI in business. Introduced in 2018, Senate Bill (SB)1001 prohibits using bots to "communicate or interact online with a person in California in order to incentivize a sale or transaction of goods or services or to influence a vote in an election without disclosing that the communication is via a bot." A bot is defined as "an automated online account where all or substantially all of the actions or posts of that account are not the result of a person."

In September 2023, California Governor Gavin Newsom signed an executive order to "to study the development, use, and risks of artificial intelligence (AI) technology throughout the state and to develop a deliberate and responsible process for evaluation and deployment of AI within state government." The executive order is designed to deploy Generative AI in an ethical and responsible manner throughout California's state government, to protect and prepare for potential arms that these AI tools can create, and to ensure that the state maintains its global leadership position in the industry.

California has been doubling down on its attempts to push the regulatory envelope further and further, given the proximity of Silicon Valley to Sacramento. In November 2023, California Consumer Privacy Agency released draft regulations on automated decision-making technology (ADMT) to provide new protections related to businesses' use of AI technologies. Consumers can opt out of, and access information to, businesses' use of ADMT, as provided under the California Consumer Privacy Act. Specifically, the Act governs use of much emerging technology in decisions related to "performance at work, economic situation, health, personal preferences, interests, reliability, behavior, location or movements." Thus, consumers are meant to have more control over the personal information that businesses collect about them. California is not the only state to take the lead to support privacy protection innovation in the face of new technologies.

In 2021, Colorado enacted SB 21-169. The law protects consumers from unfair insurance practice discrimination that could arise from algorithms using external consumer data to discriminate against protected classes. The Colorado Privacy Act, in effect in July 2023, provides consumers the right to opt out of personal data processing leading to decision-making. In addition, SB 21-169 regulates "a decision that results in the provision or denial of financial and lending services, housing, insurance, education enrollment or opportunity, criminal justice, employment opportunities, health care services, or access to essential goods or services."

The Connecticut Privacy Act, effective July 2023, also provides consumers the right to opt out of profiling, if such profiling is used to make legally binding decisions. Those implementing AI tools in decision-making must perform a risk analysis if they use AI algorithms in:

> certain profiling activities that present a reasonably foreseeable risk of unfair or deceptive treatment of or unlawful disparate impact on consumers, financial, physical or reputational injury to consumers, physical or other intrusion into the solitude, seclusion or private affairs or concerns of consumers that would be offensive to a reasonable person, or other substantial injury to consumers.

Enacted in 2019, the Illinois AI Video Interview Act requires employers in the state to:

(1) notify applicants of AI use;

(2) explain to employees how the AI works;

(3) obtain consent;

(4) only share videos of applicants with those evaluating the applicants;

(5) destroy the videos upon the applicant's request; and

(6) report demographic data of those applicants interviewed, hired, and interviewed but not hired.

Effective October 2020, Maryland law HB 120 prohibits employers from using facial recognition during pre-employment interviews, unless the applicant signs a consent waiver. Montana's SB 384, introduced in State Legislature in February 2023, regulates personal information collection and processing, profiling, and automated decision-making. SB 384 also enables individuals to opt out of profiling if AI uses the profiling in legally binding decisions.

In April 2024, Tennessee enacted legislation that imposes liability on Generative AI companies and internet platforms for the unauthorized use of a person's voice or likeness. The Ensuring Likeness, Voice, and Image Security (ELVIS) Act of 2024 went into force in July 2024, expanding the state's statutory right of publicity in a manner that could pose new risk of liability for AI tools, internet platforms that feature them, and the technology companies that use artists' voices and likenesses. The name is not by accident: Tennessee is the birthplace Elvis Presley and the site of Graceland after all. Thank you very much Ma'am. The legislation left the (State Capitol) building.

Not to be outdone, Virginia's Consumer Data Protection Act, in effect since January 2023, governs profiling and automated decision-making. It enables individuals to opt out of AI algorithms that use such actions to produce legally binding effects. The Commonwealth of Virginia has also legislated against the use of facial recognition. Enacted in December 2021, New York City Local Law 144, requires employers to conduct regular audits to ensure that automated employment decision tools are not biased. There is also the proposed New York Privacy Act. Introduced in January 2023, SB 365 requires companies to "disclose their use of automated decision-making that could have a 'materially detrimental effect' on consumers, such as a denial of financial services, housing, public accommodation, health care services, insurance, or access to basic necessities; or could produce legal or similarly significant effects."

In addition, companies must provide consumers with a way to contest negative decisions. The contesting procedure must include human review of the decision. The law also mandates that consumers may opt out of AI algorithms that use profiling to make legally binding decisions.

A bipartisan bill was working its way through Wisconsin's State Legislature which reduces the use of deep fakes and other falsely AI-generated media that could threaten election integrity. Wisconsin is taking the lead in addressing the use of AI in political campaign advertising. The bill requires that any paid advertising that contains synthetic media purchased through candidates or groups ahead of the 2024 elections must provide notice to the public that it contains misleading AI-generated content by way of a disclaimer.

In addition to the legislative work done by the states, cities have responded in a robust way to the use of AI in a variety of legal fields. For example, San Francisco banned its law enforcement officials from using facial recognition software in its operations. So has Oakland. Boston has taken a different approach, encouraging its municipal employees to use ChatGPT and other generative Artificial Intelligence. What is glaring, however, is the slow work of regulation coming from the U.S. government itself. To date, we had the Blueprint, and a framework—basically, just some general guidelines.

In December 2024, after the 2024 election and before the Trump administration, a House AI Task Force released a bipartisan report to serve as a "road map" for Congress's development of future proposals regarding Artificial Intelligence. Although not comprehensive, it is recognized as a first step towards the future of AI-related laws. In fact, Trump's transition team as well as David Sacks, nominated as President Trump's AI (and crypto) czar, met with the Task Force that wrote the report. The direction that Congress has seemingly taken is that AI needs to be regulated sector-by-sector, rather than as a whole. The report includes recommendations for government use, data privacy, national security, research and development, and more.

In his farewell address to the nation, President Joe Biden addressed concerns over potential changes in AI policy. In a last-minute Executive Order, President Biden addressed AI infrastructure, setting aside resources and federal land for AI data centers. In an effort to remain competitive in the AI tech space, the federal government also announced new regulations on the exportation of AI chips, including a three-tier system in which U.S. allies are unrestricted, and arms embargoed countries, (notably, the People's Republic of China) are barred from receiving advanced AI technology. In the waning days of the Biden administration, the White House Chief of Staff, Jeff Zients, was reportedly working with private companies to sign public pledges regarding their use of AI technology. It seemed we were back to October 2022 and the days of the Blueprint—a voluntary virtue signaling exercise to incorporate DEI and ESG issues into AI development and deployment.

Because the federal government of the United States was not willing nor able to legislate how to incentivize or punish AI companies to do their work in an ethical and responsible manner, the vacuum was filled by state and municipal governments and the judicial systems at all levels of the country. Then came the Trump Administration 2.0 and the "big, beautiful bill" that, in part, attempted to make the enforcement of any regulation of AI or automated decision-making tools by states and municipalities illegal. This hands-off approach may work for only so long as the EU and China take leadership roles in regulation, effectively boxing out U.S. companies from doing business, collecting or selling data, or undertaking research outside the United States.

V. Trump Administration 2.0

The Second Trump administration has picked up where the First Trump administration left off regarding Artificial Intelligence. The Trump Administration contends that the Biden Administration "over-regulated" the AI space, specifically referring to President Biden's October 2023 AI Executive Order. Note that there may be some overlap between the previous and current administration's AI priorities: Both agree on the importance of using federal land for data centers.

After the 2024 election, President-elect Donald Trump announced on Truth Social that he was appointing former PayPal CEO, billionaire David Sacks as his "White House AI & Crypto Czar." President Trump has directed Sacks to focus on making America a "global leader" in AI and cryptocurrency, as well as "safeguard free speech online" to avoid "big tech bias and censorship." The new administration is expected to neither sharply regulate AI, nor enforce AI-related antitrust. In fact, judging by the first four months, he is encouraging technological competition with China. The new administration is likely to strengthen AI-related export restrictions that began with President Biden's Administration. The support of big tech during the election and around the inauguration indicates that a "hands off" approach to regulating AI and big tech is the mantra, thereby allowing the industry to profit and compete without many guardrails. Like President Biden's approach to AI, the Trump administration is focusing on prioritizing support for the U.S. as the global AI leader in the AI industry for both commerce and national security reasons.

It was no surprise then that upon being sworn in as the 47th President of the United States, President Trump repealed President Biden's Executive Order 14110 on Artificial Intelligence. This was expected as the 2024 Republican National Convention Platform officially adopted President-elect Trump's plan to do just that. And then the tech bros ran amuck lobbying Congress for not just limited rules, but no rules at the state and municipal levels of government.

One of the first AI-focused executive orders in the second Trump administration has provisions to review any action taken related to the revoked executive order for conflict with the current administration's approach to Artificial Intelligence. The Executive Order Removing Barriers to American Leadership in Artificial Intelligence is not prescriptive. It is aspirational and a bit of a reach some might say. The group—which includes AI and Crypto Czar David Sacks—developed America's AI Action Plan.

OpenAI Chief Global Affairs Officer, Chris Lehane, in the wake of DeepSeek's launch in January 2025, announced on LinkedIn:

> With the US locked in a competition with the Chinese Communist Party over AI's future, OpenAI's growing collaboration with the US government will strengthen America's global position and ensure that democratic AI wins out over China's authoritarian version of the technology. Our partnership with the National Labs will advance that broader mission—and pave the way for future projects that will extend AI's benefits to as many people as possible.

This race for AI supremacy, in the face of the ascendency of China, is the *leitmotif* of the second Trump administration. The European Union, well, not so much.

Because of that race to the death with China, in May 2025 House Energy and Commerce Committee Chairman Rep. Brett Guthrie (R-Kentucky) released the markup of a new appropriations bill and budget for the fiscal year 2025. This spending bill included an amendment called Section 43201: "Artificial Intelligence and information technology modernization initiative" which provided that "no State or political subdivision thereof may enforce any law or regulation regulating artificial intelligence models, artificial intelligence systems, or automated decision systems during the 10-year period beginning on the date of the enactment of this Act."

By May 2025, more than 30 states had passed laws or resolutions relating to AI in 2024 alone, according to the National Conference of State Legislatures. As noted earlier, they include laws on the use of deepfakes in elections, discriminatory uses of AI in hiring, limits on the use of biometrics (Illinois), limits facial recognition technology in law enforcement (Virginia) and the creation of "digital replicas" of people without their permission (ELVIS Act, Tennessee).

Here is how the moratorium on state and municipal laws being enforced can play out: There still could be federal legislation and hopefully it is enlightened, streamlines and foments further competition balanced with consumer protections and civil rights. An example of legislation that could be promulgated by the federal government is the Law on Deepfakes—The Take It Down Act, which is not just about AI but also about free speech, hate speech, defamation and privacy loss angles.

Following the failure of the Senate passing a provision instituting a national ten-year ban on the state and municipal enforcement of AI tools, it may be that U.S. Senator from Texas Ted Cruz, the sponsor of that effort in the Big Beautiful Bill, may try another at such a provision. He said so.

Regardless of which way it goes, the next step from the U.S. federal government will have repercussions across the globe. Chile, Brazil and other countries around the world have been looking to the European Union as a model. Since the U.S. has Silicon Valley and the best ecosystem for technology, plus unfettered capitalism, these other countries may opt for an approach closer to what the U.S. is promoting. They certainly will not be looking to the regulatory authoritarianism of China.

It should also be noted that the EU is also having a rethink as to whether it is regulating itself out of AI relevance. It is likely that the regulatory space globally will be different in a few years as it is now.

Regardless of how this plays out, the U.S. has been the undisputed leader in AI technology development for decades, but it is not a leader in regulation. But given how regulation can send a chilling effect to new companies and drive away more established ones (to more permissive jurisdictions), maybe the wild west, *laissez faire* approach of U.S. lawmakers will continue unabated. A regime of no rules, or even a lack of regulatory clarity, can be a strategic and comparative advantage.

VI. Summary/Key Points

1. AI Regulation is complex because it involves multiple, competing objectives: fostering innovation versus preventing harm, enabling economic leadership versus preserving rights, and advancing national security versus maintaining ethical guardrails. These tradeoffs are real and unresolved.

2. Technology companies have taken the lead and driven AI innovation, but they increasingly face growing scrutiny from civil rights advocates, regulators, and state governments. Regulatory capture, lobbying pressure, media criticism, and public backlash are all at play.

3. A unified international framework for AI governance remains aspirational. The idea of a single global AI regulator looks good on paper but impractical in practice because of multiple legal systems, different political ideologies and clashing national interests.

4. On the current state of U.S. regulation:

    a. The U.S. may be winning the AI race, but it is not winning the AI regulation race, and that could be a blessing in disguise. The competition with China is heating up big time! Get your fire-retardant suits and oven mitts on.

    b. The U.S. federal government has signaled some intent to regulate: The Blueprint for an AI Bill of Rights (October 2022) and the Executive Order for Safe, Secure and Trustworthy Artificial Intelligence (Oct. 2023) were examples. The first had no legal force and the second got rescinded in 2025 by President Trump.

    c. There have been policies and initiatives to encourage AI development and risk mitigation within the federal government over the years (e.g. NIST AI Risk Management Framework, OMB's public sector AI procurement guidelines.)

5. Existing (non-AI) statutes like the FCRA, ECOA, FTCA, and CCPA already cover many AI-related practices, especially in consumer finance, credit, housing, and employment. Some agencies like the FTC have issued guidance on how these laws can regulate algorithmic decision-making. Enforcement has been sporadic.

6. Meanwhile, in the absence of federal laws, many states and cities created their own AI regulations. These include laws on facial recognition bans, biometric privacy, employment screening tools, and consumer data protection. In 2025, the Trump administration floated a 10-year moratorium on state and municipal enforcement of AI laws. The provision passed the House of Representatives but failed in the Senate.

7. With legal uncertainty and potential enforcement risk, AI compliance, audit, and risk management services are poised for growth. This will present opportunities for enterprising lawyers and law firms.

CHAPTER 6

AI Regulation in the European Union

I. Introduction

Picture the heady vibe of celebration when a space shuttle is launched successfully. The Brussels bunch—thickly knotted ties and spread collared shirts intact—is high-fiving each other, not because there is a new particle accelerator bigger than the Large Hadron Collider that speeds up fundamental physics research or because these Eurocrats and the companies they have subsidized for years have launched a new space telescope that reveals cosmic secrets or alien civilizations. Nope. They are jubilant because they wrote a piece of legislation about Artificial Intelligence (AI) and shepherded its passage into law. And it is the law in all 28—err, 27 European Union (EU) Member States. The British need not apply (it).

When it comes to making history, there is the Magna Carta, there is the Emancipation Proclamation, and then there is the "Regulation of the European Parliament and of the Council laying down harmonized rules on Artificial Intelligence and amending certain Union legislative acts," in short, the EU AI Act (the New Regulation). Will this prove to be a pyrrhic policy victory or bring forth a new era of Enlightenment? Will other countries, or even transnational organizations, use it as a model or jettison its risk-averse protections? Time will tell, but the amount of legislative initiative, drafting and redrafting efforts, and lobbying resources that were expended for such a rapidly evolving technology was impressive. Bravo. Time for an encore?

Only a few months after the first provisions went into force, Eurocrats are talking about lightening up a little, given the lack of regulation in the United States (U.S.). It may also be that U.S. President JD Vance admonished Brussels while speaking at the Munich Security Conference in February 2025, warning Europe that it could regulate itself out of relevance in the technology space. World-class technology is not something made by committee. Notwithstanding regulators' remorse, the risk mitigation lovefest that is the EU AI Act is a go.

Following this Introduction, Part II of this Chapter reviews the history behind the efforts that the EU undertook over these last few years to be the first major jurisdiction—and a supranational one at that!—to work out, put into writing, and pass into law that regulates Artificial Intelligence. Part II of this Chapter explores the history of AI within the European Union. Part III details the EU AI Act which was finally promulgated in March 2024 after a gestation period of a few years. Part IV of this Chapter examines the manner that the EU divides up its regulations according to risk allocation—from low to high. Part V of this Chapter explores the ways in which criminal law is to be affected by the Regulation coming out of the European Union. Part VI details how employment laws are to be changed and be updated under the EU AI Act. Part VII looks at the ways in which intellectual property (IP) laws are affected by the EU AI Act. Going forward, at least for the time being, the Europeans have set *the* standards when it comes to AI regulations. Whether or not these will foment AI development and deployment on the Continent, or drive it away, remains to be seen.

II. The European Union and AI: A History

The European Union may be the middle ground between the U.S. and the People's Republic of China (China), the two opposite poles along the same regulatory spectrum. There is a focus on the environment on harmonization (rather than "harmony" which is a Chinese preoccupation in its Beijing Principles which we will see in Chapter 7). There are, however, tensions between supranational rules and national rules and the need to protect citizens (across the European Union).

It is only natural that the issue of ethics came out of Europe. Whether in the caves around Piraeus or the smoky cafes of Paris, "how to be" was long the metaphysical issue for discussion and debate. We must remember that as it was the Germans and the French who gave us *droits morals* (moral rights—the personal rights a creator has to their work including artistic integrity and authorship) when it came to IP protections in the nineteenth century. More than a century later in 2014, the EU brought out Future and Emerging Technologies (FET) under Horizon 2020 as early as 2009.

Europe is the home of this culture, so it was no surprise that the faceless European bureaucrats adding Value Added Tax (VAT) to everything and regulating everything on God's green Earth were the first to get out of the gate. *Mais oui*, the EU has been a pioneer in AI and ethics discussions. European Commission (EC) President Ursula von der Leyen called for a concerted European approach in her political guidelines for 2019 to 2024 work of the EC concerning AI which included how to better regulate the use of big data for innovation. The Council of the EU also weighed in on a coordinated plan for AI adoption.

The EU was highly motivated to create AI regulations as lawmakers discerned ways to regulate uncontrolled growth. For years, the EU had diligently worked to promulgate a new AI law that sets guidelines concerning accountability, human oversight, data quality, and transparency. The EU has long sought to take the lead in regulating Artificial Intelligence.

In 2019, the EC released its report on a single market in trustworthy Artificial Intelligence. Few read it (and even fewer watched the film). Imagine what the beret-wearing, Gauloise-smoking Left Bank crowd was thinking when, less than a year later, the EC released its White Paper on AI, adding to the bounty of regulations clearly on their way. *C'est la vie.*

The EU has also long set its sights on maximizing resources and coordinating investments in the digital world. They planned to do this through Digital Europe and Horizon Europe programmes. The Commission plans to invest one billion euros annually in Artificial Intelligence. Additionally, the EU believed, and continues to believe, that both the private and public sectors must gradually increase their research and development investments. Finally, the EU hopes that the digital innovation hubs it is establishing will help small businesses and companies take advantage of digital opportunities. But do not expect another SAP anytime soon. France's bet on Mistral could be a silver lining. That is, until its headquarters burns down *á la* Crédit Lyonnais.

Sure, corporations do offer expertise on business models, finance, market awareness, technology skills and networking acumen. They are after all in the arena offering products and services and hoping to multiply their revenue streams. But the EU is about supranational governance and not so much about maximizing profits for private corporations. The EU aims to promote AI and to become a leader in AI through large investments into the different Member States of the EU while also maintaining AI that is good for society. But just ask yourself whether you can name one world-class European AI company? World-class regulations, sure. But AI tools that are ubiquitous? Not so fast, Heinrich!

III. The European Union AI Act

Enter the newest foray towards an enforceable and actionable EU law: The EU AI Act. It is the first actual law—not a treaty commitment, nor a longing or a lofty set of principles, nor guidelines, nor even a blueprint. With the EU AI Act, the EU plans to steward AI development and deployment ("use and uptake" as Recital 8 of the Regulation puts it) on the Continent. The legal basis of the law is the Article 114 of the Treaty on the Functioning of the European Union. This foundational agreement that allows taking the necessary steps to establish a well-functioning internal market. The new law also provides for subsidiarity, providing for non-exclusive competence, in order to avoid contradictory national frameworks and the functioning of a seamless internal market for Artificial Intelligence. Finally, to institutionalize a risk-based approach, there is a provision for proportionality and necessity. Only when an AI system is likely to pose high risks to safety and citizen rights, does the EU AI Act impose regulatory burdens.

All about norms, the EU has set up lofty principles for its Member States to follow. The strategy was designed to accelerate AI development and align AI policy to remove fragmentation and address global challenges. In order to achieve these goals, the EU has outlined four strategies to make the EU the jurisdiction in which excellence thrives from the lab to the market. Brussels believes that by ensuring that AI works for EU citizens and consumers, is a force for good in society and strengthens strategic leadership in high-impact industries.

After months of negotiations and nearly two years since its introduction to the European Parliament, EU lawmakers passed the first draft of the AI Act in April 2023. A little less than a year later, all 27 Member States of the EU agreed to the provisions, as amended. Included in the legislation that was first passed by Members of the European Parliament (MEPs) is a new rule that forces companies that deploy Generative AI tools to disclose any copyrighted material used to develop their respective AI systems. That is a clear win for rights holders and legacy catalog companies.

While AI systems with limited or minimal risks can be utilized with relatively fewer requirements, transparency obligations remain essential. Conversely, AI systems that pose an unacceptable risk are largely prohibited, with few exceptions, especially those involving real-time biometric identification and government social scoring. Notably, high-risk AI systems are permitted but subject to stringent regulations. These include critical sectors such as autonomous vehicles, medical devices, and infrastructure machinery. These regulations demand rigorous testing, detailed documentation of data quality, and the establishment of an accountability framework with human oversight.

AI applications that give rise to an unacceptable risk, such as the government-run social scoring system in vogue in China, are prohibited in the European Union. Legal requirements are also very specific when it comes to high-risk applications, such as a curriculum vitae-screening tools used by companies to rank job applicants. Largely escaping regulation are applications that are not listed as high-risk nor explicitly banned. With the AI Act's implementation, the EU is hoping to strike a balance between innovation and risk management to safeguard the interests and well-being of society in the realm of Artificial Intelligence.

The EU carries a big stick: Companies that do not comply with the proposed law may face fines of up to up to 7% of their total worldwide annual revenue. The European Commission is no shrinking violet. We have witnessed the Commission and its Member States dish out big fines to bigtech in the past. Just ask Amazon which in 2021 was fined €746 million ($812 million) for being in breach of the EU's General Data Protection Regulation (GDPR). Or ask Google which in 2018 was fined €4.3 billion ($4.5 billion) for violation of antitrust laws of the European Union. Ouch! That has got to sting.

Foundation models, also known as base models (we have been referring to them as large language models (LLMs)), are AI models that are pre-trained on vast amounts of data. Being versatile enough to attempt a wide range of tasks, the EU AI Act requires general transparency measures for foundation models. The creators will need to register them in the EU database, including risk assessment and mitigation measures, and must comply with design, information, and environmental requirements (Can you do that ChatGPT?).

Currently, EU lawmakers have placed General Purpose AI Systems (GPAIS) such as ChatGPT into the "high-risk" category. This would be considered a "generative foundation model," having to comply with more transparency restrictions than just a foundational model. The EU has not clarified what regulations these GPAIS manufacturers would be subject to yet. Within the EU AI Act, MEPs have instituted requirements such as compliance with what they call "additional transparency requirements," like disclosing content generated by Artificial Intelligence. This is intended to restrain the models from generating illegal content and publishing summaries of copyrighted data that may have been used in their training.

We have noted already that the EU AI Act introduces significant penalties for non-compliance. Furthermore, submitting misleading or false documentation to regulators may also lead to financial penalties. There will be a transition period of approximately two years to allow regulated parties to comply with the provisions of the Act. MEPs still want to incentivize positive AI innovation, so some exemptions to these rules include AI components that are built through open-source licenses. This would encourage AI to be tested by public authorities, before its deployment to the general public. MEPs, in the New Regulation, also want citizens to feel safe filing complaints about AI systems. The EU Parliament wants EU citizens to "receive explanations of decisions based on high-risk AI systems that significantly impact their rights." The AI Office also oversees the effective implementation of and compliance with GPAI model providers. Downstream providers can file complaints with the AI Office regarding any infringements by upstream providers. To ensure compliance, the AI Office may conduct evaluations of GPAI models, particularly when the information obtained through its information request powers is insufficient.

Finally, the role of the EU AI Office has been transformed. It is responsible for monitoring the implementation of the 'AI rulebook.' In addition to examining the use of AI by corporations, the EU AI Office also considers its utilization in the public sector and law enforcement. It operates in conjunction with other 'similar-in-spirit' regulations, such as the General Data Protection Regulation.

In sum, the inclusion of a comprehensive risk-ranking system within the AI Act marks a significant step towards effectively regulating artificial intelligence. The European Parliament's priority is to ensure that AI systems are "safe, transparent, traceable, non-discriminatory and environmentally friendly" throughout the European Union. Rather than AI operating in fully automated mode, the European Parliament has demanded that AI systems have human oversight. The legislative body also established a uniform definition for AI that is technology-neutral, so that it is future-proof and applicable to any forthcoming technologies as well.

In February 2024, the 27 Member States of the European Union overcame last minute French objections (the French government was holding out to negotiate rules friendly to their LLM AI companies) and endorsed the above referenced political deal made in December 2023 to bring the EU Act to its final phase for promulgation. It was finally passed by the European Parliament in March 2024. Now the Europeans can fight existential threats coming from AI while being Existentialists! Black turtlenecks for everyone!

IV. The Unbearable Risk of Being European

The EU AI Act includes an AI systems ranking system of four tiers: unacceptable, high, limited, and minimal (or no) risk. Each of the categories has different regulations and requirements. AI systems that carry limited or minimal risks, such as spam filters and video games, have few compliance requirements other than transparency obligations. However, AI systems that are considered to pose an unacceptable risk, like real-time biometric identification systems in public spaces or government social scoring, are by and large, not allowed (except a few carve outs). While high-risk AI systems are permitted, developers and operators must follow strict regulations. Rigorous testing, proper documentation, and an accountability framework that specifies human oversight are par for the course here. Autonomous vehicles, medical devices, and critical infrastructure machinery fall into this category. With the New Regulation, MEPs also added AI systems with the potential to influence voters in political campaigns and systems used by social media platforms to the high-risk list.

Unacceptable risk AI systems include those capable of "subliminal manipulation, exploitation of vulnerabilities, biometric categorization based on sensitive characteristics, general-purpose social scoring, real-time remote biometric identification in public spaces, assessing emotional states in certain contexts, predictive policing, and scraping facial images for databases." These applications are generally prohibited due to their potential for significant harm or violation of EU values and fundamental rights. A few exemptions are permitted for law enforcement purposes. In a limited number of serious cases, real-time remote biometric identification systems are permitted. Court approval will be required for post-facto identification using remote biometric identification systems.

High-risk AI systems are subject to stringent regulation and must meet specific requirements related to "risk management, data quality, transparency, human oversight, accuracy, registration, quality management, monitoring, record-keeping, and incident reporting." High-risk AI systems include both safety components of already regulated products (such as medical devices or machinery) and stand-alone systems in areas like "biometric identification, critical infrastructure management, education and vocational training, employment and workers management, access to essential services, law enforcement, migration, asylum and border control management, and administration of justice and democratic processes." The EU wants to make an online register public, listing all active high-risk AI systems and use-cases, as well as foundation models on the market (Article 60 of the EU AI Act).

Limited risk AI systems are those that pose a risk of manipulation or deceit, requiring transparency about the use of AI (e.g., chatbots). Users must be informed when they are interacting with an AI, and any synthetic content should be clearly labeled. Lastly, minimal risk AI systems, which comprise a majority of AI applications, such as AI-enabled spam filters, do not have specific regulatory requirements but are encouraged to adhere to general principles of human oversight, non-discrimination, and fairness.

V. Implications on the Use of AI in Criminal Law and Civil Matters

According to the *MIT Technology Review* predictive policing is banned unless used with "clear human assessment and objective facts, which basically do not simply leave the decision of going after a certain individual in a criminal investigation only because an algorithm says so." However, the EU AI Act does not apply to AI systems that are meant only for military and defense uses. In other words, we know they can have serious consequences, but pragmatism rules the roost here.

While drafting the EU AI Act, legislators debated on the best way to regulate police use of biometric systems in public places. Under the EU AI Act, EU police forces can only use biometric identification systems in public places with court approval. Police can only use biometric identification systems for a few specific crimes, such as terrorism, human trafficking, sexual exploitation of children, and drug trafficking. Also, EU police forces can only use high-risk AI systems in "exceptional circumstances relating to public security".

High-risk AI systems are those that "negatively affect safety or fundamental rights." AI systems in areas of law enforcement and assistance in legal interpretation are considered high-risk AI and will have to be registered in an EU database. High-risk AI systems will be "assessed before being put on the market and also throughout their lifecycle." This is a concept that has followed in the pharmaceutical market. New drugs are vetted before release and monitored after they are in the market. More examples of high-risk AI systems: AI systems used by the courts and dispute resolution bodies to "help them research and interpret facts and the law, or to apply the law to a concrete set of facts," according to law firm Pinsent Masons.

Concerning EU AI Act Article 6(2)(a), law firm Pinsent Masons reports that AI systems are considered high-risk if they are "intended to be used by or on behalf of law enforcement authorities, or by Union institutions, agencies, offices or bodies in support of law enforcement authorities or on their behalf to assess the risk of a natural person to become a victim of criminal offenses." Other articles expand the use of AI by law enforcement authorities as high-risk to other actions and tools. Article 6(2)(b) includes the use of "polygraphs and similar tools," Article 6(2)(d) includes using AI "to evaluate the reliability of evidence in the course of investigation or prosecution of criminal offenses." Article 6(2)(e) includes using AI in "assessing the risk of a natural person of offending or re-offending not solely based on profiling of natural persons or to assess personality traits and characteristics or past criminal behavior of natural persons or groups."

The EU AI Act will progress in stages over the course of the next three years, with different guidelines throughout. This is to help companies follow the compliance in a reasonable fashion. It is estimated that other countries outside of the EU will follow in their footsteps, making AI regulations of their own. A lot of these steps by the EU will affect consumers, in more ways than one. The main safeguards for consumers that the New Regulation, according to *European Parliament News*, include safeguards concerning "general purpose artificial intelligence; limits on the use of biometric identification systems; bans on social scoring and AI used to manipulate or exploit user vulnerabilities; and the right of consumers to launch complaints and receive meaningful explanations."

The New Regulation restricts the use of facial recognition in public places by law enforcement agencies (allowing for exceptions as noted above). This is similar to the bans by San Francisco, Oakland, and the Commonwealth of Virginia stateside. The ban by the EU would apply to all 27 Member States and a population of close to 450 million people.

The European Parliament, one of the EU institutions that worked very diligently to amend the law, installed a ban on predictive policing systems. Such systems use AI to analyze large data sets to proactively allocate resources and preemptively deploy police to crime-prone areas or predict an individual's potential future criminality. Needless to say, these systems are controversial. Is the past always the prologue to the future? Or are we to ignore flashing warning signs? Critics complain that these systems are often racist and lack transparency. We unpacked a lot of this in our *Short and Happy Guide to Artificial Intelligence for Lawyers* (a must read) which dealt with the criminal justice system and Artificial Intelligence. You should be developing a sense of the way in which the EU authorities are trying to walk a tightrope here.

The EU AI Act bans high-risk AI systems that include things such as "social scoring" systems. These pose a high-risk threat to society, classifying people by their behavior out in public using AI technology. In China, they are currently working on these social scoring systems, for example in schools, using retina scans, facial recognitions, and fingerprints. Using databases, CCTV, and the internet, the AI can infer things such as race, sex, and even political and religious beliefs. The EU has decided to ban such systems, stating that only law enforcement in specific circumstances will be allowed to use facial recognition and other similar AI software.

Moreover, one of the most discussed sections of the act is that facial recognition technology on "live crowds" is banned. Again, law enforcement will be able to use it in special situations such as a potential terrorist attack or finding a missing person. In most cases, the law enforcement will still be required to get permission to use the special AI software\. In terms of consent, transparency, and data protection in commercial situations, this is a pivotal step for consumer privacy and rights.

The EU AI Act sets the legal foundation for regulating AI systems, but it also shows a need for commitment within other legal sectors, such as product safety and liability, to regulate AI for consumers. For example, the EU has made plans to alter and add to existing product safety legislation. This will ensure that AI systems work effectively and safely, meeting high safety standards before reaching a public market. AI systems in use in critical public infrastructure such as water, electricity, and gas, will be gauged for high-risk systems. AI that is deployed in sectors such as employment, education, healthcare and banking, will be covered. Certain law enforcement, justice and border control systems will also use this standard. For example, a high-risk system banned by the AI Act's standards would be one to choose a job-candidate, or university admissions. These types of AI software can pose threats of bias and create unfair disparities.

Another critical part of the act requires AI systems deployed to the public be accurately tested for risk assessments, have human oversight, and have their usage logged. General-purpose AI (GPAI) systems, and the models they are mirrored off, will have to meet certain criteria including transparency requirements. An instance of this will be compliance with EU copyright law and publishing comprehensive notes of the content used in training the GPAI systems. EU citizens that have been affected can also request explanations about decisions made by these AI systems. The EU's official website harrumphs, "Thanks to Parliament, unacceptable AI practices will be banned in Europe, and the rights of workers and citizens will be protected." If only.

VI. The European Union and AI in Employment Matters

By now you know that the Act adopts a risk-based approach to AI governance, distinguishing different levels of risk associated with various AI applications. Specifically, AI tools designed for workplace use are categorized as "high-risk," attracting a stricter regulatory regime to ensure ethical and responsible usage.

For EU employers, the AI Act stipulates a series of obligations that must be met when employing high-risk AI systems. Firstly, there is a requirement to disclose the use of such systems to employees and their representatives, ensuring transparency in the workplace. Additionally, human oversight is mandated, necessitating adequately trained and competent individuals to monitor and manage these AI systems. This role is responsible for stopping the use of AI if discrimination or any form of bias is detected, with a protocol in place to report such issues to the system's provider, importer, distributor, and the relevant market surveillance authority.

Another key aspect of the AI Act is data retention. Employers must maintain logs generated by the AI system and preserve records for at least six months. This facilitates accountability and potential auditing processes. Additionally, adherence to data privacy laws remains paramount, in alignment with existing frameworks such as the General Data Protection Regulation.

The AI Act's scope extends beyond the European Union's physical borders. Employers outside the EU must comply with the Act if the AI system they use impacts individuals within the EU, such as job applications or the management of workers in EU Member States. Non-compliance with the AI Act is met with severe penalties, which mirror the GDPR's stringent approach. Fines range from €7.5 million to as much as €30 million, or a percentage of the company's total worldwide annual sales—1.5% or up to 6%, respectively, depending on which amount is higher.

The AI Act introduces a comprehensive set of regulations that EU employers must carefully follow. This legal framework intends to balance the benefits of AI innovation with the need to protect fundamental human rights and prevent discriminatory practices. As AI use grows within the European workspace, and the entire world, these regulations will shape the ethical and legal boundaries within which AI operates. That's because they were the OG of AI regulation.

VII. Implications for Intellectual Property Law

The EU AI Act applies to every AI system that impacts the EU residents, regardless of the place from which the AI systems are built or operated. The AI Act may apply to AI models created prior to the EU AI Act taking effect if the AI systems are "prohibited" or "high-risk" systems that are typically used by public authorities. As discussed above (and as you can now recite in your sleep), the AI Act is based on a tiered compliance framework of different risk levels on how the AI system could or is used. AI systems are prohibited if they are considered a risk to the safety, security and fundamental rights of people. According to EY, a global consultancy, AI systems considered high-risk necessitate compliance obligations related to "data governance, human oversight, cybersecurity measures, post-market monitoring, and maintenance of the required technical documentation." All other systems are considered minimal risks, which impose no additional obligations, other than the encouragement of companies to commit to the codes of conduct voluntarily.

Generative AI systems, such as OpenAI's ChatGPT, are trained through data scraped from the internet, much of which may be copyrighted. The EU AI Act, Article 3(44e), according to law firm Morgan Lewis, defines "general purpose AI system" as an "AI system which is based on a general-purpose AI model, that has the capability to serve a variety of purposes, both for direct use as well as for integration in other AI systems."

Recital 60c, which provides context on how to interpret EU AI articles, clarifies this definition, stating that "large generative AI models are a typical example for a general-purpose AI model, given that they allow for flexible generation of content (such as in the form of text, audio, images or video) that can readily accommodate a wide range of distinctive tasks," according to law firm Morgan Lewis. The law firm's also reports that Recital 60i expands the obligations for GPAI models to obtain the "authorization of the [individual] rightholder concerned" for AI training, as the "development and training of such models require access to vast amounts of text, images, videos, and other data . . . [a]ny use of copyright protected content requires the authorization of the rightholder concerned unless relevant copyright exceptions and limitations apply."

However, Recital 60i does not state if U.S. copyright law exemptions, such as fair use, are applied by the EU AI Act. According to the firm's commentary, courts may interpret the EU AI Act to mean that "only authorization of the rights holder as recognized under EU copyright law will count, particularly if read alongside Recital 60j, which, in turn, potentially seeks to apply EU copyright law outside of the EU." Recital 60j states that: "[a]ny provider placing a general-purpose AI model on the EU market should comply with this obligation, regardless of the jurisdiction in which the copyright-relevant acts underpinning the training of these general-purpose AI models take place." Morgan Lewis interprets that the AI Act may require "compliance with EU copyright law for AI training abroad . . . If this interpretation were accepted, it would suggest that the EU is seeking to export its IP laws worldwide with respect to the AI sector." That is just the sort of extraterritoriality of which the EU has long complained that the United States had been doing from its shores.

Another relevant Recital of the AI Act for IP law is Recital 60k, which states that: "providers of such models draw up and make publicly available a sufficiently detailed summary of the content used for training the general purpose model." In contrast, disclosing sources of training data is not required by U.S. copyright law.

It is also important to note that providers of GPAI models, according to the law firm Covington:

must create and maintain technical documentation of the model that includes certain minimum elements, provide detailed information and documentation to providers that integrate these models into their AI systems, adopt a policy to respect EU copyright law, and make publicly available a 'sufficiently' detailed summary of the content used for training the GPAI.

Covington also reports that the AI Act also creates transparency obligations on providers and users of GPAI models which include:

(1) providers of AI and GPAI systems generating synthetic audio, image, video, or text content,

(2) deployers of emotion recognition or biometric categorization systems,

(3) deployers of AI systems that generate or manipulate image, audio, or video content constituting a deepfake, and

(4) deployers of systems that generate or manipulate text published with the purpose of informing the public on matters of public interest.

Although the EU AI Act does provide exceptions for AI systems transparency obligations if used "for artistic, satirical, creative, or similar purposes."

What is clear, most importantly, is that transparency is of paramount importance. What is not yet clear is what happens when the rubber meets the road. Will these rules favor large organizations or will small firms (which already are being outmuscled) be able to compete effectively?

VIII. Summary/Key Points

1. Enacted in 2024, the European Union AI Act is the law for the EU's 27 Member States. There is a compliance window of 6 months to 36 months depending on the AI system's risk classification.
2. The EU AI Act prohibits use of certain types of AI systems deemed as having an unacceptable risk such as social scoring, real-time biometric surveillance, and subliminal (user) manipulation. There are exceptions for law enforcement.
3. The risk-based categorization of different AI applications (unacceptable, high, limited, and minimal risk) and pegging compliance obligations to these risk-tiers, with more stringent requirements for high-risk systems is a reasonable approach.
4. The EU AI Act exerts global influence. It has implications not just for EU-based companies but non-EU entities that deploy AI affecting EU individuals must comply. It is an example of extraterritorial jurisdiction.
5. Critics argue that the EU AI Act may inhibit innovation, particularly for startups and smaller firms unable to meet compliance demands. U.S. Vice President JD Vance publicly warned that over-regulation risks marginalizing Europe technologically.
6. Be that as it may, the EU AI Act represents the first comprehensive legislative framework governing artificial intelligence. It prioritizes transparency, accountability, and human oversight. Whether it also fosters AI innovation remains to be seen.

CHAPTER 7

AI Regulation in the People's Republic of China

I. Introduction

The ambition of the People's Republic of China (PRC or China) to become the world's leading power in Artificial Intelligence (AI) has driven the country to invest heavily, not just in development and deployment of AI tools, but also in policymaking to shape its increasing technological growth. Since the release of DeekSeek's R1 model upended the AI space in January 2025, Chinese AI companies continue to challenge the dominance of Western competitors at a fast pace. In turn, the Chinese government has implemented a number of regulatory measures that ensure both creative innovation for future leadership and necessary controls to maintain its power and influence over Chinese society. Since 2017, China has introduced a series of AI policies that aim to regulate the application of algorithmic decision-making and deep synthesis technologies, and eventually Generative AI services in various sectors of life. These efforts have generally been successful. These policies have prompted the Chinese government to enjoy the benefits of AI development while ensuring the use of this paradigm shifting technology is done within the dictates of China's ruling apparatus.

Following this Introduction, Part II of this Chapter looks at the dynamics of China's command economy and the roles that the Golden Share policy and Great Firewall of China (GFW) play in that country's AI development. Part III explores China's regulations in a geopolitical context which folds in the national industrial policy of the country coupled with its international trade and investment program, the Belt and Road Initiative (BRI, also known as the One Belt, One Road initiative). Part IV unpacks the various laws and regulations in the AI space, including the country's cybersecurity laws, which form the legal underpinnings for AI regulation, the path-breaking nature of the Beijing AI Principles, and the ethical standards that have been applied to the use of AI tools by children, the Data Security Law (DSL), and a number other rules that have emerged from Chinese authorities. Part V concludes with a global context for Chinese regulations—little of what China does is done in isolation.

II. China's Command Economy and Legislative Black Box

China's AI regulatory system operates within a broader "black box" legal framework, in which policies are often ambiguous, enforcement mechanisms done on a case-by-case basis. Decision-making processes remain largely in the hands of the government and reflect the priorities of the Communist Party of China (CPC) and not business cases. This lack of transparency and uncertainty with law enforcement raises concerns about the trajectory between innovation, censorship, and international competition. China's AI policies, not surprisingly, prioritize social stability, national security, and ideological alignment, subsequently leading to a restrictive regulatory environment.

Over the years, China has rapidly emerged as a leading figure in AI development with strong government involvement and support. The Chinese government recognizes the need for regulations on AI technologies to set obligations and restrictions for providers and users alike. Unlike Western approaches to AI governance models, the PRC's approach to AI development is tightly integrated into a national strategy through which the Chinese government aims to balance between expanding AI operations by major technology companies and greater government control of individual freedom. AI is an industry that can help Beijing secure dominance in so many other technology industries—so they are playing for keeps.

There are guidelines, measures, and principles as well as governmental and Ministerial statements that are important in China. Each has a different weight and is enforced in varying ways at carrying times. Frankly, it is all a bit of a mystery for Western experts. Viktar Fedaseyeu and Adam Yu have explained:

> Because Chinese regulators by and large strive to promote economic growth, the interplay between China's implicit and explicit regulations follows a predictable pattern. Initially, innovation (including financial innovation) is often allowed to develop with few if any explicit rules. If and when signs of misbehavior appear, regulators step in by providing implicit guidance rather than issuing explicit rules. If implicit guidance is insufficient to rein in the excesses that government officials are concerned about, explicit (and often strict) regulations follow.

So, we are talking about black boxes (AI tools) in a black box (China's opaque legal and regulatory frameworks). It sounds like what Russians call "Matryoshka dolls," (dolls within dolls) except these dolls are masked and censored.

This lack of transparency and uncertainty with law enforcement raises concerns about the trajectory and intersection among innovation, censorship, and international competition power; China's AI policies prioritize social stability, national security, and ideological alignment, all of which lead to a restrictive regulatory environment. The Chinese make the European Union look like the United States when it comes to AI regulation. Get that?

To begin to understand the AI regulations of the PRC, it is very important to understand several ideas surrounding the model of Chinese governmental operation. The first fundamental idea is the "Golden Share." The Golden Share initiative is a power instrument used by the Chinese government to maintain influence over private companies, especially major high-tech organizations. Although it accounts for only 1% ownership, this symbolic stake grants the Chinese government the authority to intervene in corporations' activities and decision-making processes to ensure those major entities align with national ideals. In short, state-based involvement provides the Chinese government with a far-reaching ability to intervene whenever it believes a corporation strays from national priorities and policies. These are the state-owned enterprises (SOEs) about which we hear so much.

The GFW is another cornerstone feature that has shaped China's regulation of internet access and provides further State control over advancements in the development and deployment of AI tools. The Chinese government implements the GFW to filter, block, and limit internet access within China's borders, effectively isolating China's digital space from global open access by restricting an increasing number of foreign websites such as the platforms of Twitter, Google, and Meta. Under the constraints of the GFW, Chinese internet users can only access and comment on content permitted by the Chinese government, rather than having open access to different information sources and shaping various perspectives. Thus, one cannot search for information about topics that the CPC finds objectionable.

After understanding the roles that Golden Share and GFW play in Chinese governmental operations, these two key concepts can help us assess China's distinctive approach to AI development, including its rapid advancements, potential applications, and the challenges associated with state-controlled regulation and oversight. Or as we like to say in our best Humphrey Bogart voice, "We'll always have Beijing."

Contrary to the common perception of Chinese policymaking as entirely top-down, the development of AI regulations has followed a dynamic and multi-stakeholder process. This iterative system, often described as a policy funnel, involves a range of actors including mid-level bureaucrats, academics, think tanks, journalists, and technology companies. Regulatory ideas often begin with real-world events or social concerns and move through stages of public discourse, intellectual debate, and technical consultation before reaching the level of formal regulation through state bodies like the Cyberspace Administration of China (CAC).

This process reveals that Chinese AI governance is not solely dictated by the CPC's ideological imperatives but is also shaped by inputs from civil society and industry. For example, media backlash against algorithm-driven news platforms and academic work on gig economy labor conditions directly influenced policy drafts. While final authority rests with party-state institutions, the participatory elements embedded in the early stages of regulation allow for greater policy adaptability. This structure reflects a hybrid model of governance, ideologically guided, yet technically consultative and responsive.

III. China's Geopolitical Agenda

It is no secret that, for decades, the PRC has been working to overtake the dominance of Western technology and become the leader in the industries of innovation for the future. AI is one such industry along with 5G, semiconductor chips, robotics, blockchain technology, and self-driving vehicles.

Indeed, the Chinese government has made AI a major priority in its "Made in China 2025" initiative from the State Council of the PRC in May 2015. In July 2017, China's State Council released the country's strategy for developing AI titled "New Generation Artificial Intelligence Development Plan" (in Mandarin, 新一代人工智能发展规划). China's goal is to become the world leader in AI by 2030. Given the disruption that DeepSeek wreaked upon the world in January 2025 and the subsequent open-source AI technologies that Alibaba and a number of SOEs have released since, this very well could happen. And the Chinese are taking this technology on the road.

In September 2013 on a visit to Kazakhstan, PRC President Xi Jinping introduced China's Silk Road Economic Belt plan. With the impulse from President Xi, the National Development and Reform Commission, the Ministry of Foreign Affairs, and the Ministry of Commerce jointly released a concrete action plan, the BRI, in March 2015 to build out the Silk Road Economic Belt. The BRI is the Chinese strategy for development and economic diplomacy that fosters mercantile connectivity and cooperation among countries around the world, by both land and sea. It seeks to connect Asian, European, and African continents and their respective trading routes (both land-based and maritime-based) through investment and other commercial vehicles. With more than 140 countries around the world linked to Chinese commerce, using Chinese technology, and eventually, Beijing hopes, Chinese currency, it is a trillion dollar plus infrastructure and investment project to rival anything the West can summon and execute.

AI systems can help scale these efforts. According to Bill Drexil and Hannah Kelly, AI is part of the Belt and Road—with the potential for being a much cheaper, quicker and more potent way for China to build its influence. The flow of data could, ultimately, be a far more powerful political tool than the flow of cars and trains. If China's build-it-first AI strategy works, it could be disastrous for American interests abroad.

In addition to pouring billions of dollars into AI companies that are SOEs, the Chinese have also worked to win the regulation race that comes with AI development and deployment. This is critical to Beijing as AI could be a threat to the control the CPC has exercised over its people, its culture, and its immense commerce. China aims to be not just the AI superpower but the AI regulatory behemoth too. And now the rules come from the 800-pound panda in the room.

IV. China's Rules and Regulations Affecting the AI Space

The PRC has invested heavily in policymaking to shape its increasing technological growth but maintain national advantages and political control. This section introduces AI development in China by highlighting essential concepts that differentiate China's uniqueness in AI from other countries. Regulation for this burgeoning industry is driven by a number of AI regulations and policies with such exciting names like the Cybersecurity Law (CSL), Beijing AI Principles, DSL, Internet Information Service Algorithmic Recommendation Management Provisions, Provision on the Administration of Deep Synthesis of Internet Information Service, Interim Measures for Generative AI Services (Interim Measures), and Trial Measures for Ethical Review of Science and Technology (Trial Measures), which are each examined hereunder for their benefits and disadvantages along with real-life applications under the Chinese government. It is no secret that there is some tension between creative innovation and the possibility of stricter government censorship on freedom of speech, greater interference with individuals' privacy, and an overall vagueness in regulation. We have seen "capitalism with Chinese characteristics." Meet AI with Chinese characteristics.

A. Cybersecurity Law

China's CSL, which went into effect in June 2017, contained provisions applying to the construction, operation, maintenance, and use of information networks, and the supervision and administration of cybersecurity in China. With some 1.4 billion, that is a lot of supervision and administration.

The CSL provides a strict data privacy law detailing guidelines for the methods by which personal data information may be collected and archived. The CSL also requires that personal and critical information collected within the PRC remain within the country. The law does allow for transfers outside of China if it is truly necessary for business requirements but to do so, the handler of said data must subject itself to a security assessment from the Chinese authorities. This security assessment consists of an initial self-assessment followed then an external assessment by the Cybersecurity Administration of China. The CSL presents a major challenge for foreign companies as they must redesign the manner in which they operate. It is not easy to work in a stricter PRC these days.

B. Beijing Principles

The Beijing AI Principles are also instructive as to the PRC's thinking on AI regulation. They set the basic principles and foundations for AI development, including being ethical, diverse, inclusive, and responsible. More specifically, the Beijing AI Principles are divided into three parts: the research and development of AI, the use of AI and the governance of Artificial

Intelligence. The Beijing Academy of Artificial Intelligence took the lead in drafting it.

In May 2019, the Beijing Academy of Artificial Intelligence (BAAI), an organization backed by the Chinese Ministry of Science and Technology and the Beijing municipal government published these Principles to foster harmony between humans and machines. They highlighted the importance of privacy, dignity, freedom, autonomy, and rights and provided guidance for the use and governance of AI including avoiding a malicious AI race, undertaking continuous research, and the monitoring of risks.

Designed as guidelines and composed of seven governance principles, the Beijing AI Principles have been the most robust AI regulation coming out of China concerning AI to date. The Beijing AI Principles included harmony and friendliness; fairness and justice; inclusivity and sharing; respect privacy; secure/safe and controllable; shared responsibility; open collaboration; and agile governance. Many of the prominent technical organizations and companies including the country's technology behemoths Alibaba, Baidu, and Tencent and the most important research centers at Tsinghua University and Peking University assisted in the development of this code of behavior.

Concerning research and development, creators should build AI products that do good, serve humanity, conform to the interests of humankind, be responsible, control the risks of AI systems, take ethical design approaches, are diverse and inclusive, and are open platforms to avoid monopolies and should share the of Artificial Intelligence. The second part—those related to usage, mandates that AI should be used wisely and properly by ensuring informed consent and incorporating education and training for stakeholders. The third part of the Beijing AI Principles that relate the governance of AI, requires that employment be optimized, harmony and cooperation be instilled, that AI adapt and moderate, and that there be adaptation and moderation of risks.

In September 2020, China's first child-oriented AI development principles, the Beijing Consensus on Artificial Intelligence for Children (the Consensus), was published. This set of guidelines was undertaken to regulate AI's impact on the most vulnerable and impressionable segment of society. The Consensus emphasized child centeredness, while protecting the rights of children and improving policy and regulatory mechanisms to these ends. In order to give a globalized context to these principles, the document states that the definition of "children," description of values and children's rights will be used as in the 1989 United Nations Convention on the Rights of the Child (UNCRC) and as per the provisions of each country or region.

Some 19 detailed principles including dignity, fairness, child first, protection of privacy and inclusion of the will of children were stipulated in the Consensus. The UNCRC was used to assist in tracking the values and enshrining children's rights provided for in this second set of rules issued by the Beijing Academy of Artificial Intelligence. Child's play? Not so much.

C. Data Security Law

In June 2021, China's National People's Congress (NPC) promulgated the DSL of the People's Republic of China. There was little transition time as the law took effect in September 2021. There was much attention paid internationally to the cross-border effects of this sweeping law, as the DSL contains rules about cross-border data transfers and restrictions on the cooperation with foreign law enforcement officials. Most pressing was the DSL's extraterritorial jurisdiction impact.

And while the DSL was more of a set of policy guidelines for future legislative development and not a detailed prescription of data handling requirements, the DSL served as a major statement about the broad vision for China's technology future and an indication of its more aggressive stance towards extraterritorial jurisdiction when it comes to the transnational and transformative prongs of the future global digital economy.

The DSL's Article 7 established a guiding principle that the DSL that was intended "to encourage the lawful, reasonable, and effective utilization of data as part of a broader goal of promoting the development of China's digital economy." The DSL provides general requirements for the Chinese State to coordinate in the development of a big data strategy and of data security standards. Article 19 of the DSL provides for a "data transaction market" to be created to ensure that data flow freely in line with the strategic goals of Beijing. As the PRC is a command economy and much of the digital economy is subject to strategic central planning, the specific measures that will be of most interest to multinational businesses operating in China. Word of advice: Hire local counsel and then hire some more.

D. *Rules and Regulations Since 2022*

New rules were released subsequently by the Chinese government including a new algorithm law which came into force in 2022. In March of that year, the CAC announced Provisions on the Administration of Algorithmic Recommendations for Internet Information, a policy designed to regulate algorithms in analyzing online content and make recommendations accordingly. This measure enhances transparency and fairness in Internet governance, strengthens cybersecurity, and ensures compliance with lawful data practices. Some important guidelines include mandating licenses for online news publications, manipulating content, and banning the use of targeted user tags in algorithm-driven recommendations.

The CAC explicitly points out in Article 13 that algorithmic service providers must obtain permits under the law to publish news content. The rule also prohibits providers from generating fake news or sharing news from unauthorized sources.

While China has strictly regulated AI technology within its own borders on news content, it takes a very different approach when using AI to shape perceptions of foreign countries.

Article 14 prohibits algorithmic recommendation services from manipulating information by blocking certain content or altering the order of search results. This regulation ensures that internet users access diverse content and form independent perspectives without excessive oversight. The government promotes this article in this way, but the government itself has violated this article. Government agencies periodically scan search queries, chat messages, and social media posts and systematically block sensitive keywords in search engines. Topics such as Taiwanese democracy, the crackdown in Xinjiang (a region in Western China which is the home of many Muslim Uighurs), and the 1989 Tiananmen Square Massacre are heavily censored, preventing users from accessing information. Chinese technology companies utilize effective means to limit access to sensitive materials because of China's strong adherence to correct political direction. Stability and control of the CPC narrative is critical to Beijing. Additionally, those people who manage search algorithms closely monitor news sites and discussion boards, particularly those covering religion and politics. As the social media movement emerges, companies are pressured to continuously expand their list of restricted terms to maintain compliance with the Chinese government's regulations. Despite the Chinese government's repeated claims of supporting free expression and open exchange of ideas, this policy on algorithmic recommendation demonstrates there may indeed be strong censorship over content.

The practical application of this article of the CAC reinforces the Chinese government's effort to limit alternative viewpoints and choice of content, which may effectively undermine the provision's original intent.

1. Deep Synthesis

The CAC also declared the Provision on the Administration of Deep Synthesis of Internet Information Service to become effective on January 10, 2023. China's regulation of deep synthesis technologies targets AI systems that generate or modify content such as images, videos, audio, or text through deep learning. The regulation was a direct response to the rise of synthetic media and deepfakes, emphasizing content labeling, ethical standards, and content moderation obligations. Service providers are required to watermark or conspicuously label AI-generated content that might mislead users or impersonate real individuals, particularly when biometric features are involved. These measures aim to prevent deception and uphold social trust, especially in politically sensitive contexts.

Moreover, the regulation imposes heightened responsibilities on platforms offering technical support for deep synthesis services. Providers must conduct regular reviews, security assessments, and file their algorithms in the national registry. These obligations extend to monitoring content that could affect national security or tarnish China's national image. While the regulation is framed as a protective mechanism for the public, it also consolidates government control over narrative formation and ideological conformity, illustrating how technological safeguards and political interests are tightly interwoven in China's AI governance model.

Article 17 of the Deep Synthesis Provision (DSP) requires service providers to label content generated or edited using deep synthesis technologies if such content could confuse or mislead the public. Although the Chinese government sets this regulation, many companies do not follow through in practice. On the contrary, the lack of labeling on AI-generated content may create opportunities for fraud.

Article 15 of the DSP mandates service providers and technical supporters to strengthen oversight by periodically reviewing, assessing, and verifying AI-generated synthetic content. Through these measures, the Chinese government seeks to protect national security and safeguard public interests by maintaining control over the ethical and legal implications of AI-generated content. This control extends to information operations, where AI-driven tools may be used to produce political propaganda against individuals.

Due to the rapid advancements in AI, China has implemented the DSP to express technological benefits with concerns over its misuse. While deep synthesis technologies enhance sectors like healthcare and education, its misuse in fraud and political stability demands extensive government oversight.

In July 2023, the CAC released its Interim Measures which provided rules to regulate those who provide Generative AI capabilities to the public in China. These included traditional AI safety measures like protections for IP, and provisions to ensure transparency and prevent discrimination. Other sections are particular to China, including the prohibition of incitement against the State and the adherence to the values of socialism. To provide Generative AI services to the public, Chinese firms must obtain a government license. Moreover, the firm must submit a security assessment if public opinion attributes or social mobilization capabilities are used in the model. Generative AI providers must also protect the integrity of state power, safeguard national unity, and avoid inciting secession.

As deep synthesis technologies continue to evolve over the years, the government's regulatory frameworks also keep growing.

In August 2023, the CAC issued Interim Measures for Generative AI Services to balance the development and deployment of Generative AI within China. The Interim Measures build upon the Deep Synthesis Provision and further expands oversight beyond deep fake content to cover all Generative AI content. This broader approach to Generative AI materials illustrates that AI's impact was wider than deceptive voice or appearance. The Interim Measures requires real-name user registration and a mechanism for reporting improper or illegal content to encourage controlled AI innovation while decreasing the potential for political disturbance and social instability.

Article 9 implies that the service provider must require users to register with their real identities before accessing generative AI application models. It is worth noticing that China had a history of enforcing real-name registration for internet services to strengthen accountability and control. Chinese AI models are not exceptions to this rule.

In addition to the real-name registration requirements under the Interim Measures, Article 15 indicates that providers should establish a complaint and reporting system. This mechanism allows users to report inappropriate content, misinformation, or rule violations promptly.

While the Interim Measures regulate AI-generated content through a real-name registration and reporting system, China's AI governance also turns to the ethical and societal impacts of advanced AI technologies. This is the space where the Trial Measures were enacted by China's Ministry of Science and Technology in March 2023. Several essential features include mandatory ethical review and annual risk assessment reports.

Besides setting up an ethical committee for "ethically sensitive" science and technology activities, the Trial Measures underscores the importance of thorough risk assessment in scientific research and technological development. This regulation not only requires the establishment of an ethics review committee but also mandates that institutions submit an annual ethics review report and an implementation report to higher authorities by March each year. These annual reports detail how institutions systematically evaluate and mitigate foreseeable risks associated with scientific research and technological developments to keep ethical considerations and risk management in check within China's regulatory boundaries. Again, the regulation fails to mention what would be the possible outcome for institutions if the government finds out violations.

The establishment of an ethics committee and the requirement of an annual report under the Trial Measures reveal China's powerful commitment to aligning AI development with social values and regulatory priorities. The Chinese government seeks to foster AI innovations within controlled limits only because it acknowledges the dangers unchecked technological growth might impose to Chinese society.

In November 2024, the CAC announced a new AI committee at the World Internet Conference with the clear intention to take leadership of the international dialogue concerning AI governance. This move occurred a mere day after, the United States-China Economic and Security Review Commission released its 2024 to the U.S. Congress.

The Chinese AI Committee is composed of 170 members, including experts from Western corporations and institutions. Through the Chinese state regulator of the internet, it is thoroughly a Chinese institution, yet it also includes representatives from Western companies and institutions, including IBM, Cisco, and SAP. Though it remains under Chinese leadership through the PRC's internet regulator, the Committee is the debut of the conference's first permanent specialized committee. The Chinese AI Committee is tasked with the development of standards and security protocols for AI development. While actual specifics remain undefined, there are increased attempts to exhibit Chinese leadership in the regulatory space. With Beijing's increasing focus on technology governance, this Committee comprises European academicians, a clear slap to the U.S. as Washington DC hits Chinese AI companies with new restrictions on investments and an on again/off again ban on the purchase of GPUs.

While all major regulations that the Chinese government have announced since 2022 have efficiently enhanced various aspects of individuals' lives, this series of regulations also presents significant obstacles and risks to the Chinese government. In addition to strengthening oversight and fostering AI advancement, these regulations raise concerns about the suppression of freedom of speech, invasion of privacy rights, and vagueness in law.

A major issue to unpack is the freedom of speech, the perennial challenge when analyzing the PRC's approach to technology. As an example, DeepSeek, the Chinese AI language model released in January 2025, has built in content control measures to satisfy China's regulatory requirements.

Although developments in Chinese AI bring numerous benefits to Chinese society, rapid progress with AI tools threatens individuals' privacy. According to China's regulatory frameworks, AI service providers shall undergo security assessments and data audits. By doing so, the Chinese government compels companies to retain extensive user data, which can be subject to government review if the government declares that companies must turn over data information. Eventually, the Chinese government grants absolute access to individuals' personal data for uses and reasons unknown to civilians. This greater discretion of reviewing personal data when the government sees fit challenges basic privacy rights.

In addition to retaining extensive user data, the interconnectivity of true identity and individuals' online accounts raises privacy concerns of anonymity. The Provision on the Administration of Deep Synthesis of Internet Information Service mandates real-name registration before interacting with AI-generated content on various platforms. This means individuals must offer authentic identity information. This provides an easier way for the Chinese government to correlate a user's online activity across different platforms, even if they use aliases as usernames.

Another drawback in China's approach to AI governance is vagueness in law provisions themselves, which gives rise to uncertainty in carrying out AI regulations. Although the Chinese government practices a series of regulations, none of these regulations specify what penalties are set for what kind of non-compliance. Instead, the common language they articulate is "pursuant to other applicable laws and regulations if any entity engaged in any violations of rules."

However, this ambiguous wording leads neither service providers nor users to know what exact consequences for their non-compliance if non-compliance occurs. This ambiguous language also makes it very difficult for individuals to consistently comply with regulation because ambiguity in legal provision suggests that those rules might be subject to change and leaves the Chinese government the sole authority with overwhelming discretion to interpret and distinguish one incident from another violation under a unified standard that could be applied to multiple occurrences.

China has implemented these different policies in an attempt to balance the tension between creative AI development and development for the PRC's drive to lead AI-related industries and the need to maintain control. However, the ultimate outcome is that individuals' personal information become increasingly transparent and subject to review by third parties, making people become more vulnerable to Chinese government's oversight with less autonomous choices. Although these aforementioned four regulations seem to address various aspects such as algorithmic recommendation, deep synthesis technology, Generative AI content, and ethical concerns on AI governance on the outset of looking, they end up serving the same purpose of "adhering to the correct direction and priorities of Chinese society." Yet, the Chinese government does not specifically set out a concrete definition for this ambiguous concept. This lack of clarity means the standard for compliance can shift over time, depending on how authorities choose to interpret the ambiguous concept. This dearth of clarity leaves the door open for various interpretations and subsequently inconsistent applications for individuals. Thus, vagueness in legal provision appears to increase uncertainty and insecurity for people when they carry out or comply with AI regulations in China.

2. License for Publishing News

The CAC explicitly points out in Article 13 of the Interim Measures that algorithmic service providers must obtain permits under the law to publish news content. The rule also prohibits providers from generating fake news or sharing news from unauthorized sources. Although this article does not specify how the government will respond to rule violations, a case involving ChatGPT use can illustrate potential penalties the Chinese government can impose on those who violate this article.

Content manipulation is an issue worldwide. Article 14 prohibits algorithmic recommendation services from manipulating information by blocking certain content or altering the order of search results. This regulation ensures that internet users access diverse content and form independent perspectives without excessive oversight. The government promotes this article in this way, but the government often acts in violation of this article. Government agencies periodically scan search queries, chat messages, and social media posts and systematically block sensitive keywords in search engines.

Issues abound with biased user tags. Article 17 mandates that algorithmic service providers must allow users to disable personalized recommendations to prevent the creation of an "information cocoon"-an environment where users are repeatedly exposed to homogeneous content based on their prior search and view history. The article promotes diverse perspectives and balanced information access by allowing users to select and delete user tags in an algorithmic recommendation service targeting personal habits. While this provision aims to enhance freedom of speech, the Chinese government seems to stay far from this principle in practice.

The CAC further declared the Provision on the Administration of Deep Synthesis of Internet Information Service to become effective in January 2023. China is no exception, as most countries benefit from the deep synthesis technologies in higher education and healthcare. In the healthcare sector, deep synthesis technologies has enabled remote consultations in regions with limited access to medical specialists, distributing efficient allocation of healthcare resources. Similarly, studies have shown that AI-powered learning environments and visual tutorial videos have significantly enhanced the learning experience for Chinese undergraduate students. While enjoying beneficial influences of the deep synthesis technologies, the Chinese government also realizes the stronger need for addressing data security and personal information protection. The DSP focuses on fraud prevention and the need for governmental control associated with deep synthesis technologies.

3. Reporting Improper or Illegal Content

In addition to the real-name registration requirements under the Interim Measures, Article 15 indicates that providers should establish a complaint and reporting system. This mechanism allows users to report inappropriate content, misinformation, or rule violations promptly. While the Interim Measures for Generative AI Services regulate AI-generated content through a real-name registration and reporting system, China's AI governance also turns to the ethical and societal impacts of advanced AI technologies. This is where the Trial Measures were enacted by China's Ministry of Science and Technology on March 1, 2023. Several essential features include mandatory ethical review and annual risk assessment reports.

4. Mandatory Ethical Review

Under the Trial Measures, any corporations engaging in "ethically sensitive" technology activities, including AI development, must establish an ethical review committee. Any AI development must obtain governmental approval before release and undergo ethics review by committees. The government is very cautious about whether current developments of algorithm applications and systems enable the ability to influence public opinion and whether AI advancement embodies socialist values. Therefore, the ethical committee primarily assesses if models are in compliance with China's legal regulations and societal priorities. When the Trial Measures only discusses requirements that service providers and users must follow, this policy does not specify any penalties for non-compliance.

Hence, China's mandatory ethical review for AI development reflects the government's effort to align technological advancements with social values and public interest. By imposing governmental approval and an ethics review committee, the policy balances responsible development and decreases risks for inappropriate applications and ethical violations simultaneously.

5. Annual Risk Assessment

Besides setting up an ethical committee for "ethically sensitive" science and technology activities, the Trial Measures also underscores the importance of thorough risk assessment in scientific research and technological development. This regulation not only requires the establishment of an ethics review committee but also mandates that institutions submit an annual ethics review report and an implementation report to higher authorities by March each year. These annual reports detail how institutions systematically evaluate and mitigate foreseeable risks associated with scientific research and technological developments to keep ethical considerations and risk management in check within China's regulatory boundaries. Again, the regulation fails to mention what would be the possible outcome for institutions if the government finds out violations.

The establishment of an ethics committee and the requirement of an annual report under the Trial Measures reveal China's powerful commitment to aligning AI development with social values and regulatory priorities. The Chinese government seeks to foster AI innovations within controlled limits only because it acknowledges the dangers unchecked technological growth might impose to Chinese society.

6. Algorithm Registry

China's algorithm registry system has emerged as a central tool in its evolving AI governance framework. Initially introduced in the 2021 algorithm recommendation regulation, the registry requires companies whose algorithms can influence public opinion or have social mobilization capabilities to submit technical documentation and undergo security self-assessments. This registry is not merely a bureaucratic formality, it serves as a regulatory checkpoint that enables the Chinese government to track and evaluate the deployment of powerful AI systems, particularly those used in content distribution and recommendation.

The registry's scope has since expanded to encompass deep synthesis technologies and Generative Artificial Intelligence. By requiring algorithmic service providers to file information on their systems, China ensures early visibility into AI applications that may pose political, social, or ideological risks. This infrastructure helps consolidate regulatory oversight and reinforces China's broader strategy of preemptively shaping the technological landscape in line with national priorities. It also institutionalizes a form of anticipatory governance, enabling authorities to intervene before AI systems become disruptive.

7. Worker Protections

Among the lesser known but significant aspects of China's AI regulation are provisions aimed at protecting gig workers, particularly those subjected to algorithmic management. The 2021 recommendation algorithm rules mandated that platforms using algorithms for scheduling or task allocation must uphold the rights of workers to fair compensation and rest. These provisions were driven by public outcry and academic attention to exploitative practices in sectors like food delivery, where algorithmic efficiency often came at the expense of labor conditions and safety.

By incorporating worker protection clauses into broader AI governance, China recognizes the material consequences of algorithmic decision-making beyond digital content. These protections signal a shift from viewing AI as purely a technical or ideological tool to acknowledging its socioeconomic impact. Although implementation remains inconsistent, the inclusion of labor rights within algorithm regulations reflects a unique attempt to align digital governance with welfare considerations, positioning China as one of the few jurisdictions to address AI's effect on workers in formal legal texts.

The major regulations that the Chinese government have announced over the years efficiently enhance various aspects of individuals' lives. These regulations also present significant obstacles and risks to the Chinese government. In addition to strengthening oversight and fostering AI advancement, these regulations raise concerns about the suppression of freedom of speech, invasion of privacy rights, and vagueness in law.

Although the Chinese government practices a series of regulations, none of these regulations specify what penalties are set for what kind of non-compliance. Instead, the common language they articulate is "pursuant to other applicable laws and regulations if any entity engaged in any violations of rules." However, this ambiguous wording leads neither service providers nor users to know what exact consequences for their non-compliance if non-compliance occurs. This ambiguous language also makes it very difficult for individuals to consistently comply with regulation because ambiguity in legal provision suggests that those rules might be subject to change and leaves the Chinese government the sole authority with overwhelming discretion to interpret and distinguish one incident from another violation under a unified standard that could be applied to multiple occurrences.

Moreover, China has implemented many different policies trying to balance the tension between creative AI development and boundaries of government control and claim these regulations target various focuses. However, the ultimate outcome is that individuals' personal information becomes increasingly transparent and subject to review by third parties, making people become more vulnerable to the Chinese government's oversight with less autonomous choices. Although four regulations seem to address various aspects such as algorithmic recommendation, deep synthesis technology, Generative AI content, and ethical concerns on AI governance on the outset of looking, they end up serving the same purpose of "adhering correct direction and priorities of Chinese society."

The Chinese government does not specifically set out a concrete definition for this ambiguous concept. This lack of clarity means the standard for compliance can shift over time, depending on how authorities choose to interpret the ambiguous concept. This unclarity leaves the door open for various interpretations and subsequently inconsistent applications for individuals. Thus, vagueness in legal provisions seems to increase uncertainty and insecurity for people when they carry out or comply with AI regulations in China.

The PRC's approach to AI regulation reflects a dilemma between fostering technological innovation and maintaining strict governmental control over content. Through a series of policies, including the Internet Information Service Algorithmic Recommendation Management Provisions, the Provision on the Administration of Deep Synthesis of Internet Information Service, the Interim Measures for Generative AI Services, and the Trial Measures for Ethical Review of Science and Technology, the Chinese government has established an overarching framework to guide AI's rapid development and deployment. These regulations address concerns over algorithmic transparency, deep synthesis content control, compliance in Generative AI, and ethical considerations to operate AI systems, all of which illustrates the PRC's strong commitment to shaping AI governance in parallel with national priorities such as societal stability. AI is part of the Made in China policy and Belt and Road initiative. And there is a budget not just for the tools themselves but for the regulation thereof.

V. Global Influence

China's AI regulations are not formed in isolation—they actively draw from international discourse and examples. Chinese policymakers, think tanks, and academics study developments in jurisdictions like the United States and the European Union, selectively borrowing concepts such as algorithmic transparency, content labeling, and rights-based frameworks. No doubt, the Chinese are catching up fast in the blink of an eye. There, they caught up again.

The issue of deepfakes is a good example. Deepfakes were first discussed in China using U.S.-sourced examples, including Defense Advanced Research Projects Agency research and media coverage from Western outlets. Chinese regulators then adapted those concerns into their own legal and ideological context, coining the term "deep synthesis" to avoid negative connotations.

This international engagement serves both strategic and practical purposes. On one hand, it enables China to stay abreast of technical standards and regulatory innovations; on the other, it helps project China as a global leader in AI governance. By refining and domesticating global ideas within its political framework, China aims to set normative precedents, particularly in the Global South where Chinese platforms and technologies are expanding. Thus, global AI governance debates are not merely parallel tracks—China's involvement is deliberate, absorptive, and increasingly assertive in shaping future norms.

DeepSeek, the Chinese-developed AI language model that surged to prominence in January 2025, represents both a technological milestone and a regulatory challenge for China's AI governance regime. Developed with substantial support from state-backed entities and aligned with national objectives, DeepSeek integrates advanced natural language processing capabilities with built-in compliance mechanisms designed to satisfy regulatory expectations, such as censorship filters and real-name verification protocols. Its release not only demonstrated China's increasing parity with Western AI leaders but also underscored the urgency of regulatory oversight in managing the sociopolitical impacts of Generative Artificial Intelligence. As such, DeepSeek serves as both a showcase of domestic innovation and a test case for the effectiveness of China's evolving rules on content control, data security, and algorithmic accountability.

Looking ahead, the evolving landscape of AI governance will require China to navigate ongoing challenges such as balancing state control with market-driven innovation, addressing ethical concerns, and adapting to international AI standards. Maybe by then, there will be more provisions to help figure out the manner in which AI guidelines work in the People's Republic of China.

VI. Summary/Key Points

1. China's involvement in AI regulation has significantly increased, going from general policy statements to a detailed legal framework governing algorithmic operations, data handling, content generation, and ethical review.
2. AI regulation itself is now a competitive arena as much as AI technology itself. Starting with the Beijing Principles to the rise of DeepSeek, China is positioning itself as both a technology and normative leader. China appears to be catching up in both arenas. The real key will be whether Chinese authorities actually enforce their rules and guidelines.
3. China's mandatory ethical review for AI development reflects the government's effort to align technological advancements with social values and public interest. By imposing governmental approval and an ethics review committee, the

policy hopes to balance responsible development and decrease risks for inappropriate applications and ethical violations simultaneously.

4. Children-focused AI regulation demonstrates the government's intent to protect vulnerable users while reinforcing "harmony" and ideological alignment early on.

5. China's AI regulatory system operates within a broader "black box" legal framework, where policy grey areas can exist, enforcement can be discretionary, and decision-making processes remain largely in the hands of the government. Political flexibility trumps legal clarity.

6. The cumulative effect of China's plethora of AI regulations across cybersecurity, data control, algorithmic transparency, and narrative enforcement is to permit innovation only within State-approved limits.

CHAPTER 8

National AI Regulation Around the Globe

I. Introduction

The tech bros took over the Artificial Intelligence (AI) Action Summit in February 2025 held at the Grand Palais in Paris. It was a victory lap of sorts to celebrate their new preeminence after the second Trump administration inauguration and a recognition of their vaulting to political heights. One of their own, Elon Musk, a former AI skeptic, was heading up the U.S. Department of Government Efficiency (DOGE) and using AI to make cuts across the United States (U.S.) federal government. This was far different than the previous global conclaves of government leaders dealing with "safety" and "security" in Bletchley Park in the United Kingdom (U.K.) in 2023 and in Seoul a year later.

By the time the 1,000 technology executives, regulators, political leaders and entrepreneurs met in Paris, the world was still waiting for sustainable rules for the deployment and use of AI tools. That has not changed since the first summit in Bletchley Park, but elsewhere things had changed a whole lot. The U.K. has a new Prime Minister, the U.S. has inaugurated President Donald Trump for a second non-consecutive term, Nobel Prizes have been awarded to AI scientists, OpenAI is almost a for profit entity, and an AI company from the People's Republic of China (China or PRC) has completely upended the marketplace and stock market valuations of leading Western companies in the space.

Clearly, the world of AI moves faster than the themes and worries of annual summits. Declarations from past conclaves are mere footnotes in the rearview mirror of this moment's concern. But we also cannot be legislating based on the latest fad.

Enlightened, forward-thinking legislation, synchronized across jurisdictions, rather than pie in the sky guidelines, principles, consensus points, or blueprints are required now. Not a year from now. But now.

* * * *

In November 2023, the then U.K. Prime Minister Rishi Sunak brought together political leaders from 28 countries around the globe. With the sponsorship of the United Nations (U.N.), the AI Safety Summit was tasked to develop a common understanding about shared risks and opportunities that AI poses. The results of the Summit were codified in the "landmark" *Bletchley Declaration*. According to the Prime Minister Sunak:

> We agreed and published the first ever international statement about the nature of all those risks [concerning AI]. It was signed by every single nation represented at this summit covering all continents across the globe. . .and including the US and China. Some said, we shouldn't even invite China. . .others that we could never get an agreement with them. Both were wrong. A serious strategy for AI safety has to begin with engaging all the world's leading AI powers.

It has been highly instructive as to what really came of these global efforts once national industrial policy, geopolitical rivalries, and technology nationalism factor into such "kumbaya" moments. After all, different countries have different priorities when it comes to technology. We covered the U.S. in Chapter 5 and the European Union (EU), a leading supranational organization, in Chapter 6 of this *Short and Happy Guide*. Other countries, like China (as explored in Chapter 7 herein), which also lead in AI research and use, have different ideas and policies than, say, Bolivia or Laos. The latter are net technology importers while the former are technology exporters. In examining the different approaches, one must also ask whether these countries enforce intellectual property (IP) rights, whether there is a national industrial policy in play, and whether public-private partnerships can provide local solutions for local consumption and potential export. So, yes, different countries have different trajectories, velocities, and priorities, some of them not so transparent.

This Chapter provides a survey of the regulatory work that a plethora of national governments of sovereign States (other than the U.S., the EU, and China) that dot the earth have undertaken concerning Artificial Intelligence. Part II of this Chapter explores the national responses that have emerged from sovereign States dealing with the development and deployment of AI tools. While it is not exhaustive, it does provide a general lay of the land, demonstrating how national strategies have blended with actual legislation, of which there is not yet much. There is some overlap in the reach of data protection and cybersecurity laws around the world with the early national regulation of AI tools in some countries.

Chapter 4 examined a few different supranational efforts. The EU AI Act, as unpacked in Chapter 6, is noteworthy because it was the first set of laws—real laws—to be promulgated and put (soon) into force. In the end, the "risk approach" of the EU does seem most prudent. Some of the EU's Member States have been trying on their own too: Germany, U.K. and France introduced their own AI strategies.

The majority of the other ones that are explored in this Chapter combine national strategies, data privacy measures, other consumer protection laws, ethical guidelines and principles and, in a few places, the beginnings of actual legislation concerning the design and use of AI tools. Part II of this Chapter unpacks the leading attempts by countries to plant their flags in the regulatory space with a mixture of these initiatives.

Part III of this Chapter explores the geopolitical ramifications of such divergent policies on AI development and deployment. Except for the EU, to date the foundational work that may one day lead to a full regulatory response (e.g. enforceable laws) has been limited to the release of guidelines, principles, frameworks and blueprints. In the U.S., federal direction has been meted out in piecemeal fashion over the years. This *laissez faire* approach has resulted in several states inside the U.S. and municipalities around the country providing their own solutions to fill the regulatory vacuum. Indeed, this is a legal maze! In China, authorities from the central government have provided some cohesive guidelines for their respective scientists, investors, universities, and corporations to develop and deploy AI tools, but China is a legal "black box" (just like AI is a black box). So, there is not much transparency, an objective that AI regulations must meet, as was explored in Chapter 3 of this *Short and Happy Guide*.

II. Country-Specific Focus on AI Guidelines

The AI industry, like all other breakthrough technology spaces, is hotly contested. Just like blockchain, 5G, semi-conductor chips, autonomous vehicles, robotics. There is also the shadow of the geopolitical rivalry between the U.S. and China. AI is one of those flash points. There will be *their* (Chinese) AI and *our* AI, just like there is their 5G technology and *our* 5G technology and *their* walled garden internet and *our* internet.

A. Australia

The Australian government has produced Australia's AI Ethics Framework and provides guidelines for the responsible design, development, and implementation of AI technologies. It aims to ensure that AI is used in a way that is ethical, safe, and beneficial for society. This Framework emphasizes the importance of ethical considerations in AI, such as fairness, transparency, and accountability. Through this Framework, Australia has developed 8 AI ethics principles to ensure the above-mentioned goals. It is important to note that these principles, which apply to Australian businesses and governments, are entirely voluntary at the time of this writing. So much for enforceable rules.

The Australian government created the Consultation Process concerning Generative AI Systems to engage with various stakeholders in the development of AI regulations. It focuses on creating a code of practice for Generative AI systems, reflecting the Australian government's approach to collaboratively shaping the regulatory environment for Artificial Intelligence. This consultation process signifies the Australian government's recognition of the importance of diverse perspectives in crafting effective and inclusive AI policies. In February 2025, the Privacy Commissioner of Australia released a joint statement with the privacy commissioners of South Korea, France, Ireland and the U.K. on building trustworthy data governance frameworks to encourage development of innovative and privacy-protective Artificial Intelligence. Human oversight and transparency will be goals for the national AI regulations that are in the process of being drafted. In the meantime, put some shrimp on the barbie.

B. Brazil

Can AI samba? Many countries are working on AI-based legislation, but only a few of them have enacted laws regarding data privacy and implemented protections against Artificial Intelligence. According to the Organisation for Economic Cooperation and Development (OECD), Brazil is currently working on a comprehensive Draft AI Law, while the General Data Protection Law (LGPD), the Brazilian Strategy for Artificial Intelligence (EBIA), and the Brazilian Internet Law (Marco Civil), are a few pieces of the latest implemented AI legislation.

The LGPD is Brazil's first comprehensive data protection regulation. Enacted in 2020, the LGPD became enforceable in August of 2021. The LGPD broadly aligns with the EU's General Data Protection Regulation (GDPR). The LGPD came into force to regulate the processing of personal data, including data used for AI applications. The law establishes guidelines for the collection, storage, processing, and sharing of personal data, and requires that organizations obtain explicit consent from individuals before collecting and using their data. This is known as the "opt-in" theory users see on their browsers, to protect personal privacy and data.

In addition to the LGPD, Brazil has also created the Brazilian Strategy for Artificial Intelligence (EBIA). Launched in 2021, the EBIA is guiding the development and use of AI in Brazil. According to the Brazilian Ministry of Science, Technology, and Innovation (MCTI), the strategy establishes guidelines for the ethical and responsible use of AI and provides recommendations for research, development, workforce training, and entrepreneurship in the field. Brazil plans to add AI and programming courses to its teaching curriculum and retrain teachers. The EBIA aims to guide the Brazilian government in the direction of conscious and principled use of Artificial Intelligence. The EBIA structures its intelligence plan on five principles defined by the OECD for responsible management of AI systems. These include inclusive growth, sustainable development, and well-being; human-centered values and fairness; transparency and explainability; robustness, security and safety; and accountability, according to the Brazilian Ministry of Science, Technology and Innovation. Once enacted, the law will include AI governance structures and policy monitoring models and provide for the sharing of tools and techniques with AI across countries.

The Marco Civil establishes rights and guarantees for all users of the internet in Brazil. This includes the flow of users' communications through the internet and their stored private communications, attempting to protect the confidentiality of people's data. The Marco Civil helps govern free speech, privacy, and net neutrality, according to the Council on Foreign Relations (CFR). The Marco Civil also aids courts in their decisions on internet protection and safety as well. The CFR also notes extreme positive impacts from the Marco Civil just a year after its enactment. CFR states lower courts still insist on injunctions ordering the takedown of online services, but many appellate courts have been consistent in reversing these decisions by citing the Marco Civil.

Brazil's Senate Committee has published a Draft AI Law. Over 900 pages, the report attempts to create a comprehensive AI law for the country. The Draft AI Law draws on the OECD countries and the ways they are regulating (or planning to regulate in most cases) the field of Artificial Intelligence. It provides a framework for legislators to define the principles of AI and create risk assessment practices, ranking certain AI systems as "unacceptable" or "high risk." There is also the Brazilian AI Plan 2024-2028, launched in July 2024, the product of a collaboration with the private sector and various institutions, is designed to position Brazil as a global leader in AI technology, not just its regulation.

C. Canada

Canada's approach to regulating AI is encapsulated in the Artificial Intelligence and Data Act (AIDA), part of the Digital Charter Implementation Act, 2022. AIDA represents Canada's first comprehensive legislation designed to govern AI's development and use, intending to protect Canadians, ensure the responsible development of AI, and position Canadian firms and values prominently in the global AI landscape. The Act adopts a risk-based approach, aligning with international norms such as the EU AI Act and the OECD AI Principles, and focuses on ensuring that high-impact AI systems adhere to Canadian safety and human rights standards. AIDA's implementation is expected to follow a structured timeline involving extensive consultations and the development of regulations, with the Act anticipated to come into force no earlier than 2025.

Under AIDA, entities responsible for AI systems must assess whether their systems are "high-impact", establish risk mitigation plans, and maintain transparency by publishing plain-language descriptions of the AI systems' intended use and risk mitigation measures. The Minister of Innovation, Science, and Industry is empowered to enforce the Act, with the ability to demand audits, halt the operation of AI systems posing imminent harm, and issue fines for non-compliance. Penalties for infringements can reach up to $10 million or 3% of global revenues for businesses, with provisions for criminal offenses related to AI systems that cause serious harm or substantial economic loss.

The AIDA is part of a broader legislative reform addressing AI and privacy, including updates to federal and provincial privacy laws that will impact AI use in business operations. The regulation's most stringent requirements apply to "high impact" AI systems, which will be determined based on factors such as the potential for harm, the scale of use, and the system's impact on human rights. The Act emphasizes developing and operating AI systems in a transparent and accountable manner and considers the risks to individuals' privacy and safety from the outset.

In anticipation of AIDA's formal regulations, Canada has introduced a Voluntary Code of Conduct for the responsible development and management of advanced Generative AI systems. This initiative, announced in September 2023, aims to establish common standards and bolster public confidence in AI systems, ensuring that Canadian companies can demonstrate their commitment to responsible AI development. This voluntary code is temporary until AIDA's regulations are fully enacted, underscoring Canada's proactive stance on fostering ethical AI development and management practices.

D. Chile

Chile was the first Latin-American country that sought to regulate Artificial Intelligence. Its initiatives are influenced by discussions from the EU, as the *chilenos* establish a risk-based regime. According to the Latin American Artificial Intelligence Index (CENIA, 2023), Chile is in the top spot in the region regarding Artificial Intelligence. There is a goal to achieve accountability, fairness, confidentiality, and data protection implications in the use of AI technologies in judicial systems.

In October 2024, Chile's Congress launched a National AI Policy and introduced an AI bill following the recommendations of the United Nations Educational, Scientific and Cultural Organization (UNESCO), aimed at regulating and promoting the ethical and responsible implementation of Artificial Intelligence. The bill includes provisions for sandboxes support small and medium enterprises (i.e. controlled test environments where new AI applications can be developed)

The bill proposes that no royalties for copyrighted works used in the development of AI systems for non-profit or research use:

> Any act of reproduction and extraction of legitimately published works for the purposes of text and data mining is lawful, without remuneration or obtaining authorization from the owner, provided that this use is carried out without profit and for research purposes. Owners may choose, in relation to the previous paragraph, to seek their rights.

The bill also assigns AI oversight to the personal data protection agency and proposes the establishment of a permanent technical advisory council for the technology. By the time this *Short and Happy Guide* gets published, the law should be out of Congress and in the President's office for signature.

E. France

France introduced French Intelligence Artificielle in 2017. In March 2018, French President Emmanuel Macron, presented a 5-year national AI plan. The French AI strategy is called AI for Humanity, developed from the AI policy report created by French Member of Parliament (MP) and famous mathematician, Cédric Villani, also known as the Villani Report. The French AI strategy has three main objectives including: the improvement of AI education and training ecosystem to develop, retain and attract world-class AI talent; the establishment of an open data policy for the implementation of AI applications and pooling of assets; and the development of an ethical framework for a transparent and fair use of AI applications.

In 2022, the 4th generation of a multi-year National Investment for the Future Program was created, with a sub-program on AI and several other sub-programs related to the actions of National AI Strategy. Focusing on the AI for Humanity framework, one goal of the French government is to reduce the skill gap between AI and the labor market by diversifying AI in education. The French AI strategy is focused on a deeper understanding of future labor demand and skill requirements to effectively prepare for transitioning professionals. The objective of the French National Research Institute for the Digital Sciences (Inria) is to strengthen the "entire French AI sector, accelerate technology spinoffs or transfers, and develop cooperation programmes with the industry."

Using AI ethically, in safe, fair, and transparent ways, is also of crucial importance to the French government. The Villani Report created a "digital technology and AI ethics committee in charge of leading public discussion in a transparent way, and organized and governed by law," according to Inria, leading to the creation of a pilot National Digital Ethics Committee (CNPEN) to coordinate ethics and Artificial Intelligence. France would like to consider itself a leader in AI ethics, as well as innovation. Concerning the latter, the prominence of Arthur Mensch, co-founder of Mistral, France's strongest AI start-up, at the February 2025 Paris Summit was a tell. The young technology pioneer has been working hand in glove with French President Emmanuel Macron on France's AI strategy and helped lead discussions on AI regulation in general preferring a more relaxed approach. Macron himself has pushed policies that will bring innovation to his country, fashioning himself as the "AI President."

F. Germany

Germany launched national strategies called Industry 4.0 and Human Brain Plan in 2012 and 2013. In 2018, Germany created the Data Ethics Commission to identify AI ethics and principles. The Commission had a year to decide on the principles and were guided on seven guiding motifs. The seven guiding motifs include: ensuring the human-centered and value-oriented design of technology; fostering digital skills and critical reflection in the digital world; enhancing protection for individual freedom, self-determination, and integrity; fostering responsible data utilization that is compatible with the public good; introducing risk-adapted regulation and effective oversight of algorithmized systems; safeguarding and promoting democracy and social cohesion; aligning digital strategies with sustainability goals; and strengthening the digital sovereignty of both Germany and Europe. The general ethics and legal principles include human dignity, self-determination, privacy, security, democracy, justice and solidarity, and sustainability.

G. India

Currently, the Republic of India (India) does not have any specific laws regulating the development and deployment of Artificial Intelligence. AI in India is governed by a set of existing laws and guidelines related to information technology (IT), data privacy, social media, and Responsible Artificial Intelligence. The Information Technology Act, enacted in 2000, and its associated guidelines issued by the government, form the primary legislation in India related to digital commerce, cybercrimes, and social media.

The NITI Aayog, the Indian government's main policy think tank, launched the National Strategy for Artificial Intelligence in 2018. The strategy focuses on using AI for economic growth and social development, looking at sectors such as healthcare, education, agriculture, and infrastructure. Building upon this, the draft principles of Responsible AI were released by NITI Aayog in February 2021, which analyzes the ethical considerations of AI systems, both at the system level (e.g. related to the technology) and societal level (e.g. impact of use of AI). This was followed up by guidance in August 2021, on implementing these principles and emphasized the collaboration between the public, private and research organizations.

In 2023, the government enacted the Digital Personal Data Protection (DPDP) Act, which modernizes the country's data privacy and data protection regime. It is not exclusively focused on AI, but works to protect personal data and create a legal framework for processing data.

The banking sector regulator, the Reserve Bank of India, has issued guidelines on the use of AI in the financial and banking services industry that underscore the need for responsible AI use, accountability, and transparency. The regulator for the Indian capital markets, the Securities and Exchange Board of India, requires quarterly reports on the usage of AI systems and also warns against misrepresentation of their benefits to the public.

In March 2024, the government mooted a proposal to more stringently regulate Large Language Models (LLMs) (such as requiring permission before releasing them) but quickly dropped the idea in response to industry and consumer feedback. With the exception of rules against deep fakes and obligations on intermediaries such as social media platforms regarding content moderation and due diligence, India's approach to AI can be characterized as more hands-off, with the aim of fostering innovation and letting the AI ecosystem flourish.

H. Israel

In January 2020, the Israeli Ministry of Innovation, Science, and Technology and the Legal Counsel and Legislative Affairs Department of the Ministry of Justice released the Principles of Government Policy on Artificial Intelligence (Policy Document), a legal framework outlining Israel's approach to the regulation and ethics of Artificial Intelligence. It was designed to guide the use of AI technology while addressing the significant challenges, including issues related to privacy, cybersecurity, and bias. It emphasizes the importance of responsible innovation, balancing the need to protect individual rights while fostering an environment that supports the development and advancement of AI technology. The document also highlights the need for collaboration between government, industry, and academia to achieve these goals.

The Policy Document works through collaboration with a multitude of stakeholders, including the Ministry of Innovation, Science and Technology, the Israel Innovation Authority, the Ministry of Justice, the Israeli National Cyber Directorate, the Israel National Digital Agency, and the Privacy Protection Authority. Following in the footsteps of the OECD AI Recommendations, the Policy Document is informed by these principles for responsible AI innovation. The Policy Document notes regulatory and ethical issues. These include discrimination; human oversight; explainability; disclosing AI interactions; reliability, robustness, security, and safety; accountability and legal liability; and privacy.

While the Policy Document thoroughly addresses key areas with its principal focus points, it also explores several specific ideas, enriching its comprehensive approach to the subject matter. One of the Policy Document's ideas includes an AI Policy Coordination Center and the creation of an "expert-based inter-agency body." The group is to offer guidance to sector-specific regulatory authorities, work towards inter-agency collaboration, update national AI strategies and give recommendations for them accordingly, and represent Israel in international AI discussions. The Policy Document also maps AI uses and challenges. By creating a catalog for the uses and challenges of AI technologies, the Policy Document hopes to be more transparent. Lastly, the Policy Document recommends creating a dialogue and collaboration platform, bringing communication and creativity to regulators and stakeholders from various sectors. With the open exchange of ideas and information, the Policy Document hopes to foster trust and connections between these groups.

I. Japan

Japan is already known as a liberal jurisdiction concerning enforcement of IP rights for training Generative Artificial Intelligence. It did not get there by accident. In 2019, Japan published the Social Principles of Human-Centric AI (Social Principles) as goals for implementing AI into Japanese society. The Social Principles reflect three basic principles: diversity and inclusion, human dignity, and sustainability. At this writing, Japan does not currently have any binding AI regulations, but in July 2021, the AI Governance in Japan report from the Ministry of Economy, Trade, and Industry (METI) noted "legally-binding horizontal requirements for AI systems are deemed unnecessary at the moment." Like the EU's GDPR and India's DPDP Act, Japan created the Act on the Protection of Personal Information (APPI) in 2022, which focused on generalized data protection for its citizens.

Japan is also working on an initiative called Society 5.0. in which the Japanese government defines as a "human-centered society that balances economic advancement with the resolution of social problems by a system that highly integrates cyberspace and physical space," according to the Cabinet Secretariat of Japan. The country has also created the Council for Social Principles of Human-Centric Artificial Intelligence. According to the Cabinet Secretariat of Japan, this Council promotes the implementation of social principles of human-centric AI throughout Japan and creates a platform for interaction among stakeholders to address ethical, legal, and social issues related to Artificial Intelligence.

It appears that Japan is taking more of a "soft law" approach to AI regulations like India and in contrast to Israel. While Japan works on investing in AI research, innovation hubs, and so on, AI regulatory groups appear to be on the "back-burner." It looks like the flexible IP regulations for Generative AI might be a competitive advantage for its national AI industry.

Japan has shifted from strict and specific regulation on AI to a general sector-specific framework, its promotion for self-regulated risk management within business, and its call for greater transparency and effective guidance. Japan has followed its allies in loosening AI regulations to encourage more innovation rather than focusing on the potential risks and dangers AI can bring to society. Those countries all realize that while strict regulations can effectively mitigate risks and maintain control of AI development, strong regulations stifle creative innovation, ultimately causing more harm than good for society.

An Interim Report from February 2025, released by the country's AI Strategic Council, emphasizes Japan's decision to rely on existing sector-specific laws rather than imposing a unified set of AI regulations. The Japanese government recognizes that there are no comprehensive AI laws that can govern all AI applications across various fields because different industries face unique challenges when implementing AI into practice. A single set of regulations to govern all AI applications will likely prove impractical and ineffective in maximizing AI's potential to drive development in specific areas, like healthcare and finance. A sector-specific approach ensures AI integration meets needs across various fields, whereas a unified regulation only provides broad guidance, leaving specific challenges unaddressed.

The Interim Report also reflects the Japanese government's reliance on businesses to independently operate AI risk management under the existing laws given the vacuum created by a lack of broad-based regulation. Japan recognizes that startup companies and other branches of business are key drivers of innovation. By opting for self-regulation, corporations can innovate more rapidly and efficiently, while complicated government bureaucracies could slow down AI development. For example, Open AI and Google's robotics AI models are both refined and adjusted according to internal safety protocols, so there is no need to go through complex assessments again for developing newer versions. This easier process allows businesses to move faster than government bodies in implementing AI applications as society changes.

Japan proposes guidance on the interpretation of existing laws as well as directions for legislative measures in the area of copyrights and other IP rights and so on with the new business-friendly approach to AI regulation. This change allows businesses to leverage their professional expertise in AI development while operating within a regulatory framework. It was not by accident that Microsoft CEO Satya Nadella commended Japan's flexible copyright laws, which allow the use of copyrighted content for the training of AI models.

This all demonstrates that the Japanese's business-led approach to regulating AI can foster innovations with more flexibility by accommodating technological advancements with existing measures without imposing restrictive governmental control. If the Japanese government announces new AI regulation laws instead of integrating existing laws into AI applications to maintain national control, these could fail to address the challenges AI development poses to various industries and could also reduce AI's effectiveness in supporting each sector of the economy in which AI tools are being applied. Compared to central government agencies, companies themselves have stronger incentives to self-regulate risk management to maintain consumers' trust and prevent reputational damage. Finally, a time for *company men* to shine again.

In the end, like other countries, Japan is attempting to promote transparency while still ensuring effectiveness. By moving away from closed, non-transparent discussions to promote a transparent multi-stakeholder process, Japan can bring together knowledge and expertise from a wide range of industries instead of a unified government control of AI, by non-expert bureaucrats. This more transparent, open-minded approach to regulate AI development allows for continuous feedback on AI policies. Subsequently, it is more efficient for the government to adjust solutions in response to industry developments and societal needs. In addition, this transparent, business-led approach to AI regulation opens a possibility for companies in other countries to develop and refine their own AI models, which are tailored to their particular needs. Thus, a new approach with greater transparency ensures that Japanese regulations on AI remain adaptable over time under the existing laws.

J. The Kingdom of Saudi Arabia

Perhaps the largest advancement in Saudi Arabia in AI currently revolves around a proposed new Intellectual Property Law (New IP Law), one of the first IP laws in the Middle East to encompass IP created by Artificial Intelligence. Working to promote innovation and protect creativity, the principles set out guidelines protecting IP created with AI technology. The proposed law states that IP is to be owned by the individual who used the AI to contribute to its creation. If the AI is made independently without significant human contribution, then the IP would enter the public domain. The New IP Law strives towards Saudi Arabia's broader intentions to maximize the contributions of data and AI to its Vision 2030 objectives and to, in the words of the Saudi Data and AI Authority (SDAIA), "promote the Kingdom as a global leader in data and AI."

The SDAIA has created several regulatory arrangements with the Council of Ministers of the Kingdom: In January 2024, the Generative Artificial Intelligence Guidelines for Government, then for the Public were published. The government guidelines provide mandatory regulations for the use of governmental data, for

Generative AI tools including transparency and reliability, privacy, social and environmental benefits.

The Public Guidelines explain "how to comply with AI ethics principles, the risks of AI and how to mitigate them." In addition, the National Data Management Office of Saudi Arabia (NDMO) has created the Data Management and Personal Data Protection Standards, with enforcement scheduled for September 2024. Similar to the GDPR of the EU, the policies and regulations included in this are data classification, personal data protection, data sharing, freedom of information, and open data policies. The SDAIA explains that the Saudi Arabian government "aims to implement the best global practices for national data management and governance policies and controls, protect personal data, and increase the value learned from it in order to make strategic decisions, anticipate the future, and uphold the highest standards of accountability and transparency." Building on these practices, the Saudi government is committed to data management and regulation that secures personal data and harnesses works toward informed policymaking.

K. Singapore

In 2019, Singapore launched its National AI Strategy (NAIS), setting goals of progressive use of AI to "transform the economy." The Singaporean government created about 150 research teams and 900 startups working on Artificial Intelligence. In 2023, Singapore deployed the Singapore National AI Strategy 2.0 (NAIS 2.0), in its "ongoing pursuit of setting the pace." The country lists three shifts they expect to make from the first NAIS to their 2.0 version. These include From Opportunity to Necessity, From Local to Global, and From Projects to Systems. Starting with From Opportunity to Necessity, the Singapore's government stated that "we must master AI, rather than think of it merely as an accessory or a luxury." The city state remarks that as the AI landscape grows, the need for serious development and deployment in Singapore does as well. Next the From Local to Global is in the name: Singapore must operate from a global point-of-view, rather than a domesticated outlook. Lastly the third shift listed is "From Projects to Systems," and cites the need to update infrastructure, create solid foundations, and to "manage the impact of AI" throughout Singapore.

The NAIS 2.0 has two main goals: Excellence and empowerment. Singapore makes it clear throughout this AI framework that it wants to be at the forefront of Artificial Intelligence. Committing to excellence in AI as its first goal, the country hopes to "advance in the field and maximize value creation." The second goal is empowerment, recognizing the trust issues and biases that come with AI systems. The Singaporean government states, "We intend for AI to be the great equalizer, which equips our people and businesses with the capabilities and resources to thrive in an AI-enabled future." The NAIS 2.0 has formed 15 actions to support these goals over the next three to five years, emphasizing Singapore's vision of "AI for the Public Good, for Singapore and the World."

Another AI initiative is the partnership between the AI Verify Foundation (AIVF) and the Infocomm Media Development Authority (IMDA), working on a Model AI Governance Framework for Generative Artificial Intelligence. It builds on a previous blueprint, the Model Governance Framework, that covers traditional AI and was last updated in 2020. The regulation looks at existing models of governance framework to discover new issues emerging from the use of Generative Artificial Intelligence. It promotes creating a trusting environment where users can feel confident in the AI they are using. The Model AI Governance Framework for Generative AI (MAIGFGI) promotes principles of explainability, transparency, and fairness in AI decisions. This initiative reflects the country's commitment to leading in the responsible use of AI, encouraging global talks among policymakers, the industry, and the research community. At the time of this writing, the MAIGFGI was expected to be completed by mid-2024.

The IMDA and Personal Data Protection Commission (PDPC), according to the World Economic Forum (WEF), have taken a first step in "identifying and defining an objective and verifiable way to validate the performance of AI systems." Titled AI Verify, the "international pilot" strives to set standards in the industry for ethical AI practices. The "AI Toolkit" mirrors legal frameworks from the EU and the OECD, according to the Singapore Personal Data Protection Commission. AI Verify has four main goals including: "to enhance the MVP to ensure it meets industry needs;" "to contribute to the development of international AI standards;" "to facilitate the interoperability of AI governance frameworks;" and "to build an AI testing community together." According to the WEF, the AI system will not set ethical standards. Instead, it will validate internationally accepted standards (that Singapore aligns with as well) for companies, to build trust and transparency in the field of Artificial Intelligence. The country hopes to build trustworthy AI while setting standards internationally. But for all this policy work in the background, self-regulation is still the ethos, with an understanding that regulation will be inevitable.

Another way Singapore is leading is in AI education, particularly in reskilling workers above 40 years old. The Ministry of Economy and Smart Singapore are offering mid-career level workers subsidies to learn Artificial Intelligence skills. Young Ph.D. students also are being funded with a view to securing Singapore's place as a leader in the AI space.

L. South Korea (the Republic of Korea)

The national AI strategy for the Republic of Korea (South Korea) includes a vision for the role of AI in the era of the Fourth Industrial Revolution and involves various government ministries working collaboratively. Plans like the 'National Strategy for Artificial Intelligence and the 6th National Informatisation Master Plan are geared towards leveraging AI for an intelligent, hyper-connected, information-based society. These strategies underscore South Korea's commitment to fostering a sustainable and responsible AI ecosystem that aligns with global trends and standards.

There is no AI-specific regulation in South Korea but AI is regulated through sector-specific regulations and guidelines. The Act, Promotion of the Data Industry and Activation of Data Use (the Data Industry Act), came into effect in April 2022. It prohibits the unjust use of data assets produced by others and enables protection of data assets. The Unfair Competition Prevention Act was correspondingly amended to add a new provision to define unjust data use and considers such usage as falling under unfair competitive practices.

An amendment to the country's current Personal Information Protection Act gives citizens the right to seek an explanation, in scenarios involving automated decision making with significant impact. The National Human Rights Commission of Korea announced guidelines for AI in May 2022, which call for transparent and accountable use of AI, risk-level based classifications for AI, and evaluating the impact of AI on human rights.

There is a pending Bill on Fostering the AI Industry and Security Trustworthy AI, which if enacted will be the overarching framework for AI governance. The Bill has a "first allow usage first, regulate next," ethos. An amendment to the Copyright Act, that governs the use of copyrighted materials for AI and data mining, is also pending in the National Assembly at this writing.

M. The United Arab Emirates

The United Arab Emirates (UAE), too, is working towards furthering the country's AI goals in both research and reputation building. The UAE has created an AI Council to protect and instill proper use of AI and its regulations. The UAE has formed the Artificial Intelligence and Advanced Technology Council (AIATC), responsible for formulating and executing strategies and policies concerning research, financial investments, and infrastructure development. In addition to the AIATC, the UAE has created the Council for Artificial Intelligence and Blockchain. The UAE Council works to develop policies for an AI-supportive environment, enhance their research sector, and foster collaboration between public and private entities, including international institutions. The Council states that they hope to "accelerate the adoption of AI."

The UAE AI Council was created to strategize AI throughout the United Arab Emirates. It has created three phases for this including the foundation phase, AI activity phase, and leadership phase. There are four objectives at the foundational stage: Talent, research, infrastructure and data, and legislative environment. The activity phase has four objectives as well, including increasing the UAE's competitive assets through AI, developing AI's ecosystem, adopting AI throughout government services to benefit all, and helping strong governance and regulation.

To create AI regulations, the UAE Council has formed the National Strategy for Artificial Intelligence 2031. The Strategy's goal is to bring AI to crucial areas, such as education and infrastructure, address environmental concerns, and more to improve quality of life in the United Arab Emirates. The UAE government hopes to be at the forefront for AI development and deployment. The UAE government has fomented developments in the private sector (including a $US1.5 billion investment in G42 from Microsoft) to ensure that the country will play a leading role.

The Emirates' Technology Innovation Institute, released an open source LLM called "Falcon" in 2023. It definitely wins the prize for the coolest name for an AI tool. One of the first countries in the world to release an open-source Generative AI model. This is a signal of the UAE's advancement in the Middle East.

N. The United Kingdom

The U.K. has released its own Robot and Artificial Intelligence and Growing the Artificial Intelligence Industry in the U.K. in 2016 and 2017 respectively. The United Kingdom has continued to grow its AI programs since releasing a 10-year national AI strategy. This strategy included three major goals, which included: investing in, and planning for, the long-term needs of the AI ecosystem, with the objective of making the U.K. a computer science and AI superpower; supporting the transition to an AI-based economy; and taking an informed and balanced approach to regulating AI technologies, by encouraging innovation whilst protecting public and fundamental values.

The U.K. has adopted three principles creators should keep in mind when designing, developing, and deploying AI projects. The three principles include accountability, transparency, sustainability, and fairness. These principles are supplemented by four principles for building a culture of responsible innovation, which include: considering the impact the design may have on the wellbeing of stakeholders and communities (ethically permissible); considering the potential discriminatory effects on individuals and social groups, mitigating biases, and being aware of fairness issues throughout the design and implementation lifecycle (fair and non-discriminatory); guaranteeing as much as possible the safety, accuracy, reliability, security and robustness of the product (worthy of public trust); prioritizing the transparency of design and implementation of the model; and the justification and interpretability of its decision and behaviors (justifiable).

O. Others

Antarctica? Huh? We are just checking if you are still awake amid this mind-numbing regulatory discussion. There is a moratorium on mining on this continent, but not data mining.

Of course, we have not covered every country, but for a broader survey, please see the important work of the OECD AI Policy Observatory available online. The reference link is in Appendix A.

III. Geopolitical Ramifications of Measures to Reign in Artificial Intelligence

Indeed, keep in mind that all countries have different priorities and different needs because they are at different stages of development. Only the EU has put it all in writing with enforceable laws, as we saw in Chapter 6 of this *Short and Happy Guide*. The otherwise lack of concreteness or at least legislation, leaves the field empty for non-mandatory, consensus-based guidelines, principles, framework or other loose (or more likely, non-) enforcement.

The U.S. government should consider pass legislation that implements a comprehensive national strategy for both the private and public sectors concerning AI, creates a strong set of enforceable regulations for the research and development of the field, and rigorously promotes international partnerships with like-minded countries and their corporations. Some worry that this may be too little, too late.

In international trade circles, we have seen a whole host of regulations on sanitary and phytosanitary standards, technical standards, customs procedures, as part of the process of harmonizing laws to be compliant with the WTO legal regime and other trade agreements. Why not harmonized AI regulations? After all, so much research is transnational that such convergence is practical. Let the best idea win, including that idea.

Notwithstanding this emerging geopolitical competition between the U.S. and China, ethics matter. The key question is whether to start a global AI arms race or prevent it from starting? It is important to note that in 2015 top scientists published a letter with a "launch on warning" use of nuclear weapons. AI should not be about surveillance or warfare, but medical advances (drug discovery), population planning, business planning, and a more equitable distribution of resources instead. We can be a better, safer and fairer society in every country through Artificial Intelligence.

Governments and international agencies, alike, need to discuss the bad uses of AI technologies and prevent them. That is the reason why the "risk approach" of the EU seems most prudent. A group of technology leaders signed a letter asking big tech to take a 6 month pause in AI technology rollout to sort out some regulatory framework in the United States. Meanwhile, China keeps moving forward with development and regulatory measures.

Just like France's Civil Code (courtesy of Napoleon) was copied (or imposed via colonization) on much of its part of the developing world, the EU's AI Act could prove to be a template for the regulation of the riskiest AI on the planet. It did not take long for the GDPR, the long impugned (4 years of negotiation, 6 years of implementing before it went into force) data protection regulation of the EU, has been replicated (in parts and in overall substance) as far afield as California and India. The alternative reality is that presented by the Communist Party of China—The Beijing Principles underwritten and expanded (imposed) by the Belt and Road Initiative, a trade, investment and infrastructure scheme linking together over 70 countries around the world.

The U.S. government, however, may provide another alternative, but they are a little slow on the development of ethics at a national level, never mind in the legal reform bazaar that is "convergence" (or treaty compliance) as part of the globalization of law. There have been a few clarion calls for an independent, international institution to be tasked to supervise AI development and use. In a free market for AI private projects, capital is forming in the United States with China gaining ground. The Europeans remain a distant third (but are first when it comes to legislation).

So, who in the end is "winning" this race (to AI and AI regulation)? And what if by "winning," the geopolitical champion does not apply the same ethical standards as the runner up contestant? In other words, winning the AI race does not necessarily mean winning the AI ethics race. Each aspiring global AI leader has different objectives and ways to get to those objectives. The incentivizing factors for each country, too, may be different. Implementing ethics creates transaction costs just like human rights do. It is costly to translate South African laws into its many official languages and to build transgender bathrooms, never mind outfitting them with environmentally sound plumbing equipment. Sure, ethics matter in the end. But they are a cost of and to business.

Meanwhile, China keeps moving forward with development and regulatory measures. There is much power in being the first mover in terms of patents, economic growth and industry domination. But there is also first mover status in terms of regulation.

Ultimately, regulation must balance multiple objectives: citizen rights, consumer welfare, technology innovation, economic interests, national security, and geopolitical interests, among others. It needs to consider the current and the future. Its scope is local and global. As such, AI rules should align with existing regulatory ethos, institutions, and capacities. AI regulation must be strategic rather than being trend-chasing or based on the newest AI system gathering headlines.

There is little doubt that AI has to be included in international trade agreements going forward. The problem is whether it fits within the definition of "goods" or "services." If AI is seen as software as a service, then the General Agreement on Trade in Services would be the covered agreement to dictate terms of trade. If AI is built into products like autonomous vehicles or other kinds of robotics, then AI would fit more cleanly into the universal rules for trade in goods under the plurilateral or covered agreements that make up the World Trade Organization Agreement of 1994. The regulation of digital goods through data sovereignty laws is a necessary next step. The USMCA was the first trade agreement to feature digital goods. There was one other that is coming close internationally—in the World Intellectual Property Organization. But it is still unclear how technology nationalism, data privacy, cyber security, and national industrial plans will all intersect here.

Undoubtedly, considerable efforts are needed to ensure that AI systems are transparent, explainable, and unbiased. Even more efforts need to be undertaken to provide comprehensive rules that work across countries and their varied national legal systems for the use of AI around the globe. Smart regulation should be the answer.

IV. Summary/Key Points

1. There is an intrinsic difficulty in legislating a technology like Artificial Intelligence that admittedly has a dark underbelly:

   a. How do governments foster innovation versus stifle it through overregulation?

   b. There is also the tension between the hubris of tech overlords and the overzealousness of regulators which results in them often speaking past each other.

2. The market caps of some technology companies active in AI are greater than the Gross Domestic Products of mid-sized countries. Sure, we should not be comparing GDP (a flow variable) with market cap (a stock variable), but it is a fun way to illustrate the immense power of technology companies. They may have more say in shaping AI regulation than many sovereign countries.

3. The United States is not the only country figuring out how to best regulate Artificial Intelligence. There is regulatory experimentation and improvisation happening across the world.

4. Different countries' national AI strategies aligned to their respective priorities. AI regulation is shaped by these national AI strategies and their existing legal norms, systems and structures.

5. There is a parallel race afoot: A race to regulate Artificial Intelligence (alongside the AI technology race itself).

6. We provided a tour of different regulations and called out their similarities and distinct features. You'll note that they fall into a few broad approaches: *Laissez faire*, restrictive, AI-specific and hybrid.

7. With the paucity of formal, legislated, national, and supranational solutions devoid of any meaningful and effective sanctions for non-compliance, it is time to take smart regulation seriously. Yeah, more regulation is coming.

8. Self-regulation appears to be the default starting point for many countries (i.e. Singapore, Japan, and the United States).
9. Regulatory models are multidimensional. It is not just a straight line that distinguishes risk-mitigation from a sectoral approach to regulation. The EU approach is more in line with the "nanny state,"; another competing variation of regulation is Beijing's command economy model. Finally, there is the current wild west, *laissez faire* approach of the United States.

CHAPTER 9

The Wise Counsel of Bar Associations

I. Introduction

As you will have noted through this *Short and Happy Guide*, aside from the European Union (EU) we are still at the early (even confused) stage of regulations from governments about the development and use of Artificial Intelligence (AI) tools. In the United States (U.S.), the federal government has yet to pass legislation that regulates AI tools, but July 2025's National AI Action Plan does present a way forward. It was as if the federal government was planning to have a plan for legislation.

For lawyers, it is now up to individual law firms and bar associations to fill in the gaps that our elected officials and other regulators are slow, or unwilling, to close. Lawyers to the rescue!!! (Try not to laugh). This is the space into which purveyors of governance, especially professional associations, are stepping. It may sound odd, but it is bar associations that are doing the work that needs to be done.

According to a 2024 study done by *American Lawyer*, big law firms are forming policies and training around the use of Generative Artificial Intelligence (called GAI in the Opinion). The study states: "Most firms are not using the technology on client information, but an increasing number of firms are using it for research and drafting. Training is as important as policies, several top information officers said, due to generative AI's propensity to hallucinate."

While some major law firms have published information about their area of practice in AI (such a potentially lucrative area for billable hours!), only a few have posted publicly specific policies on the use of Responsible Artificial Intelligence. For example, many large-scale firms have AI listed on their respective websites. But these are listed as a practice area, not explaining their respective policies on Responsible Artificial Intelligence. This is not a bait and switch, just an additional review stream. Some are creating an AI policy to train lawyers on the responsible use of Generative Artificial Intelligence. Some firms simply state that they do not allow for the use of Generative AI in the firms' practices.

At this writing, it appears many large, medium, and small firms are exercising caution when it comes to the use of Generative AI in their practices. Many large to medium scale firms are working on Responsible AI policies, but these appear to be more "in-house" private discussions and based on clients wishes.

A. The Formal Opinion of the American Bar Association

In July 2024, the Standing Committee on Ethics and Professional Responsibility of the American Bar Association (ABA) released a Formal Opinion (the Opinion) regarding the use of AI tools such as Generative AI by lawyers. We are not sure if the Opinion has been optioned for a full-length film or Broadway musical, but we can always hope. Key areas in the Opinion include, but are not limited to:

B. Competence (ABA Model Rule 1.1)

The ABA requires lawyers to provide competent representation to clients, keeping up to date with "the benefits and risks associated" with the relevant technologies. AI tools too. The ABA Committee stresses that lawyers must practice due diligence, evaluate, and understand the limitations of Generative AI, such as its tendency to have "hallucinations, providing ostensibly plausible responses that have no basis in fact or reality." Such a duty of competence is consistent across both U.S. and foreign jurisdictions.

C. Confidentiality (ABA Model Rule 1.6)

A lawyer's duty to safeguard confidential client information is paramount to ensure lawyer-client trust. The Opinion emphasizes that a lawyer must be cognizant of the requirements under Model Rules 1.6, 1.9(c), and 1.18(b) when using Generative Artificial Intelligence. Concerning whether information relating to client representation is adequately protected, the Opinion states a lawyer must evaluate the sensitivity of the information, the likelihood of disclosure, the challenges of implementing safeguards, and the manner in which the challenges could impede the lawyer's ability to represent the client effectively.

Before utilizing Generative AI, a lawyer must review the terms of services and vet the tool's cybersecurity to ensure compliance with high-security standards. To prevent the inadvertent breach of confidentiality, the Opinion reiterates a lawyer's duty to ensure secure data privacy, providing a warning that these practices apply not only to external risks of violation but also to unauthorized access from within the firm. Given that some AI tools train on the data that is provided to it, lawyers are in a difficult position in the use of these tools, given this critical duty of confidentiality.

D. Communication (ABA Model Rule 1.4)

The Opinion addresses the interplay between Model Rule 1.6 (Confidentiality) and Model Rule 1.4 (Communication.) When Rule 1.6 does not mandate disclosure or informed consent, lawyers must still consider their obligations under Rule 1.4. A lawyer must consult and disclose the use of AI tools where it may have a material impact on the decisions in the representation. Citing Model Rule 1.4(a)(4), the Opinion states that "lawyers must disclose their GAI practices if asked by a client how they conducted their work, or whether GAI technologies were employed in doing so, or if the client expressly requires disclosure under the terms of the engagement agreement or the client's outside counsel guidelines."

E. Supervision (ABA Rules 5.1 and 5.3)

Rules 5.1 and 5.3 require lawyers to supervise subordinate attorneys and nonlawyer assistants within the firm and ensure adherence to professional conduct rules. Not only do lawyers have to supervise the use of Generative AI tools, the Opinion makes clear that this extends to the actual AI tools themselves. Managerial lawyers must establish clear firm policies outlining the permissible use of Generative AI tools and implement adequate training for subordinate attorneys and nonlawyers. The Opinion identifies key elements for training programs to ensure that those employed or contracted receive adequate education concerning the ethical and practical applications of permissible Generative AI tools.

Lawyers cannot delegate ethical responsibilities to the actual tools; however, lawyers have additional supervisory duties when relying on third parties outside the firm which use Generative AI tools in assisting in legal representation. The Opinion states prior guidelines for outsourcing legal and non-legal services to third-party providers also apply to Generative AI tools and providers. Lawyers remain accountable for ensuring the Generative AI tool and providers comply with applicable professional standards. Simply outsourcing these duties is not an option. A lawyer must ensure that their third-party providers, agents, assigns and contractors perform their work competently and protect client confidentiality. The Opinion provides a number of steps to follow to verify such compliance. From Wall Street to Main Street, the duty is the same, even if the billing rate is far different.

F. Misrepresentation (ABA Model Rules 3.1, 3.3, and 8.4)

Per ethical obligations concerning meritorious claims and candor toward the tribunal, the ABA states: "A lawyer must thoroughly review all AI-generated content in court submissions to ensure accuracy." The Opinion also notes that "[s]ome courts have responded by requiring lawyers to disclose their use of Generative Artificial Intelligence." Kudos to our judges for enforcing this on the officers of the court.

In order to mitigate false or misleading information, a lawyer should review and verify the existence and accuracy of Generative AI outputs and citations. Thus, according to the Opinion, "output from a GAI tool must be carefully reviewed to ensure that the assertions made to the court are not false." We call this the Lawyer in the Loop, a concept we introduced in our first book in this series, *A Short and Happy Guide to Artificial Intelligence for Lawyers*. This applies to everyone, from public defenders to mergers and acquisitions hot shots.

G. Reasonable Fees (ABA Model Rule 1.5)

Lawyers must ensure their fees are reasonable. The Opinion spends a great deal of time unpacking how Generative AI affects fees and the manner in which lawyers should charge their clients when Generative AI tools are used. It is as if lawyers are for profit actors, looking for ways to earn a living. Go figure. Go seven figures!

The Opinion states lawyers may charge for time spent inputting information into Generative AI and reviewing accuracy and compliance; however, lawyers should not charge for the time saved by using Generative AI tools. Additionally, the ABA Standing Committee stresses lawyers should not charge clients for time spent learning the use of Generative AI tools, as maintaining competence in relevant technology is part of the professional responsibility of attorneys. Lawyers are encouraged to practice clear communication with clients about the basis of their fees and expenses related to Generative AI tools to promote transparency and maintain client trust.

II. State Bar Associations in the United States

As Generative AI continues to proliferate in the legal profession, some state bar associations have taken preliminary action to address the topic by establishing task forces while others have taken the lead on the heels of the ABA's Opinion 512. States like California, New York, New Jersey, and Florida have been at the forefront of providing guidance for the use of Generative AI by lawyers in their respective states.

A. California

Spearheading the effort to address the use of AI in the practice of law in California, the California State Bar Association (California Bar) has provided a comprehensive guide and emphasizes competence and confidentiality while promoting transparency by urging lawyers to disclose the use of AI with clients. The California guide warns of the "lack of clarity as to how it works," expressing the risk of over-reliance on Generative AI due to the tools' ability to output responses in a "manner that projects confidence and effectively emulates human responses" while many of the guidelines available by the California Bar align with those of other state bar associations, California's recommendations are notably detailed and provide more elaborate directives on confidentiality, communication, and billing practices.

The California Bar's Committee on Professional Responsibility and Conduct has created the Practical Guidance for the Use of Generative Artificial Intelligence in the Practice of Law (Guidance). The Guidance covers potential problem areas with Generative Artificial Intelligence. The California Bar states: "The manner in which a lawyer's professional obligations will apply to the use of generative AI depends on many factors, including the type of product being used, the client, matter, practice area and firm size." Under the California rules on competence and diligence, attorneys are expected to fact-check any information when using Generative AI, and receive client consent under confidentiality rules.

B. Florida

In January 2024, the Florida Bar published its Ethics Opinion paralleling that of California and New York. The Florida Bar also cautions lawyers of AI's "infancy." Like the ABA's Ethics Opinion, the Florida Bar goes a step further by suggesting lawyers should obtain informed consent before using these tools. Most recently in January of 2025, the Florida Bar took the next step by the relaunch of a comprehensive guide as a resource for lawyers exploring the use of AI developed by the Special Committee on AI Tools and Resources. It also provides a comparison chart of general versus legal AI models as well as a chart comparing the largest Generative AI models.

C. Illinois

Although the Illinois State Bar Association has not published an official Opinion, the Illinois Supreme Court released a new policy in 2024. The Court's new policy conveys an enthusiastic outlook on the implementation of AI, concluding the policy with a promising note: The Court encourages the development of technologies that enhance service to all court users and promote equitable access to justice. To facilitate this, the judicial branch will support ongoing education on emerging technologies, including Artificial Intelligence. The Court embraces "the advancements of artificial intelligence (AI). . .and remains steadfast in its commitment to upholding the highest ethical standards in the administration of justice" Notably, the Court distinctly addresses the use of AI by litigants, attorneys, judges, judicial clerks, research attorneys, and court staff providing similar support "may be expected, should not be discouraged, and is authorized provided it complies with legal and ethical standards." The Court continues to specifically state: "Disclosure of AI use should not be required in a pleading." Additionally, the Court promises to stay up to date with the advancement of technology and regularly reassess policies aimed at "prioritizing public trust and confidence in the judiciary and the administration of justice."

D. New York

Following in California's footsteps, in August 2024, the New York Bar Association published Formal Opinion 2024-5 (New York Opinion) tailored specifically to New York Rules of Professional Conduct and practices. Regarding Generative AI, the New York Opinion notes "addressing developing areas, lawyers need guardrails and not hard-and-fast restrictions or new rules that could stymie developments." New York provides that even if a lawyer is competent in the use of technology, a lawyer's "professional judgment cannot be delegated" to a Generative AI tool. Regarding candor, the NY Opinion explicitly notes that "if an attorney suspects that their client may have provided the lawyer with Generative AI-created evidence (including "deepfakes"), a lawyer may have a duty to further investigate." The New York Opinion addresses Rule 7.1 and Rule 7.3, prohibiting the use of Generative AI in marketing and solicitation. This explicit focus on marketing and solicitation distinguishes New York from that of other state bar associations.

In a different report back in April 2024, the New York State Bar Association Task Force on Artificial Intelligence provided guidance on the need to proceed with caution on AI, particularly about the use of Generative AI by lawyers. The report also highlighted the need to bring lawyers and judges up to speed on AI, the need to identify the risks of AI which are not currently addressed by AI and ultimately, reflecting on the role of law in the governance for Artificial Intelligence. The Task Force also suggested that the New York State Bar Association examine the role that law must play in governing Artificial Intelligence. That will not be too difficult. They can just read this *Short and Happy Guide*.

As New York moves, so moves the rest of the world. In general, bar associations all over the globe are waking up to the reality that ChatGPT is a toy with which lawyers cannot be trusted. This is sad but a little true. Just ask former Trump fixer and lawyer Michael Cohen. Google it or check out Chapter Two of our *Short and Happy Guide to Artificial Intelligence for Lawyers*.

E. Pennsylvania

The Pennsylvania Joint Opinion 2024-200 (2024) (PA Joint Opinion) provides detailed ethical guidelines distinguishing itself from other state bar associations by particularly emphasizing the significance of technological competence. The PA Joint Opinion cites Florida, New York, California, New Jersey, and Michigan stating: "In every jurisdiction that has issued guidance or made recommendations concerning the use of AI, there is one common theme: Lawyers must recognize the risks and benefits of AI technology. If they choose to use AI, particularly Generative AI, they must understand its strengths and weaknesses and employ it consistent with their ethical obligations under the Rules of Professional Conduct."

F. Texas

The State Bar of Texas has a proposed Opinion, opening the document with the question: What ethical issues are raised under the Texas Disciplinary Rules of Professional Conduct by a lawyer's use of generative artificial intelligence in the practice of law? The proposed Opinion addresses: Competence, confidentiality, oversight and supervision, and fees.

G. Washington DC

Ethics Opinion 388 (DC Opinion) provides additional applicable model rules to the ABA's Opinion 512. It lists Rule 1.1 (Competence), Rule 1.2 (Scope of Representation), Rule 1.5 (Fees), Rule 1.6 (Confidentiality of Information), Rule 1.16 (Client File), Rule 3.3 (Candor to Tribunal), Rule 3.4 (Fairness to Opposing Party and Counsel), Rule 5.1 (Responsibilities of Partners, Managers and Supervisory Lawyers), Rule 5.3 (Responsibilities Regarding Nonlawyer Assistants), Rule 8.4 (Misconduct) Like Florida, the DC Opinion also provides training tools to help lawyers stay up to date on their website.

III. Other Countries' Bar Associations

A. The European Union

The European Union (EU) stands at the forefront of AI regulations, with its EU AI Act, as we explored in Chapter 6 of this *Short and Happy Guide*. The EU has created a comprehensive, horizontal framework that classifies AI by risk level. The EU AI Act is shaping international discourse with some countries and jurisdictions even explicitly referencing it or using it as a guidance for their own regulatory and policy framework. The AI Act does not specifically address professional responsibility rules for lawyers; however, "high-risk" AI systems are subject to meticulous compliance obligations and regulatory scrutiny which would likely apply to lawyers also. Some of the provisions that will likely apply include transparency, accountability, and human oversight. As of now, bar associations in EU Member States anticipate issuing guidance which will integrate the EU AI Act into existing professional conduct rules.

In conjunction with the anticipated changes, Article 22 of the EU's General Data Protection Regulation (GDPR) prohibits solely using automated decision-making that significantly affects individuals, absent explicit consent or other legal basis. This regulation may impact how lawyers can use AI tools, instilling anti-discriminatory practice. Several European bar associations rely greatly on Article 22 to prevent unmonitored AI applications from making or guiding critical decisions in legal practice. The privacy and security provisions of the GDPR serve as a robust regulatory framework. Consequently, even before the AI Act's finalization, European lawyers were still subject to data protection regulations that mandate meticulous handling of client data, especially in situations in which automated processes pose a risk of infringing confidentiality or individual rights.

The Council of Bars and Law Societies of Europe (CCBE) acts as a central coordinating body that formulates common positions. Frequently publishing position papers or guidance to clarify the impact of EU-level regulations for the legal profession. The CCBE has released considerations on the legal aspects of AI, a detailed guidance on GDPR compliance for lawyers and firms, which emphasizes the importance of communication, competence, and privacy, a statement on the use of AI in the justice system, and lastly, a position paper strongly supporting ethical safeguards that ensure AI does not replace human judgment in judicial decision-making and lawyering—advocating transparency, explainability, accountability, and supervision.

B. Argentina

In 2024, the Ministry of Justice issued Order No. 111/2024 which established the Comprehensive National AI in Justice Program. This initiative indicates a growing emphasis within the public sector on promoting and regulating the use of Artificial Intelligence.

There is no current law that specifically governs AI usage by lawyers in Argentina; however, lawyers and law firms are using AI tools in their daily practice. Argentina is actively debating the regulation of AI, with a focus on balancing technological innovation with data protection and privacy. Recent developments include an amendment project to the Personal Data Protection Law, Resolution 2/2023 recommendations for reliable AI, and a program for transparency and data protection in AI use. These initiatives align with international efforts to promote ethics in AI, highlighting Argentina's commitment to Responsible Artificial Intelligence.

In 2024, the Supreme Court of the Province of San Juan approved the Acceptable Use Protocol for Generative AI, a protocol for using this tool in the judiciary. The protocol, mandatory for all judicial agents, complements existing regulations on information technology use. Mandating ethical and responsible use of generative AI within the judicial system. The Protocol prohibits personal use, inappropriate content, data manipulation, and unauthorized access, emphasizing data anonymization to protect confidentiality.

The Bar Association of the City of Buenos Aires provides specialized training and periodic courses on the application of AI in the practice of law. One of your intrepid authors provided a workshop to some 200 lawyers at the Federal Bar Association of Buenos Aires in July 2024.

Other professional associations in the region also provide training and conferences geared towards AI-related topics, including the Bar Association of Lomas de Zamora, Bar Association of La Plata, and the Bar Association of the Judicial Department of Azul. Lastly, and most notable, the Corrientes Bar Association has developed the first postgraduate degree in Medical Law and Artificial Intelligence.

In summary, notable developments include the publication of a guide on responsible AI use, the creation of a national AI program in justice, and the approval of a protocol for Generative AI use. And lastly, the National Tax Court's launch of an AI-assisted jurisprudence search system, marking a monumental step towards improving access to justice.

C. *Australia*

Australia has demonstrated a judicial intervention in regulating AI in the legal context. In November 2024, the Chief Justice of New South Wales (NSW) issued the Generative AI Practice Note SC Gen 23 and revised in January 2025 (NSW Practice Note) banning the use of AI in drafting critical evidence documents and prohibiting judges from using AI tools to draft or edit judgments. Such judicial driven mandates illustrate a concern over "black box" AI systems and reflect a desire to preserve the integrity and autonomy of judicial decision-making. Meanwhile, in Victoria, parties must disclose to each other the use of Generative AI when preparing cases, while Queensland adopts a more lenient approach where lawyers are encouraged but not required to disclose its use. Australian legal bodies place a heavier emphasis on transparency. On the legislative front, the federal government published the Safe and responsible AI in Australia: Proposals Paper (Proposals Paper). The proposal aims to establish binding horizontal standards for all high-risk AI technologies. Much of the Proposals Paper is significantly influenced by the EU AI Act, which is referenced numerous times throughout the proposal. As these 'guardrails' are introduced, we may see the implications of AI in the legal sector addressed.

Although Australia's legal ethics model, governed by the Australian Solicitor's Conduct Rules (ASCR), does not explicitly address artificial intelligence, it does encompass a range of ethical considerations that are relevant to AI applications. The rules imposed are like those of the ABA, including competence, diligence, and confidentiality (ASCR Rules 3-10). Recognizing the significance of technological literacy, the Law Council of Australia has emphasized that solicitors are obligated to protect against confidentiality breaches and effectively utilize emerging technologies, such as AI tools.

Various law societies have published guidelines and discussion papers regarding the ethical responsibility of technology in the practice of law. The common prominence being a lawyer's accountability for ensuring clients are not misled by automated advice and lawyer's duty to stay accountable for all work produced whether by AI or other. The societies urge lawyers to ensure clear data security measures using AI vendors and maintain transparency with clients about the use of such technology.

D. Brazil

Brazil does not have any applicable legislation specifically addressing the use of AI by lawyers, "since AI regulation is still being discussed by the Brazilian National Congress." However, the Brazilian Bar Association (OAB) has taken initiative in addressing the use of AI by Brazilian lawyers. In 2018 the Bar created the Artificial Intelligence Coordination to regulate the use of AI in the legal sector. Notably, Brazilian Statute Law requires legal activities and consultations are only permissible by a lawyer registered with the National Bar Association.

The OAB approved recommendations for Generative AI, key aspects of the recommendations include the need for lawyers to supervise AI applications, ensure transparency in client communications, uphold confidentiality and service quality, and remain updated on technological advancements.

Most recently, Brazil's Senate approved a regulatory framework under the AI Act (Bill No. 2338/2023), echoing the EU risk-tired regulatory scheme. The drafted legislation combined with Brazil's comprehensive General Data Protection Law known as Lei Geral de Proteção de Dados (LGPD) suggests foreseeable professional guidelines will likely emerge.

A Brazilian regulation for the use of AI by the Judiciary has been instituted. At this writing, AI has already been adopted in at least half of the Brazilian courts, with at least 47 having AI programs and systems in use or under development, including the Supreme Court and the Superior Court of Justice.

E. Canada

Canada has not enacted explicit rules regarding the use of AI by lawyers; however, the Federation of Law Societies of Canada (FLSC) provides Model Rules of Professional Conduct. The FLSC amended rule 3.1-2 to add technological competence to the existing rules which also highlighted a lawyer's duty of confidentiality. The FLSC and various law societies have hosted conferences, discussions, and provided ethical guidance and training to ensure legal practitioners remain informed on the use of Artificial Intelligence. The key takeaway: A lawyer must understand the ways in which AI tools process data and produce outcomes to guard against inadvertent disclosure of confidential information and algorithmic bias.

On the provincial level, law societies have taken measures to clarify ethical boundaries. The five Canadian law societies of Alberta, Manitoba, Saskatchewan, Ontario, and British Columbia have published their own guidance and white papers on the use of Generative AI by lawyers. The Law Society of Ontario (LSO), of which one of your authors is a proud member, has provided guidance regarding Rule 6.1-1 emphasizing a lawyer is completely responsible for the output of their legal work and must directly supervise non-lawyers. In 2019 the Technology Task Force established by the LSO released a report warning that some AI tools may go "beyond merely performing support functions" demanding heightened and adequate lawyer supervision. In 2023, the Law Society of British Columbia published a Guidance on Professional Responsibility and Generative AI, underscoring competence, confidentiality, and information security, and human oversight, further reinforcing the principle of a 'lawyer in the loop.'

In conjunction with the law societies, the Canadian Bar Association (CBA) has issued guidelines on the use of Generative AI. Key areas of focus being competence, understanding AI's limitations rather than understanding the technology itself, maintaining confidentiality, supervising and guarding against potential biases, urging lawyers not to delegate core legal judgment to automated systems. The guide addresses "hallucinations," reiterating the importance of verifying machine outputs. Most notably, the CBA provides a toolkit covering an array of topics and guidance in relation to the use of AI in legal practice.

Further bolstering transparency and fairness, the Federal Court of Canada has introduced disclosure requirements for parties that rely on AI generated content in court filings or submissions. The court pays homage to the "human in the loop," urging verification of any AI-created content. It mandates that "the first paragraph of the text in that document must disclose that AI has been used to create or generate that content."

Law societies in Canada overall guidelines echo those of many global bar associations in recognizing that AI should enhance and not replace a lawyer's professional judgement and responsibility.

F. Chile

Currently there are no specific regulations regarding the use of AI by lawyers. However, in October 2024, Chile's Congress launched a National AI Policy and introduced an AI bill following the United Nations Education, Scientific and Cultural Organization's recommendations, aimed at regulating and promoting the ethical and responsible implementation of Artificial Intelligence.

One of the objectives noted in the National Artificial Intelligence Policy is to incorporate AI as a cross-cutting discipline in professional training, regardless of whether the career is related to technological areas or not. This indicates the legal field is no exception and training will likely be mandated, requiring lawyers to be competent in the technology.

For the time being, Chilean lawyers are expected to follow existing rules in the Código de Ética Profesional (Professional Ethics Code) set out by the Chilean Bar Association. The Code emphasizes confidentiality, loyalty to the client, and competence. Given that federal decisions are now being made in accordance with the EU's framework, it is likely that lawyers will be bound by stringent data security policies and risk assessment which will require careful vetting of AI systems and a need for human oversight.

The Chilean Bar Association has already been proactive in keeping lawyers informed through organizing talks and workshops. Additionally, in Chile, some universities provide training programs, seminars, and diploma courses aimed at lawyers to develop specialized AI professionals, building on Chilean lawyers' renowned drive for constant professional development and renewal.

G. China (People's Republic of China)

Currently there are no existing AI specific professional conduct rules or comprehensive guidelines. No Chinese bar association or lawyer regulatory body has yet issued a comprehensive, AI-specific professional code or guideline comparable to the considerations that are ongoing in jurisdictions such as the U.S. or the European Union. According to the IBA's 2024 ANLBS Handbook, China has "no planned, discussed or implemented sectorial statutory regulations on the use of AI in the legal profession or services that are traditionally rendered by lawyers."

In China, the legal profession is mainly governed by the Ministry of Justice (司法部), the All China Lawyers Association (中华全国律师协会, "ACLA"), and local (provincial/municipal) lawyers associations. They apply longstanding confidentiality, competence, and integrity rules which are supplemented by the Personal Information Protection Law (PIPL) and cybersecurity regulations. Many of the general ethics rules, professional codes, and new AI regulations (particularly those related to data privacy, cybersecurity, and Generative AI) impact lawyers.

In July 2023, China implemented the official Interim Administrative Measures for Generative Artificial Intelligence

Services which was finalized and came into effect in August of 2023. Under these sets of rules, lawyers are required to disclose when using Artificial Intelligence.

AI is being used in Chinese courts to process documents, identify legal issues, and even suggest opinions and judgments. In some cases, AI is providing non-human judges for citizens to submit and resolve cases digitally. Although China has advanced "Smart Courts" which streamline administrative tasks. China's official policy consistently notes that final judicial decisions remain under human control, even if AI automates procedural steps.

Although AI tools are being utilized in automating some judicial processes, it does not participate in the actual making of judicial decisions and attorneys still must file and argue the cases. Even with the advancement of AI, under the current legal framework, it is prohibited to entirely automate court decisions without human oversight.

The Beijing Bar Association, the Shanghai Bar Association, and Guangdong Lawyers Association have not released any professional conduct guidelines pertaining to the use of AI by lawyers. However, these Bar associations frequently host seminars and issue alerts regarding new legal technologies.

Under China's current AI regulatory framework, AI technologies are regulated by type. This contrasts with the approaches taken in other jurisdictions, such as the EU and United States. Evidenced by smart court initiatives and judicial interpretations from the Supreme People's Court, there seems to be a national push towards the use of AI driven tools in the legal sector. Given this larger push, it is likely AI specific rules for lawyers may be forthcoming in the near future.

H. France

French bar associations have shown a growing awareness of the implications of AI in legal practice, with efforts largely led by the Conseil National des Barreaux. Primarily contributing to debates through organizing conferences discussing AI and formulating proposals.

Although no laws directly address the ethical use of AI by lawyers, existing core professional duties include competence, confidentiality, and independence, overlaid with the General Data Protection Regulation. Emphasizing legal advice must remain supervised, meaning lawyers may not delegate their work to Artificial Intelligence.

Uniquely, France has legislated a criminal penalty for AI-driven analysis of judges' behavior. In a groundbreaking intervention aimed at curbing the increasing litigation analytics and prediction industry, the French Government has enacted Article 33 of the 2019 French Justice Reform, a prohibition on the publication of statistical data pertaining to judges' decision-making patterns.

Violators could face up to five years in prison. Although these restrictions do not directly govern lawyers' uses of AI, they strongly influence the deployment of predictive analytics in litigation strategy.

I. Germany

There are currently no specific AI laws targeting legal professionals, like many countries, Germany's approach involves applying existing professional practice rules for lawyers when using Artificial Intelligence.

German attorneys' professional obligations are outlined in the Bundesrechtsanwaltsordnung (BRAO) and the Berufsordnung für Rechtsanwälte (BORA). While AI usage is not explicitly regulated, these statutes indirectly influence its application. As a member of the European Union, Germany's regulations will likely align with the EU framework and follow the EU's AI Act.

The Bundesrechtsanwaltskammer (The German Federal Bar, BRAK) published a position paper in 2021 supporting a tiered "risk-based" regulation of AI. Underscoring the importance of balancing innovation with strict adherence to professional and ethical practice of law. It emphasized the importance of maintaining human oversight, transparency of AI usage, competence, integrity, compliance with data protection regulations such as the GDPR, and ongoing training for lawyers. Germany's position is that while AI can support decision-making, replacing judicial decisions is generally prohibited, with the exception for voluntary automated decisions in civil and administrative cases.

The primary objective and function of German bar associations is to safeguard the high quality and reliability of legal services. The Bar Association is tasked with monitoring the progression of AI through review of new developments and ensuring high quality of human legal advice.

The German law for legal services does not allow the fully automated provision of legal services. However, using AI to assist lawyers is permissible under German law. The report emphasizes that AI can only provide limited assistance to lawyers and cannot act on their behalf. This demonstrates a strong emphasis on maintaining a "human in the loop" oversight.

The Federal Government of Germany advocates for "ethics by, in, and for design" in Artificial Intelligence. "It highly recommends engaging in dialogue with other leading regions to reach an agreement on joint guidelines and ethical standards on AI." Germany anticipates the development of a legal and ethical framework that aligns with European guidelines. This framework will consider the recommendations of the national Data Ethics

Commission, which emphasize transparency, verifiability, and the predictability of AI systems.

The final consensus is that attorneys must remain fully responsible for the professional work product and cannot delegate final decision-making to an algorithm without appropriate human oversight.

J. Japan

The Japan Federation of Bar Associations (JFBA) develops regulations and ethical guidelines which are found in the Basic Regulations on the Duties of Practicing Attorneys. Although the rules do not specifically address the use of AI by lawyers, they emphasize duties such as confidentiality, competence, diligence, and data security. In 2023, the JFBA participated in the G7 Bars' Statement on Artificial Intelligence, confirming a shared commitment to ethical frameworks and Japan's commitment to collaborating with bar and law societies.

Consistent with data protection norms in the Act on the Protection of Personal Information, lawyers in Japan must be vigilant with handling client information. Ongoing initiatives by the JFBA demonstrates that the development of AI tools for analyzing and predicting judgments is likely; that is, as long as human oversight remains central. Additionally, lawyers must comply with confidentiality rules outlined in the Attorney's Act. Official guidelines bind lawyers to the duty to preserve client confidence and heavily emphasize that attorneys themselves must remain in control.

K. New Zealand

Currently there is no overarching regulation specifically governing AI use by lawyers in New Zealand, however law societies have released guidelines reiterating practitioners' expectancy to adhere to existing professional obligations when using AI tools while still maintaining responsibility for the accuracy and validity of AI-generated content.

New Zealand's legal profession is regulated by the Lawyers and Conveyancers Act of 2006 and the associated Lawyers and associated Conduct and Client Care Rules, these rules govern competence, confidentiality, and client loyalty.

In March 2024, the New Zealand Law Society Te Kāhui Ture o Aotearoa published the Generative AI Guidance for Lawyers (the NZ Guide), aimed to assist lawyers in navigating the use of AI in their work. The NZ Guide warns that "although Gen AI has significant potential for the legal profession, there are also risks and ethical issues that need to be carefully managed." The NZ Guide substantially draws on England and Wales resources, an example of the ways in which countries look to each other for help in developing guidance on the ethical use of AI in the practice of law.

The overall tone of the guidance provides an enthusiastic outlook for the upcoming scalability of AI in the legal field while also warning practitioners about ethical uses of such tools in legal practice. Key concerns regarding the use of AI in practice highlighted by the Law Society include following strict data privacy and security measures, ensuring and maintaining the quality services without compromise, supervising AI outputs, and remaining the final say in giving legal advice. Adopted from the Law Society of England and Wales, the Guide provides a checklist for practitioners to reference when considering the use of AI tools.

L. Singapore

Singapore is renowned for technological innovation, in contrast to the EU AI Act, Singapore has taken a more flexible approach. While Singapore has yet to implement AI legislation, it has initiated responsible AI frameworks and toolkits to warrant the ethical and effective deployment of AI, including the Model AI Governance Framework, which was updated in 2020 to enhance usability and relevance.

Speaking to the professional responsibilities of lawyers, Singapore's Chief Justice Sundaresh Menon shared his views at the Litigation Conference held in April 2024, stating that "[l]egal professionals must also uphold their professional responsibilities when using AI tools, such as by verifying the accuracy of AI-generated output and ensuring that confidential client information is not included in prompts to public generative AI tools."

In 2023, Singapore courts partnered with Harvey, a cutting-edge AI tool in the legal field, to test Generative AI to assist self-represented individuals in small claims courts. Since lawyers in Singapore are not allowed to represent parties in small claims consultations or hearings. The initiative demonstrates Singapore's willingness to experiment with AI in the judicial process without displacing legal representation and improving access to justice.

The Law Society of Singapore has addressed technological adoption through its publication, Guide on the Adoption of LegalTech for Law Practices, advising lawyers to protect confidentiality and verify accuracy of AI-generated outputs. Ultimately, Singapore's approach balances its tech-forward ethos while recognizing the paramount importance of attorneys adhering to ethical standards and maintaining client trust.

M. South Korea (the Republic of Korea)

There are no specific regulations regulating the use of AI by lawyers in the Republic of Korea (Korea). Existing rules under the Attorney-At-Law Act stringently restrict non-lawyers from providing legal services. They highlight the duty of oversight by lawyers. The Korean Bar Association (KBA) enforces the regulations under the Act and the KBA's Code of Ethics underlines an attorney's obligation to maintain confidentiality and integrity.

"Any AI-driven service that might encroach upon the exclusive domain of licensed attorneys could be deemed unauthorized if it performs functions akin to those restricted to lawyers." Korea raises concerns about unauthorized "legal robots" or "chatbots" that promise free or low-cost advice. Delegating legal work to non-lawyers is strictly prohibited.

While the Korean government has published a national AI strategy and ethical guidelines, these do not specifically regulate how lawyers must use Artificial Intelligence. The Ministry of Science and Information and Communication Technology has discussed implementing binding AI ethics standards in the future, but no formal legislation focusing on the legal profession is in place or formally scheduled.

N. The United Arab Emirates

The United Arab Emirates (UAE) has adopted a forward-looking approach to AI at the government level. In 2017, it appointed a Minister of State for Artificial Intelligence and launched the UAE Strategy for Artificial Intelligence 2031, with the objective of promoting AI across various industries. While the UAE has published an array of decrees and guidelines regarding regulation of AI, there are currently no regulations specifically addressing the legal profession's utilization of Artificial Intelligence. However, the broader AI strategy and its associated guidelines encompass several components that have clear implications for lawyers' professional responsibility, particularly concerning confidentiality, data security, non-discriminatory or biased use of AI tools, oversight, and transparency.

There is no explicit rule on AI in any federal professional code; lawyers are bound by stringent confidentiality obligations and can face sanctions for breaching these duties. In Dubai, for instance, the Code of Professional Conduct for Legal Consultants (administered by the Dubai Legal Affairs Department) emphasizes the lawyer's duty to maintain confidentiality and competence in all aspects of practice.

While not directly binding on lawyers, of the eight principles outlined in the UAE's AI Ethics Framework, "fairness in system operations, accountability mechanisms, and transparent decision-making process" are relevant when using AI in legal practice. Similarly, the quality control and oversight requirements outlined in the framework—"making important decisions must undergo regular quality check" applies to a lawyers' obligation to supervise AI outputs to ensure accuracy and legal compliance.

The UAE has placed significant fines and even jail time for AI-driven discrimination and non-compliance with ethical guidelines and this directly affects lawyers and requires regular audits of AI tools being used by a lawyer.

So, even without explicit AI regulations for lawyers, existing UAE rules and professional standards already create important guardrails for confidentiality, competence and supervision, accuracy and reliability, and informed consent.

Lawyers must preserve client confidences under UAE law. Uploading client data to AI platforms (especially if cloud-based or located outside the UAE) raises data privacy and security risks. AI tools should supplement—not replace—human lawyer judgment.

Practitioners must ensure that they remain competent to evaluate AI-generated work products. Attorneys remain responsible for the factual and legal accuracy of their filings, advice, and communications, regardless of whether they used AI in the drafting or research process. While not explicitly mandated in current UAE regulations, some attorneys adopt international best practices by informing clients if significant AI tools are used in handling their matters, particularly where sensitive data is concerned.

O. The United Kingdom

Alongside U.S. bar associations and Canada's various provinces, the Law Society of England and Wales has formally published a guideline for the ethical use of AI by solicitors.

England and Wales exemplify a jurisdiction whose primary regulatory bodies explicitly encourage "lawtech" adoption, including AI, while insisting that core professional duties remain unchanged. The Law Society of England and Wales and the Bar Standard Board (BS) provide guidance addressing Generative AI in the legal profession, reminding solicitors that the principles of the Solicitors Regulation Authority's (SRA) Code of Conduct for Solicitors such as competence, supervision, data security and confidentiality continue to apply. This guidance's "Ethical Considerations" section refers to the U.K. government's AI White Paper's ethical considerations regarding the use of Generative AI tools. The principles outlined are safety, security, robustness, appropriate transparency and explainability, fairness, accountability and governance, and contestability and redress.

Interpreting existing ethical rules and providing checklists, the Law Society of England and Wales published their Generative AI: The Essentials. This guidance covers risk assessment, data security, and reiterates the need to maintain a 'human in the loop.' Unauthorized entities and non-lawyers provide certain legal services. Although such providers exist outside the SRA's purview, in-house solicitors within those entities remain personally bound by professional rules. Therefore, individual solicitors must ensure AI-based services do not compromise client data or deviate from SRA outcome-based standards.

P. *Uruguay (the Oriental Republic of Uruguay)*

Uruguay's Bar Association (Colegio de Abogados del Uruguay) provides a Code of Ethics, emphasizing confidentiality, independence, and competence. However, Uruguay's Bar Association and regulatory authorities have not yet issued regulations specifically addressing AI use by legal professionals. Under the Code of Ethics, attorneys must protect client confidence, act independent, and maintain competence.

Regarding the responsible application of AI, Maximiliano Maneiro, Sub-director of the Information Technologies area at Uruguay's Agency for e-Government and the Information and Knowledge Society AGESIC, expressed that the government "prefer an AI that is more explainable than one that performs well."

Q. *Concluding Thoughts*

This survey shows that the use of AI in the legal profession is a thorny issue but at the same time, it is an idea whose time has come (or, for some, it is long overdue). The different professional bodies and bar associations are trying to balance tightrope talk: Using AI to make legal practice better while not subverting the professional obligations and duties of their members. It is said that the courts can stay anything. Except perhaps that irresistible itch of lawyers to use ChatGPT for their briefs.

IV. Summary/Key Points

1. The American Bar Association's Formal Opinion sets the national baseline for how lawyers should approach Generative Artificial Intelligence. It frames AI-related responsibilities through existing rules on competence, confidentiality, communication, supervision, misrepresentation, and

reasonable billing. Lawyers remain accountable even when the machine does the typing, and the thinking.

2. State bar associations are also developing their own rules and opinions on use of artificial intelligence. California leads with detailed guidance; New York and Florida follow closely with formal opinions and task forces. Other states are cautious but gradually catching up.

3. Most state bar associations are in agreement that AI tools are in their "infancy." But early adoption doesn't mean ready forgiveness. Diligence and ethical duties still apply: even if your AI insists it passed the bar.

4. The bar associations in many other countries have endeavored to provide regulations for their members, but their successful adoption depends on whether the bar associations have mandatory membership and enforceable sanctions for those who violate the rules. In many countries, membership in national or local bar associations is voluntary.

5. There is universal consensus that the lawyer must still be in the loop. Across jurisdictions, the recurring theme is that AI may assist, but not replace, professional legal judgment.

CHAPTER 10

A Call to Action

I. Who Won't Get Fooled Again?

The classic rock band The Who released the song "Won't Get Fooled Again" on the 1971 album *Who's Next*, a few years after the band's appearance at the Woodstock festival. Guitarist and principal song-writer Pete Townsend wrote the song's lyrics about the vagaries of political change:

We'll be fighting in the streets

With our children at our feet

And the morals that they worship will be gone

And the men who spurred us on

Sit in judgement of all wrong

They decide and the shotgun sings the song. . .

I'll tip my hat to the new Constitution

Take a bow for the new revolution

Smile and grin at the change all around

Pick up my guitar and play

Just like yesterday

Then I'll get on my knees and pray

We don't get fooled again

The band finishes the song after lengthy guitar, keyboard, and drum solos with the lyrics:

Meet the new boss

Same as the old boss

The classic rock song's lament maps well to the evolving world of Artificial Intelligence (AI). Let us unpack this for a moment:

1. AI was supposed to free up our time and fire up our creativity so that we can play guitar, paint, or write. Now no one needs to worry about that: Turns out AI can do it better than we can anyway. We may still have free time but not necessarily gainful employment.

2. AI has become a kind of religion. There are high priests and doomsayers, there are prophets and profits.

3. We are going to be fooled again—and repeatedly, thanks to misinformation, deep fakes, and synthetic data. Add 300 million knowledge workers whose jobs will be reconfigured (see below). That's a whole lot of change all around.

4. Ethics and values are struggling to keep pace. What matters is compute power, output efficiency and an absence of guardrails to rein in the excesses.

5. There is frenetic change all around us and we do not fully comprehend the consequences of what we are unleashing.

After all, the advent of AI may entail many things for our societies: Robots automating jobs out of existence, chatbots creating liability for corporations based on website Question and Answer functions, and AI tools deployed to trick voters and change election results. And that's only on Monday. Just wait for Thursday.

* * * *

We are right to be concerned given that Goldman Sachs predicted in March 2023 that some 300 million knowledge-jobs—those jobs done in front of a computer, could be displaced over the next several years. The International Monetary Fund released a study in January 2025 that AI will affect almost 40 percent of jobs around the world. Some of those jobs will be replaced, others will be complemented by AI tools, but disruption is definitely in the offing. Eduardo Porter wrote in March 2024 in *The Washington Post* that:

> There is good reason to believe that artificial intelligence is coming for our jobs. That's, after all, what information technology has been doing for decades. The tech plutocrats apparently agree that human employment will become the stuff of folklore. They probably don't mind that all wealth in this world will accrue to the lucky few who own the AI patents. They seem willing to share some of it with regular people through some universal basic income scheme.

TechCrunch ran a story in May 2025 that a study by Giskard, a Paris-based company that creates holistic AI benchmarks, found that chatbots are hallucinating when asked to provide short answers. Hallucinations are not harmless but can have serious consequences. AI tools can foment instability through misinformation, leading to mistrust and the end of social cohesion.

For lawyers, the use of AI could mean problems with the bar associations that license us. It could lead to lawsuits by clients when the data we provide AI tools to help with our work ends up divulging confidential information to AI systems which train on said data.

For the rest of us it could mean that we will get fooled again. Technology is advertised as a good thing—to free us from mundane job tasks so we can sing, write and paint. But what happens when AI tools can sing, write and paint better than we can? Enter the regulators.

II. A Comparative Approach to AI Regulation

Our brief comparative survey of AI regulation across the European Union (EU), the United States (U.S.), and the People's Republic of China (China) (and many places in between) has revealed the emergence of divergent governance models, each shaped by distinct legal traditions, industrial policy goals, and political economies. Despite their variance, several core regulatory themes emerge that define the contemporary global discourse on AI governance. These include state intervention in the form of algorithmic transparency and liability rules, the emerging centrality of risk-based frameworks, sector-specific regulatory calibration, data privacy safeguards, and the broader geopolitical tension between national industrial strategies and the aspirations for international harmonization.

A. *State Intervention: Transparency, Accountability, and Governance*

Across jurisdictions, a key axis of regulatory attention lies in ensuring algorithmic transparency, non-discrimination, and clear lines of liability. As we noted in Chapter 6 of this *Short and Happy Guide*, the EU AI Act represents the most comprehensive legal instantiation of these concerns, with its layered obligations for high-risk systems including documentation, human oversight, and post-market monitoring. The United States, in contrast, has oscillated between soft law initiatives like the Blueprint for an AI Bill of Rights during the Biden administration and sectoral statutes, although some subsequent Biden executive orders suggested a pivot towards more enforceable oversight mechanisms (at least for the federal government)—now rescinded under the second Trump administration. China's regulatory apparatus emphasizes algorithmic accountability through licensing and state audits, albeit with limited procedural transparency. It also has to do with "social cohesion," a euphemism for centralized control and market authoritarianism. Meanwhile, Japan prefers a guidance-driven, industry-led model with minimal direct state enforcement, relying instead on business-led ethical review. Other countries are building from their respective national AI strategies to more sector-focused initiatives that have some legal weight. Eventually.

B. *Risk Mitigation as an Organizing Principle*

As we saw in Chapter 6, the EU has decisively centered its AI strategy around a risk-based classification schema, distinguishing AI systems into categories of unacceptable, high, limited, and minimal risk. This typology not only rationalizes state intervention but provides a scalable model adaptable to technological evolution. The US's adaptive enforcement approach, promoting voluntary compliance for low-risk AI while enhancing scrutiny of high-risk systems, aligns conceptually, though it lacks the legal force of the EU framework. China's classification is implicit, determined through opaque assessments of "social harmony" and "security," while Japan has refrained from imposing an ex-ante classification regime, trusting instead in industry discretion and sectoral adaptation.

C. *Sectoral Regulation and Proportionality*

The regulatory regimes under review diverge significantly in the role they assign to sectoral laws. The U.S. and Japan lean heavily into pre-existing sector-specific regulations—such as the U.S.'s Health Insurance Portability Act of 1996 for health and the Fair Credit Reporting Act of 1970 for finance—arguing that contextual adaptation yields more tailored outcomes. The EU, despite its preference for harmonization, also integrates sector-specific compliance under its high-risk classification, while China enforces rules differently across sectors, especially emphasizing content governance, education, and public opinion manipulation.

D. *Data Privacy and Protection*

Data protection continues to be a critical area of overlap and divergence. The General Data Protection Regulation (GDPR) remains the global benchmark for data privacy, with the EU ensuring interoperability between its AI and data protection regimes. Japan's Act on the Protection of Personal Information offers a more flexible, innovation-friendly model, while the U.S. lacks a comprehensive federal privacy law, though state-level statutes and sectoral rules attempt to fill the gap. China, on the other hand, enshrines data control in the service of national security, giving the state expansive surveillance and censorship powers under the Data Security Law and Cybersecurity Law. Brazil has a very robust data protection law too. There are lots of different varieties.

E. *National Security, Industrial Policy, and Global Fragmentation*

AI regulation has become a geopolitical tool—an extension of national industrial strategy as much as a safeguard against technological risks. The EU seeks to bolster its digital sovereignty and internal market competitiveness through regulatory leadership. The U.S. model reflects a deep ambivalence—balancing national security imperatives, such as export controls and restrictions on cross-border data flows, with an enduring faith in market-driven innovation. China tightly fuses AI regulation with its national security and ideological objectives, explicitly prioritizing state control and sovereignty over global collaboration. Japan positions itself strategically seeking to attract capital and talent through deregulatory openness while emphasizing human-centric AI values.

F. Public Versus Private Sector Innovation Leadership

Underlying these regulatory approaches is a tension between public sector stewardship and private sector primacy in AI innovation. The EU and China adopt a more *dirigiste* model—strong state oversight with the intent to shape industrial outcomes. Japan and the U.S., by contrast, entrust much of the AI value chain to private enterprise, with public policy playing a reactive or supportive role through tax incentives, research funding, or voluntary codes of conduct. Yet both models face scrutiny: the EU risks stifling innovation with overregulation, while Japan and the U.S. contend with under-regulation and ethical blind spots.

G. The Elusive Quest for Global Norms

Despite efforts like the Bletchley Declaration, G7 Hiroshima Process, and the Organisation for Economic Cooperation and Development (OECD) AI Principles, there remains no binding global AI treaty or universally accepted model. This is not due to lack of interest but because of irreconcilable differences in regulatory philosophy, values, or national strategic interests. International institutions are hindered by soft law fatigue-producing frameworks that lack enforcement, funding, or even legitimacy. Instead, regional blocs and bilateral arrangements are likely to dominate future norm diffusion, raising questions about interoperability, compliance costs, and digital protectionism.

In sum, AI regulation is coalescing around a shared vocabulary of transparency, fairness, safety, and human oversight, but the institutional responses to these shared concerns remain highly divergent. The EU's regulatory maximalism offers a rights-based, precautionary template; the U.S. oscillates between innovation-first permissiveness and ethical vigilance; Japan exemplifies techno-liberal pragmatism; China demonstrates authoritarian stewardship. The world is unlikely to converge on a singular regulatory architecture. Instead, a pluralistic, competitive ecosystem of regulatory models will persist, shaped by national interests, market dynamics, and the evolving capabilities of AI systems. Risk-based regulation may provide the *lingua franca* of global AI governance, but translation across jurisdictions will remain a contested and politically charged endeavor.

What is clear with the three different approaches (U.S., EU, and Chinese) to AI regulation, and the fact that there are technologists, investors and ethicists from each of those three jurisdictions working on AI systems around the world, is that there will need to be some convergence or practical overlay to work well within all three approaches. We—your intrepid co-authors—believe that we have a way to do just that.

III. A Flexible AI Governance Framework

Contemporary AI regulation is excessively blunt and broad, often engendering more problems than it resolves. A principal deficiency of policymakers' preoccupation with a binary risk categorization of AI is the negligence of the exogenous factors of who is deploying the AI and their motivation, both of which are frequently more determinative of actual risk than the AI's intrinsic characteristics. To rectify this oversight, we propose the Actor-Intent Matrix for AI (AIM-AI) Governance Framework, a contextually sensitive regulatory paradigm that calibrates AI oversight based on these considerations.

The AIM-AI Governance Framework (AIM-AI Framework) is an intent-based regulatory structure that classifies AI applications into four distinct governance zones: SAFE-AI, for unrestricted applications; FAULT-AI, for applications requiring calibrated constraints; ABUSE-AI, for prohibited applications; and REBEL-AI, for applications that necessitate case-by-case adjudication. This Framework is constructed upon a comprehensive analysis of legal literature, regulatory reports, and contemporary AI controversies, to demonstrate its capacity to furnish proportional, context-sensitive AI regulation. In doing so, it aims to protect democratic institutions, technological advancement, and fundamental rights. As AI governance approaches an inflection point, the AIM-AI Framework offers a pragmatic and ethical regulatory model adaptable to the fluid complexities of Artificial Intelligence.

The AIM-AI Framework aims to reform AI regulation by instituting contextually appropriate accountability, fostering innovation, and furnishing a legal mechanism for ambiguous cases. We advocate for a reflective approach to AI policy formulation.

A. Enter the Matrix

The swift advancement of AI technologies has provoked worldwide discourse on governance and regulation. Governments, industries, and civil organizations are deliberating pivotal issues, specifically the necessity, scope, and methodology of AI governance. The heterogenous regulatory reactions to these deliberations have failed to uniformly address the multifaceted and progressive character of AI applications. The AIM-AI Framework posits that an effective AI regulatory framework necessitates a paradigm shift from monolithic regulatory models to a context-specific, adaptive framework that acknowledges the nuanced intricacies of AI deployment and its diverse users. This regulatory strategy is contingent on the nature of AI utilization and the cadre of its users, grounded on the doctrine of exogenous factors.

The cornerstone of the Framework is a dual classification model that discerns AI applications as either beneficial or detrimental, acknowledging the subjective nature of these qualifiers, and categorizes AI users based on their objectives and ethical standards. This dual classification yields four governance scenarios: AI applications that are beneficial and deployed by benign users, AI applications that are detrimental albeit deployed by benign users, AI applications that are detrimental and deployed by bad faith users, and AI applications that are beneficial but deployed by bad faith users. Each scenario gives rise to distinct governance challenges that mandate bespoke regulatory instruments.

The AIM-AI Framework is an adaptive, structured model that can be contrasted with existing one-size-fits-all AI policies. It evaluates AI according to a dual-layered governance approach that examines both the user and the intent pursued in utilization. By grounding AI regulation in actor-intent analysis, the AIM-AI Framework can be contextually aligned with legal, ethical, and societal requirements, thereby ensuring that AI remains an instrument for progressive innovation.

B. Four Governance Zones

The AIM-AI Framework is a structured, adaptive regulatory model that is contingent on two pivotal factors: the actor deploying the AI and the intent and impact of the AI's usage. This dual-focused approach facilitates a calibrated regulatory response that is neither excessive nor insufficient, but proportional. The framework strikes a balance between security and innovation and can be readily integrated with prevailing regulatory standards such as the EU AI Act, the OECD AI Principles, and America's AI Action Plan.

The AIM-AI Framework is operationalized through four distinct governance zones, each delineating the AI applications within them. These zones are associated with several simplified and self-explanatory acronyms—SAFE-AI, FAULT-AI, ABUSE-AI, and REBEL-AI—to make them more accessible to policymakers and to facilitate regulatory discourse.

1. SAFE-AI

This zone pertains to AI applications that are deployed responsibly and ethically, yielding positive social, economic, and environmental impacts. These applications are governed by a light-touch regulatory regime that encourages innovation and adoption.

2. FAULT-AI

This zone addresses instances where AI tools, despite being deployed by well-intentioned actors, lead to unintended harm. The regulatory approach here is stringent, focusing on algorithmic bias audits, impact assessments, and consumer protection laws.

3. ABUSE-AI

This zone is concerned with AI applications that are exploited by bad faith actors for nefarious purposes such as fraud, cybercrime, and political destabilization. The regulatory response is one of strict prohibition and enforcement.

4. REBEL-AI

This zone pertains to AI applications that, although deployed by actors deemed 'bad' by legal or societal standards, eventuate beneficial social outcomes. These applications necessitate a nuanced regulatory approach that includes case-by-case evaluations and potential legal carve-outs.

See Appendix B for an overview of the sub-components of these four governance zones.

C. *Benefits of the AIM-AI Governance Framework*

The AIM-AI Framework represents a paradigm shift in AI governance by offering a regulatory regime that is adaptive, precise, and balances innovation and risk mitigation. This framework enhances public trust and accountability and provides legal and ethical safeguards for controversial AI uses. The self-descriptive labels for each scenario and the available policy levers provide a pragmatic instrument for regulators.

1. Adaptability

   The AIM-AI Framework provides a dynamic regulatory environment that keeps pace with the rapidly evolving AI landscape. For example, AI-powered facial recognition, which has beneficial applications in finding missing persons (SAFE-AI), can also be used for mass surveillance and political repression (ABUSE-AI). The AIM-AI Framework allows a nuanced regulatory approach, permitting ethical uses while restricting harmful applications.

2. Precision

   The AIM-AI Framework allows proportional regulatory interventions based on risk. This avoids overregulation and encourages low-risk, beneficial AI applications. For instance, an AI application in healthcare should face streamlined approvals compared to AI-powered autonomous weapons.

3. Balanced Innovation and Risk Mitigation

   The AIM-AI Framework allows pro-growth policies for beneficial AI applications while appropriately regulating harmful AI uses. It encourages ethical AI development and protects fundamental rights. For example, AI-driven hiring algorithms (FAULT-AI) require algorithmic bias audits to prevent discrimination, while AI-powered virtual assistants (SAFE-AI) require proportionally minimal regulatory oversight.

4. Alignment with Global AI Governance Standards

   The AIM-AI Framework is compatible with existing and emerging AI governance frameworks, making it a practical model for international AI regulation. It aligns with risk-based global AI models (e.g., EU AI Act) and standards-based approaches (e.g., OECD AI Principles).

5. Improved Public Trust and AI Accountability

   The AIM-AI Framework enhances public trust in AI by establishing clear governance mechanisms that prioritize transparency and accountability. It mandates explainability standards for AI applications that affect human rights (FAULT-AI and ABUSE-AI categories) and holds corporations and governments accountable for AI-driven decisions.

6. Legal and Ethical Safeguards for Controversial AI Uses

   The AIM-AI Framework provides a structured approach to evaluating ethically ambiguous AI applications. It prevents AI-driven censorship and provides a legal framework for assessing controversial AI applications. For example, AI-powered whistleblowing tools exposing corporate corruption, which may be legally sensitive but ethically justifiable.

7. Practicality

   The AIM-AI Framework is structured yet flexible, making it usable by policymakers, regulators, businesses, and civil society groups. It provides policymakers with a clear AI classification system for targeted regulation and gives businesses a compliance roadmap to navigate AI laws efficiently.

The AIM-AI Framework enhances AI accountability by introducing mandatory fairness audits, explainability standards, and liability laws as appropriate. It can strengthen democratic norms by preventing AI-generated election fraud while ensuring AI-driven journalism is not unfairly censored. The AIM-AI Framework provides a scalable AI governance model that aligns with legal, ethical, and human rights principles.

D. Next-Gen National AI Governance

The AIM-AI Framework is a future-proof AI governance model. Its scalable and globally relevant framework helps governments, businesses, and civil society navigate the complex AI governance landscape effectively.

AI is rapidly becoming a critical component of national economies, governance structures, and societal functions. However, the absence of comprehensive and adaptive national AI policies creates significant gaps in oversight, leaving beneficial AI applications over-regulated while allowing harmful AI use cases to slip through regulatory loopholes.

The AIM-AI Framework classifies AI applications into four governance zones, each with specific regulatory sub-components that define oversight mechanisms, liability models, and enforcement strategies. Governments can use this as a starting point to develop a national AI governance framework (or enhance existing AI governance models by using AIM-AI principles).

When used as a blueprint for governance, the AIM-AI Framework can deliver multiple benefits to different stakeholders. For governments, a structured policy toolkit can be instituted to support AI-driven economic growth without compromising ethics or security. Businesses also gain as developers when there is a clear compliance roadmap for AI projects, ensuring fair regulation without stifling innovation (the latter being a major concern for AI entrepreneurs). For international organizations, there is much to be gained here too: A universal AI governance framework adaptable to different legal, cultural, and economic contexts is good for everyone—corporations and citizens alike.

Implementing the AIM-AI Framework requires national AI governance institutions and oversight bodies. Governments should establish an AI Regulatory Commission (AIRC) (or designate an existing body performing the AI governance function) to create and enforce AIM-AI policies, ensuring AI governance remains adaptive, enforceable, and technologically up to date.

AIRC responsibilities include classifying AI applications under AIM-AI categories based on real-world deployment and conducting periodic AI risk assessments to update policies as AI technologies evolve. It also coordinates with cybersecurity agencies to detect and prevent AI misuse and oversees whistleblower protections.

Such an approach signifies proactive AI risk mitigation rather than reactive legal enforcement. It also promotes responsible use, safety, and regulatory compliance.

E. Scaling AI Governance and Future Directions

This Part outlines key areas where the AIM-AI Framework can be integrated with existing regulatory systems, expanded to address emerging challenges and create a more globally scalable governance model.

First, there is much opportunity to integrate the AIM-AI Framework with AI risk-based models already being adopted. Existing AI governance models, such as the EU AI Act, OECD AI Principles, and National Institute of Standards and Technology AI Risk Management Framework, adopt a risk-based classification approach. The AIM-AI Framework can be combined with these models to create a dual-layered regulatory approach that accounts for both actor intent and AI risk level.

The AIM-AI Framework provides a foundational scaffolding for AI regulation by categorizing AI applications based on actor intent and usage impact. However, as AI technology continues to evolve, so too must the governance structures.

AI is increasingly a target for cyberattacks, and malicious actors can exploit AI vulnerabilities for potential data poisoning attacks (through the act of feeding AI false data). There are also dangers of model inversion attacks, wherein sensitive information is extracted from AI systems. Also, there is a risk of adversarial AI attacks whereby AI is tricked into incorrect outputs, jeopardizing the trustability of AI systems.

This calls for the development of a set of National AI Cybersecurity Standards to ensure a country's institutions, corporations, non-profit organizations, other community actors, and individuals are safe. This can be achieved by expanding the AIM-AI Framework to include risk-management protocols for AI security. Moreover, AI security audits should be mandated so that AI models in critical industries (such as healthcare, finance, and defense) undergo periodic security checks.

In the end enforcement becomes paramount through global cooperation, compliance requirements and a regime of sanctions and penalties for bad actors, bad behavior, and bad governance. AI regulations must go beyond guidelines and include enforceable mechanisms that prevent AI misuse and regulatory arbitrage (where companies relocate to jurisdictions with weaker AI laws). This may require:

- Developing AI-Specific Legal Penalties: Expand AIM-AI to define specific criminal offenses for AI exploitation, particularly in ABUSE-AI cases.
- Cross-Border AI Law Enforcement: Strengthen international cooperation for AI crimes, ensuring bad actors cannot evade responsibility.
- Sanctions and Trade Restrictions for AI Misuse: Countries can restrict AI technologies that violate human rights, democracy, and cybersecurity norms.

In the near future, governance will become increasingly important as AI technologies proliferate.

The AIM-AI Framework is designed to evolve with AI advancements, ensuring that regulation remains proactive, adaptive, and globally aligned. In the future we expect the AIM-AI Framework to evolve into a more comprehensive AI governance system. There, now you have it. Use it, don't lose it.

IV. The Bots Cannot Win

We have a new version of "Won't Get Fooled Again." And it goes like this:

We'll be fighting in the feeds

With our children down in the weeds

And all the rights that we held dear are gone

While the tech bros soldier on,

Crooning, there's nothing wrong,

They preside and the algorithm swipes the song

A long trip to UBI—still no fair distribution

A hard blow if you're not part of the solution

There's much chagrin at the change all around

Lost my job today

Guess I'll play air guitar all day

Till it hits me: AI is here to stay

Let's get retooled again

[AI-created guitar solo]

Meet the new bots.

Same as the old boss.

If this sounds dystopian, just remember: The bots didn't ask for power—we gave it to them because the terms of service were too long to actually read.

APPENDIX A

Sources and References

Our Commentary in Popular Media

Some of the information and arguments developed in this *Short and Happy Guide* were based on various opinion pieces, together and separately, the authors have published in a number of print and online platforms. These include, but are not limited to:

James Cooper & Kashyap Kompella, *Why AI should be a hallmark of US foreign assistance*, THE HILL (Feb. 18, 2025), https://thehill.com/opinion/technology/5149319-us-soft-power-ai-foreign-aid/.

James Cooper & Kashyap Kompella, *China's DeepSeek may erase America's lead in AI. And wreck your 401(k)*, U.S.A. TODAY (Jan. 29, 2025), https://www.usatoday.com/story/opinion/2025/01/29/deepseek-ai-nvidia-stock-openai-google-meta/77992395007/.

James Cooper & Kashyap Kompella, *The U.S. response to Chinese advances in artificial intelligence*, ATLANTA JOURNAL-CONSTITUTION (Jan. 28, 2025), https://www.ajc.com/opinion/opinion-the-us-response-to-chinese-advances-in-artificial-intelligence/EE3ICC4XP5HONOCQQ2FXHQSSEY/.

James Cooper & Kashyap Kompella, *Memo to the new czar of artificial intelligence: How to maintain U.S. leadership*, PASADENA STAR NEWS (Dec. 17, 2024), https://www.pasadenastarnews.com/

2024/12/17/memo-to-the-new-czar-of-artificial-intelligence-how-to-maintain-u-s-leadership/.

James Cooper & Kashyap Kompella, *Is International Regulation of AI Moving in the Right Direction or Moving at All?*, LAW.COM (Oct. 31, 2024), https://www.law.com/legaltechnews/2024/10/31/is-international-regulation-of-ai-moving-in-the-right-direction-or-moving-at-all/.

James Cooper & Kashyap Kompella, *El imperativo de la inteligencia artificial para los sistemas jurídicos de América Latina*, ESTADO DIARIO (Chile), (Oct. 17, 2024), https://estadodiario.com/columnas/el-imperativo-de-la-inteligencia-artificial-para-los-sistemas-juridicos-de-america-latina/.

James Cooper & Kashyap Kompella, *Regulating Digital Assets: Can the United States Avoid Being a Legislative Luddite*, LEGAL TECH NEWS (Mar. 20, 2024), https://www.law.com/legaltechnews/2024/03/20/regulating-digital-assets-can-the-united-states-avoid-being-a-legislative-luddite/.

Kashyap Kompella & James Cooper, *Politics with AI: We Must Be 'We, The People,' Not 'We the Bots'*, THE MESSENGER (Sept. 1, 2023), https://web.archive.org/web/20240117052253/https://themessenger.com/opinion/politics-with-ai-we-must-be-we-the-people-not-we-the-bots.

Kashyap Kompella & James Cooper, *Mis-Regulating Artificial Intelligence Could Be Highly Hazardous*, THE MESSENGER (June 9, 2023), https://web.archive.org/web/20230609101514/https://themessenger.com/opinion/mis-regulating-artificial-intelligence-could-be-highly-hazardous.

James Cooper & Kashyap Kompella, *AI Regulation is Not a Silver Bullet*, THE HILL (June 5, 2023), https://thehill.com/opinion/technology/4034754-ai-regulation-is-not-a-silver-bullet/.

James Cooper & Kashyap Kompella, *Opinion: Artificial Intelligence Can Make Hiring More Inclusive, But Regulation is Necessary*, SAN DIEGO UNION-TRIB. (Apr. 26, 2023), https://www.sandiegouniontribune.com/opinion/commentary/story/2023-04-26/opinion-artificial-intelligence-hiring-job-applications-chatgpt-regulation-san-diego.

Fernando Garibay, Kashyap Kompella & James Cooper, *AI-Generated Music Is Officially a Hit—How Will it Change the Music Industry?*, THE HILL (Apr. 26, 2023), https://thehill.com/opinion/technology/3971398-ai-generated-music-is-officially-a-hit-how-will-it-change-the-music-industry/.

Kashyap Kompella & James Cooper, *ChatGPT Blues: the Coming Generative AI Gerrymandering of the American Mind*, THE HILL (Mar. 13, 2023), https://thehill.com/opinion/technology/3890357-chatgpt-blues-the-coming-generative-ai-gerrymandering-of-the-american-mind/.

Kashyap Kompella & James Cooper, *Artificial Intelligence and the Looming Misinformation Society*, THE HILL (Dec. 19, 2022), https://thehill.com/opinion/technology/3780759-artificial-intelligence-and-the-looming-misinformation-society/.

James Cooper & Kashyap Kompella, *Practice Tips: AI and Threats to the Criminal Justice System*, L.A. LAWYER 13 (Oct. 2022), https://lalawyer.advanced-pub.com/?issueID=40&pageID=11.

James Cooper & Kashyap Kompella, *No, China Is Not Winning the AI Race*, THE HILL (Feb. 3, 2022), https://thehill.com/opinion/technology/592270-no-china-is-not-winning-the-ai-race?rl=1.

The authors also published a law review article that covers, in part, some of Chapter 10's AIM-AI Governance Framework:

James M. Cooper & Kashyap Kompella, The Artificial Intelligence Trolley Problem: Governance in the Post-Chevron World, 28:2 SMU Sci. & Tech. L. Rev. (forthcoming, Spring 2026).

The authors have also published some of their ideas in a thematic issue coordinated by Singapore Management University's (SMU) Centre for Digital Law on "Operationalising Responsible AI in Public Administration:"

Kashyap Kompella & James M. Cooper, Horses for Courses: Regulating Artificial Intelligence Based on Who Uses It and In What Ways, Not Just What It Does, CAMBRIDGE FORUM ON AI: LAW & GOVERNANCE (forthcoming, Spring 2026).

The authors have published a book chapter as part of the 9th Asian International Economic Law Network (AIELN) Conference in June 2025 at Senshu University in Tokyo, Japan:

James M. Cooper & Kashyap Kompella, *A Race to the Bottom?: A Comparative View Artificial of Intelligence Regulation*, in Geopolitical Risks and Geoeconomics in International Economy Law, (Junji Nakagfawa, ed.) (Springer, forthcoming, 2026).

This *Short and Happy Guide* has also been informed by James M. Cooper's law review article:

James M. Cooper, *Are 'Friends' Electric? A Comparativist Approach to Guidelines for the Development and Implementation of Artificial Intelligence in the People's Republic of China and the United States of America*, 42 BOST. U. INT'L L. J. 119 (2024).

Finally, this *Short and Happy Guide* has also been informed by Kashyap Kompella's consulting practice, his public service, and his teaching including at the Institute of Directors, New Delhi and at the BITS School of Management (BITSoM), Mumbai.

References

Chapter 1: AI Governance and Regulation in 30 Minutes or It's Free

Ian Duncan, David J. Lynch, & Dana Munro, *Port strike freezes shipping on East Coast, dealing blow to economy*, WASH. POST (Oct. 1, 2024), https://www.washingtonpost.com/business/2024/10/01/port-strike-shutdown-east-coast-dockworkers-union/.

Heidi L. Frostestad, *AI Regulation in the ChatGPT Era: Cross-border Cooperation and Hope in a Sudden Storm*, 32 INDIANA J. OF GLOBAL L. STUD. 1 (2024).

Rebecca Falconer, *Newsom vetoes controversial AI bill*, AXIOS (Sept. 30, 2024), https://www.axios.com/2024/09/30/california-ai-safety-bill-governor-newsom-veto.

Eduardo Porter, *Dockworkers are trying to stop automation. They will fail*, WASH. POST (Oct. 15, 2024), https://www.washingtonpost.com/opinions/2024/10/15/dockworkers-automation-unions-jobs.

David J. Lynch & Julie Zauzmer Weil, *Dockworkers union asserts 'absolute, airtight' anti-automation stance*, WASH. POST (Oct. 5, 2024), https://www.washingtonpost.com/business/2024/10/05/port-strike-workers-jobs-automation-union/.

Will Henshall, *Elon Musk Tells Rishi Sunak AI Will Eliminate the Need for Jobs*, TIME (Nov. 2, 2023), https://time.com/6331056/rishi-sunak-elon-musk-ai/.

Jackie Davalos & Leon Yin, *AI Detectors Falsely Accuse Students of Cheating—With Big Consequences*, BLOOMBERG (Oct. 18, 2024), https://www.bloomberg.com/news/features/2024-10-18/do-ai-detectors-work-students-face-false-cheating-accusations?srnd=homepage-americas.

The U.N. Guiding Principles on Business and Human Rights (Ruggie Principles) (2011), https://www.ohchr.org/sites/default/files/documents/publications/guidingprinciplesbusinesshr_en.pdf.

FTC v. Rite Aid Corporation, FTC Matter/File Number 2023190, Docket Number 2:23-cv-5023, Eastern District of Pennsylvania, (Mar. 8, 2024), https://www.ftc.gov/legal-library/browse/cases-proceedings/2023190-rite-aid-corporation-ftc-v.

Christian Edwards & Katie Hunt, 'Godfather of AI' shares Nobel Prize in physics for work on machine learning, CNN (Oct. 8, 2024), https://www.cnn.com/2024/10/08/science/nobel-prize-physics-hopfield-hinton-machine-learning-intl/index.html.

Jennifer Corn, *AI pioneer quits Google to warn about the technology's 'dangers,'* CNN (May 3, 2023), https://edition.cnn.com/2023/05/01/tech/geoffrey-hinton-leaves-google-ai-fears.

Karen Hao, *Artificial Intelligence: We read the paper that forced Timnit Gebru out of Google. Here's what it says*, MIT TECH REV. (Dec. 4, 2020), https://www.technologyreview.com/2020/12/04/1013294/google-ai-ethics-research-paper-forced-out-timnit-gebru/.

Karen Hao, *Artificial Intelligence: Training a single AI model can emit as much carbon as five cars in their lifetimes*, MIT TECH REV.

(June 6, 2019) https://www.technologyreview.com/2019/06/06/239031/training-a-single-ai-model-can-emit-as-much-carbon-as-five-cars-in-their-lifetimes/.

No quick tech fixes for AI bias against women job applicants, Essex Un. News (Apr. 3, 2024), https://www.essex.ac.uk/news/2024/04/03/no-quick-tech-fix-for-ai-bias-against-women-job-applicants.

Chapter 2: AI Regulation: Concepts and Debates

Thorin Klosowski, *The State of Consumer Data Privacy Laws in the US (And Why It Matters)*, N.Y. TIMES (Sept. 6, 2021), https://www.nytimes.com/wirecutter/blog/state-of-privacy-laws-in-us/.

Craig Stedman, *Definition What is data governance and why does it matter?*, TECHTARGET (2024), https://www.techtarget.com/searchdatamanagement/definition/data-governance.

5 Data Governance Examples: Case Studies from Airbnb, Uber, and More, ATLAN (May 25, 2023), https://atlan.com/data-governance-examples/.

AI, Data Governance and Privacy, ORG. FOR ECON. COOPERAT'N & DEV'T., No. 22 (June 2024), https://www.oecd.org/content/dam/oecd/en/publications/reports/2024/06/ai-data-governance-and-privacy_2ac13a42/2476b1a4-en.pdf.

EU AI Act, European Union (Updated 2024), https://eur-lex.europa.eu/legal-content/EN/TXT/?uri=CELEX:32024R1689.

California Consumer Privacy Act, CAL. LEG. INFO. (2018), https://leginfo.legislature.ca.gov/faces/codes_displayText.xhtml?division=3.&part=4.&lawCode=CIV&title=1.81.5.

Can I Use Someone Else's Work? Can Someone Else Use Mine?, U.S. COPYRIGHT OFF. (2024), https://www.copyright.gov/help/faq/faq-fairuse.html.

Andrew M. Parks, *Unfair Collection: Reclaiming Control of Publicly Available Personal Information from Data Scrapers*, MICH. L. REV. (Mar. 2022), https://michiganlawreview.org/journal/unfair-collection-reclaiming-control-of-publicly-available-personal-information-from-data-scrapers/.

Erez Hasson, *Is Web Scraping Illegal? Depends on Who You Ask*, IMPERVA (Dec. 7, 2023), https://www.imperva.com/blog/is-web-scraping-illegal/.

Compulsory License Regime: The United States, PURDUE UNIV., (Nov. 22, 2017), https://blogs.lib.purdue.edu/patents/2017/11/22/compulsory-license-regime-the-united-states/.

Rhiannon Williams & James O'Donnell, *We finally have a definition for open-source AI*, MIT TECH. REV. (Aug. 22, 2024), https://www.technologyreview.com/2024/08/22/1097224/we-finally-have-a-definition-for-open-source-ai/.

Why open-source is crucial for responsible AI development, WORLD ECON. FORUM (Dec. 22, 2023), https://www.weforum.org/stories/2023/12/ai-regulation-open-source/.

Francisco Eiras et al., *Risks and Opportunities of Open-Source Generative AI*, CORNELL UNV., (May 29, 2024), https://arxiv.org/pdf/2405.08597.

Charles Owen-Jackson, *Open source, open risks: The growing dangers of unregulated generative AI*, IBM (June 7, 2024), https://www.ibm.com/think/insights/unregulated-generative-ai-dangers-open-source.

Industrial policy, ORG. FOR ECON. COOPERAT'N & DEV'T., (2024), https://www.oecd.org/en/topics/policy-issues/industrial-policy.html.

Anna Ilyina et al., *Industrial Policy is Back But the Bar to Get it Right Is High*, IMF (Apr. 12, 2024), https://www.imf.org/en/Blogs/Articles/2024/04/12/industrial-policy-is-back-but-the-bar-to-get-it-right-is-high.

Naveen Siddiqui & Andrew Lautz, *Industrial Policy: Path to U.S. Competitiveness or Pitfall?*, BIPARTISAN POLICY CTR. (Oct. 3, 2023), https://bipartisanpolicy.org/blog/industrial-policy-path-to-u-s-competitiveness-or-pitfall/.

CHIPS Act (2022), 15 U.S.C. § 4651 et seq.

National Artificial Intelligence Research And Development Strategic Plan 2023 Update, NITRD (May 23, 2023), https://www.nitrd.gov/

national-artificial-intelligence-research-and-development-strategic-plan-2023-update/.

Artificial Intelligence for the American People, THE WHITE HOUSE (2024), https://trumpwhitehouse.archives.gov/ai/.

David Shepardson, *Trump revokes Biden executive order on addressing AI risks*, USA TODAY (Jan. 20, 2025), https://www.usatoday.com/story/money/2025/01/20/trump-revokes-biden-executive-order-ai-risks/77842476007/.

The Communications Act of 1934, enacted as part of the Communications Decency Act of 1996, 47 U.S.C. § 230, P.L. 118-137.

Adam Candeub & Euegene Volokh, *Interpreting 47 U.S.C. § 230c(2)*, 1 J. FREE SPEECH L. 175 (2022), https://heinonline.org/HOL/LandingPage?handle=hein.journals/jfspl1&div=9&id=&page=.

What is generative AI?, IBM, https://research.ibm.com/blog/what-is-generative-AI (last visited Feb. 5, 2025).

AI is poised to drive 160% increase in data center power demand, GOLDMAN SACHS (May 14, 2024), https://www.goldmansachs.com/insights/articles/AI-poised-to-drive-160-increase-in-power-demand.

Katie Tarasov, *Generative AI requires massive amounts of power and water, and the aging U.S. grid can't handle the load*, CNBC (July 28, 2024), https://www.cnbc.com/2024/07/28/how-the-massive-power-draw-of-generative-ai-is-overtaxing-our-grid.html.

What is LLM (Large Language Model)?, AWS (2024), https://aws.amazon.com/what-is/large-language-model/.

Harshal Dharpure, *Generative vs. Rule-Based Chatbots*, MEDIUM (Apr. 16, 2024), https://medium.com/@harshaldharpure/generative-vs-rule-based-chatbots-694e8c28ec87.

Conversational AI on Gen App Builder unlocks generative AI-powered chatbots and virtual agents, GOOGLE CLOUD (July 18, 2023), https://cloud.google.com/blog/products/ai-machine-learning/generative-ai-powered-chatbots-and-virtual-agents.

EMA & HTA Guidance on Use of Large Language Models, NSF (Sept. 26, 2024), https://www.nsf.org/life-science-news/ema-hta-guidance-on-use-of-large-language-models.

Guru Sethupathy, *An Executive's Guide to the Risks of Large Language Models (LLMs)*, FAIRNOW (May 14, 2025), https://fairnow.ai/executives-guide-risks-of-llms/.

Understanding the US 'AI Bill of Rights'—and how it can help keep AI Accountably, WORLD ECON. FORUM, (Oct. 14, 2022), https://www.weforum.org/stories/2022/10/understanding-the-ai-bill-of-rights-protection/.

Kashyap Kompella, *How CIOs can reduce AI's environmental impact*, TECH TARGET (Feb. 7, 2025): https://www.techtarget.com/sustainability/feature/How-CIOs-can-reduce-AIs-negative-environmental-impact.

What is business intelligence?, IBM (2025), https://www.ibm.com/think/topics/business-intelligence?utm_content=SRCWW&p1=Search&p4=43700068092239030&p5=p&p9=58700007560265568&gad_source=1&gclid=CjwKCAiAw5W-BhAhEiwApv4golwJec5HzxN1dxAb2QlgNleuDSFvnbSEFc9hw_P6GGXSTvBdxLu5fBoCxqwQAvD_BwE&gclsrc=aw.ds.

Minna Lo Naranjo, Leonidas Theodosiou, & John Ceccio, *Generative AI and Antitrust Enforcement: Understanding the GenAI 'Stack'*, MORGAN LEWIS (Jun. 12, 2024), https://www.morganlewis.com/pubs/2024/06/generative-ai-and-antitrust-enforcement-understanding-the-genai-stack.

Antitrust, CORNELL LEGAL INFO. INST. (2025), https://www.law.cornell.edu/wex/antitrust.

Lina M. Khan, *Amazon's Antitrust Paradox*, 126 YALE L. REV. 710 (2017), https://www.yalelawjournal.org/pdf/e.710.Khan.805_zuvfyyeh.pdf.

Algorithms and Collusion: Competition policy in the digital age, ORG. FOR ECON. COOPERAT'N & DEV'T. (2017), https://www.oecd.org/content/dam/oecd/en/publications/reports/2017/05/algorithms-and-collusion-competition-policy-in-the-digital-age_02371a73/258dcb14-en.pdf.

Artificial Intelligence and Antitrust: When Do Algorithms Violate Competition Laws?, QUINN EMANUEL TRIAL LAWYERS (2025), https://www.quinnemanuel.com/media/vdwbb1ag/client-alert-artificial-intelligence-and-antitrust-when-do-algorithms-violate-competition-laws.pdf.

Andrew Lacy et. all, *Antitrust and Competition Technology Year in Review 2024*, GOODWIN (Mar. 7, 2025), https://www.goodwinlaw.com/en/insights/publications/2025/03/insights-technology-antitrust-and-competition-2024-year-in-review.

Anticompetitive Practices, F.T.C. (2025), https://www.ftc.gov/enforcement/anticompetitive-practices.

Paul Kirvan, *Data Sovereignty*, TECHTARGET (2025), https://www.techtarget.com/whatis/definition/data-sovereignty.

Carlos Saura García, *Digital expansionism and big tech companies: consequences in democracies of the European Union*, HUMANIT. SOC. SCI. COMMUN. 11, 448 (Mar. 22, 2024), https://www.nature.com/articles/s41599-024-02924-7.

Toussaint Nothias, *An intellectual history of digital colonialism*, JOUR. OF COMM. (Mar. 13, 2025), https://academic.oup.com/joc/advance-article/doi/10.1093/joc/jqaf003/8078024?searchresult=1.

Catriona Gray, *More than Extraction: Rethinking Data's Colonial Political Economy*, 17:2 INT'L POL. SOC. 4 (Jun. 2023), https://academic.oup.com/ips/article/17/2/olad007/7094587.

Sean Fleming, *What is digital sovereignty and how are countries approaching it?*, WORLD ECON. FORUM (Jan. 10, 2025), https://www.weforum.org/stories/2025/01/europe-digital-sovereignty/.

The Digital Personal Protection Act, INDIA MINISTRY OF LAW AND JUSTICE, No. 22 (2023), https://www.meity.gov.in/static/uploads/2024/06/2bf1f0e9f04e6fb4f8fef35e82c42aa5.pdf.

Brazilian General Data Protection Law (LGPD, English translation) iAPP (Oct. 2022), https://iapp.org/resources/article/brazilian-data-protection-law-lgpd-english-translation/.

Definition of National Security, CORNELL UNIV. LEGAL INFO. INST. 10 U.S.C. § 801(16) (2025), https://www.law.cornell.edu/definitions/

uscode.php?width=840&height=800&iframe=true&def_id=10-USC-1888418286-325139519&term_occur=999&term_src=.

Justice Manual: Title 9: Criminal 9-90.000—National Security, U.S. DEPT. OF JUST. (2025), https://www.justice.gov/jm/jm-9-90000-national-security.

Marios Tokas, *The concept of the level playing field in International Economic Law*, 27:3 J. OF INT'L ECON. L., 558 (Sept. 2024), https://academic.oup.com/jiel/article/27/3/558/7749854.

Cybersecurity, U.S. DEPT. OF HOMELAND SEC. (2025), https://www.dhs.gov/topics/cybersecurity.

Erol Yayboke et. all, *The Real National Security Concerns over Data Localization*, CTR. FOR STRAT. & INT'L ST. (Jul. 23, 2021), https://www.csis.org/analysis/real-national-security-concerns-over-data-localization.

China's digital data sovereignty laws and regulations, INCOUNTRY STAFF (Aug. 20, 2024), https://incountry.com/blog/chinas-digital-data-sovereignty-laws-and-regulations/.

Michelle Kurilla, *What Is the CHIPS Act?*, COUNCIL ON FOR. RELAT'NS (Apr. 29, 204), https://www.cfr.org/in-brief/what-chips-act.

Statement on the Purpose of a Corporation, Business Roundtable, Aug. 2019, https://opportunity.businessroundtable.org/our commitment/.

OECD Guidelines on Multinational Enterprises, ORG. FOR ECON. COOPERAT'N & DEV'T., (June 8, 2023, https://www.oecd.org/en/publications/2023/06/oecd-guidelines-for-multinational-enterprises-on-responsible-business-conduct_a0b49990.html.

Chapter 3: AI Ethics

Artificial Intelligence Ethics/Responsible Artificial Movement

Future of Life Institute, *Pause Giant AI Experiments: An Open Letter*, (Mar. 22, 2023), https://futureoflife.org/open-letter/pause-giant-ai-experiments/.

Jan Hatzius et al., *The Potentially Large Effects of Artificial Intelligence on Economic Growth (Briggs/Kodnani)*, GOLDMAN SACHS: ECONOMICS RESEARCH (Mar. 26, 2023, at 9:05 PM EDT), https://www.gspublishing.com/content/research/en/reports/2023/03/27/d64e052b-0f6e-45d7-967b-d7be35fabd16.pdf.

Definitions of Ethics

Ethics, CORNELL L. SCHOOL: LEGAL INFO. INST., https://www.law.cornell.edu/wex/ethics (last visited Dec. 22, 2024).

American Association for the Advancement of Science (AAAS), *Artificial Intelligence and the Courts: Materials for Judges*, at 9 (Sept. 2022), https://www.aaas.org/ai2/projects/law/judicialpapers?adobe_mc=MCMID%3D28184402771370035972070700203311801975%7CMCORGID%3D242B6472541199F70A4C98A6%2540AdobeOrg%7CTS%3D1664555375.

Artificial Intelligence Ethics

United Nations Educational, Scientific and Cultural Organization (UNESCO), *Recommendation on the Ethics of Artificial Intelligence*, UNESDOC DIGITAL LIBRARY (adopted on Nov. 23, 2021), https://www.unesco.org/en/artificial-intelligence/recommendation-ethics.

Transparency

George Lawton, *AI Transparency: What Is It and Why Do We Need It?*, TECHTARGET (Sept. 10, 2024), https://www.techtarget.com/searchcio/tip/AI-transparency-What-is-it-and-why-do-we-need-it.

Fairness

Genevieve Smith, *What does "Fairness" Mean for Machine Learning Systems?*, BERKELEY HAAS: CTR. FOR EQUITY, GENDER & LEADERSHIP (2020), https://haas.berkeley.edu/wp-content/uploads/What-is-fairness_-EGAL2.pdf.

Guidelines vs Regulations

François Candelon, et al., *AI Regulation Is Coming*, HARV. BUS. PUBL'G: AI AND MACHINE LEARNING, (Sept.—Oct. 2021), https://hbr.org/2021/09/ai-regulation-is-coming.

Regulatory Capture

Andrea Saltelli, et al., *Science, the Endless Frontier of Regulatory Capture*, 135 FUTURES, (Jan. 2022), https://www.sciencedirect.com/science/article/pii/S0016328721001695.

Reliability

Asset Reliability, C3 AI GLOSSARY, https://c3.ai/glossary/artificial-intelligence/reliability/ (last visited Dec. 22, 2024).

Clare Duffy, *Three More Execs Out at OpenAI, Including Technology Chief Mira Murati*, CNN BUS. (Sept. 25, 2024), https://www.cnn.com/2024/09/25/tech/openai-technology-chief-mira-murati-leaving/index.html.

Joe Salas, *OpenAI, Meta, and Anthropic Partner with US Military and Its Allies*, NEW ATLAS (Dec. 11, 2024), https://newatlas.com/military/openai-meta-anthropic-partner-with-us-military-allies/.

IBM

IBM, *IBM's Principles for Trust and Transparency*, (May 30, 2018), https://www.ibm.com/policy/wp-content/uploads/2018/06/IBM_Principles_SHORT.V4.3.pdf.

Francesca Rossi, *How IBM Is Working Toward a Fairer AI*, HARV. BUS. REV. (Nov. 5, 2020), https://hbr.org/2020/11/how-ibm-is-working-toward-a-fairer-ai.

Philip Pullella & Jeffrey Dastin, *Vatican Joins IBM, Microsoft to Call for Facial Recognition Regulation*, REUTERS (Feb. 28, 2020), https://www.reuters.com/article/us-vatican-artificial-intelligence/pope-to-endorse-principles-on-ai-ethics-with-microsoft-ibm-idUSKCN20M0Z1/.

Microsoft

Brad Smith, *Meeting the AI Moment: Advancing the Future through Responsible AI*, MICROSOFT (Feb. 2, 2023), https://blogs.microsoft.com/on-the-issues/2023/02/02/responsible-ai-chatgpt-artificial-intelligence.

Microsoft, *Microsoft Responsible AI Standard, v2*, MICROSOFT CORP. (June 2022), https://cdn-dynmedia-1.microsoft.com/is/content/microsoftcorp/microsoft/final/en-us/microsoft-brand/documents/Microsoft-Responsible-AI-Standard-General-Requirements.pdf?culture=en-us&country=us.

Google, *AI Principles Progress Update 2023*, GOOGLE AI, https://ai.google/static/documents/ai-principles-2023-progress-update.pdf (last accessed Dec. 30, 2024).

OpenAI

OpenAI Charter, OpenAI (2025), https://openai.com/charter/.

Safety, OpenAI (2025), https://openai.com/safety/.

OpenAI's safety committee to oversee security practices as an independent body, REUTERS (Sept. 16, 2024), https://www.reuters.com/technology/artificial-intelligence/openais-safety-committee-oversee-security-practices-an-independent-body-2024-09-16/.

Tom Chavez, *OpenAI & The New York Times: A Wake-Up Call For Ethical Data Practices*, FORBES (Jan. 31, 2024), https://www.forbes.com/sites/tomchavez/2024/01/31/openai--the-new-york-times-a-wake-up-call-for-ethical-data-practices/.

James Dargan, *Sam Altman Discusses AI Ethics, Governance & the Future of OpenAI*, AI INSIDER (Nov. 25, 2024), https://theaiinsider.tech/2024/11/25/sam-altman-discusses-ai-ethics-governance-the-future-of-openai/.

Meta

Connect 2024: The responsible approach we're taking to generative AI, META (Sept. 25, 2024), https://ai.meta.com/blog/responsible-ai-connect-2024/.

Rebecca Picciotto, *Facebook-parent Meta breaks up its Responsible AI team*, CNBC (Nov. 18, 2023), https://www.cnbc.com/2023/11/18/facebook-parent-meta-breaks-up-its-responsible-ai-team.html.

James Barney, *Are Meta's AI Profiles Unethical?*, TOWARDSDATASCIENCE (Jan. 9, 2025), https://towardsdatascience.com/are-metas-ai-profiles-unethical-a157ec05a58f/.

Anthropic

Will Henshall & Billy Perrigo, *Time 100 AI: Dario and Daniela Amodei CEO & President, Anthropic*, TIME (Sept. 7, 2023), https://time.com/collection/time100-ai/6309047/daniela-and-dario-amodei/.

Claude's Constitution, CLAUDE (May 9, 2023), https://www.anthropic.com/news/claudes-constitution.

Anthropic: *Your partner in safer, more responsible AI*, ANTHROPIC (2025), https://assets.anthropic.com/m/3845cfe7bf8f2e47/original/Anthropic-Safety-and-Security-info-sheet.pdf?utm_source=chatgpt.com.

Sigal Samuel, *It's practically impossible to run a big AI company ethically*, VOX (Aug. 5, 2024), https://www.vox.com/future-perfect/364384/its-practically-impossible-to-run-a-big-ai-company-ethically?utm_source=chatgpt.com.

DeepMind

Ben Wodecki, *DeepMind Sparrow: The AI Agent that Won't Give Inappropriate Answers*, AI BUS. (Sept. 30, 2022), https://aibusiness.com/nlp/deepmind-sparrow-the-ai-agent-that-won-t-give-inappropriate-answers.

Amelia Glaese et al., *Improving alignment of dialogue agents via targeted human judgements*, DEEPMIND (Sept. 20, 2022), https://arxiv.org/pdf/2209.14375.

Perplexity

AI and Ethics: The Perplexity Plagiarism Controversy, VIINYX AI (Jul. 5, 2024), https://www.viinyx.com/blog/ai-ethics-perplexity-ai-controversy.

Diana Wolf T., *Perplexity AI Under Fire for Unethical Practices*, LINKEDIN (Jun. 20, 2024), https://www.linkedin.com/pulse/perplexity-ai-under-fire-unethical-practices-diana-wolf-torres-fsfjc/.

Wes Davis, *The New York Times warns AI search engine Perplexity to stop using its content*, THE VERGE (Oct. 15, 2024), https://www.theverge.com/2024/10/15/24270774/new-york-times-cease-and-desist-letter-perplexity-ai-search-engine?utm_source=chatgpt.com.

Apple

Blanca Begert, *Apple signs on to Biden's responsible AI guidelines*, POLITICO (Jul. 26, 2024), https://www.politico.com/news/2024/07/26/apple-biden-ai-00171502?utm_source=chatgpt.com.

Apple Intelligence and privacy on iPhone, APPLE (2025), https://support.apple.com/guide/iphone/apple-intelligence-and-privacy-iphe3f499e0e/ios?utm_source=chatgpt.com.

Walmart

Nuala O'Connor, Our Responsible AI Pledge: Setting the Bar for Ethical AI, WALMART (Oct. 17, 2023), https://corporate.walmart.com/news/2023/10/17/our-responsible-ai-pledge-setting-the-bar-for-ethical-ai.

AI Governance Podcast—Responsible AI at Walmart, EnzAI (Jan. 5, 2025), https://www.enz.ai/post/ai-governance-podcast---responsible-ai-at-walmart.

Adobe

Responsible AI at Adobe, ADOBE (2025), https://www.adobe.com/trust/responsible-ai.html.

Grace Yee, *Reflecting on our five-year journey with our AI Ethics principles*, ADOBE BLOG (Oct. 14, 2024), https://blog.adobe.com/en/publish/2024/10/14/reflecting-our-five-year-journey-with-our-ai-ethics-principles.

Our Commitment to AI Ethics, ADOBE (Oct. 2024), https://www.adobe.com/content/dam/cc/en/ai-ethics/pdfs/Adobe-AI-Ethics-Principles.pdf.

NVIDIA

Nikki Pope, *What is Trustworthy AI?* NVIDIA (Mar. 1, 2024), https://blogs.nvidia.com/blog/what-is-trustworthy-ai/?utm_source=chatgpt.com.

Midjourney

Mackenzie Ferguson, Midjourney Unveils AI Image Editor: Web-Based Creativity Revolution or Ethical Dilemma?, OPENTOOLS (Oct. 21, 2024), https://opentools.ai/news/midjourney-unveils-ai-image-editor-web-based-creativity-revolution-or-ethical-dilemma.

Chapter 4: International Bodies and Agencies

White & Case, *AI Watch: Global Regulatory Tracker*, https://www.whitecase.com/insight-our-thinking/ai-watch-global-regulatory-tracker (last visited Aug. 21, 2025).

Alem Tadeneke, WORLD ECON. FORUM, (June 15, 2023), https://www.weforum.org/press/2023/06/world-economic-forum-launches-ai-governance-alliance-focused-on-responsible-generative-ai/#:~:text=URL%3A%20https%3A®®www.weforum.org®press®2023®06®world.

AI Governance Alliance: Briefing Paper Series, WORLD ECON. FORUM, (Jan. 18, 2024), https://www.weforum.org/publications/ai-governance-alliance-briefing-paper-series/.

A Blueprint for Equity and Inclusion in Artificial Intelligence, WORLD ECON. FORUM, (June 29, 2022), https://www.weforum.org/publications/a-blueprint-for-equity-and-inclusion-in-artificial-intelligence/.

GPAI Global Partnership, OECD, https://oecd.ai/en/about/about-gpai (last visited on Aug. 28, 2025).

IEEE Ethically Aligned Design: https://standards.ieee.org/wp-content/uploads/import/documents/other/ead_v2.pdf (last visited Aug. 28, 2025).

Hiroshima AI Process

Group of Seven, *The Hiroshima AI Process: Leading the Global Challenge to Shape Inclusive Governance for Generative AI*, GOV'T OF JAPAN, (Feb. 9, 2024) https://www.japan.go.jp/kizuna/2024/02/hiroshima_ai_process.html.

AI Observatory, ORG. FOR ECON. COOPERAT'N & DEV'T., https://oecd.ai.

United Nations

Global Cooperation: Davos 2025: Special Address by António Guterres, Secretary-General, United Nations, WORLD ECON. FORUM (Jan. 22, 2025), https://www.weforum.org/stories/2025/01/davos-2025-special-address-by-antonio-guterres-secretary-general-united-nations/.

Other International Treaties

The Council of Europe Framework Convention on AI and Human Rights, Democracy, and the Rule of Law, CETS No. 225, Vilnius Sept. 5, 2024, https://www.coe.int/en/web/conventions/full-list?module=treaty-.

Florence G'Sell, *Regulating Under Uncertainty: Governance Options for Generative AI,* STANFORD CYBER POLICY CTR. (2024) https://fsi9-prod.s3.us-west-1.amazonaws.com/s3fs-public/2024-09/GenAI_Report_Florence-GSELL.pdf (last visited Oct. 21, 2024).

AI Safety Institutes

The Global Landscape of AI Safety Institutes https://alltechishuman.org/all-tech-is-human-blog/the-global-landscape-of-ai-safety-institutes (last visited Aug. 28, 2025).

AI Safety Is Becoming AI Security: https://www.centeraipolicy.org/work/ai-safety-is-becoming-ai-security (last visited Aug. 28, 2025).

Tackling AI security risks to unleash growth and deliver Plan for Change, https://www.gov.uk/government/news/tackling-ai-security-risks-to-unleash-growth-and-deliver-plan-for-change (last visited Aug. 28, 2025).

U.S. Artificial Intelligence Safety Institute, https://www.nist.gov/aisi (last visited Aug. 28, 2025).

Chapter 5: AI Regulation in the United States

Introduction (Smith and Altman Quotations)

Will Oremus & Andrea Jiménez, *House GOP eyes moratorium on state AI laws*, WASH. POST (May 13, 2025), https://www.washington

post.com/politics/2025/05/13/house-reconciliation-bill-state-ai-preempt/.

Stock market flash crash: https://www.nytimes.com/2023/05/23/business/ai-picture-stock-market.html.

AI Bill of Rights, WHITE HOUSE, (Oct. 2022), https://bidenwhitehouse.archives.gov/ostp/ai-bill-of-rights/.

For FTC investigations of 5 AI companies announced in January 2024, see *FTC Launches Inquiry into Generative AI Investments and Partnerships*, FTC (Jan. 25, 2024), https://www.ftc.gov/news-events/news/press-releases/2024/01/ftc-launches-inquiry-generative-ai-investments-partnerships.

Governor Gavin Newsom, Governor Newsom Signs Executive Order to Prepare California for the Progress of Artificial Intelligence (Sept. 6, 2023), https://www.gov.ca.gov/2023/09/06/governor-newsom-signs-executive-order-to-prepare-california-for-the-progress-of-artificial-intelligence/.

A New Landmark for Consumer Control Over Their Personal Information: CPPA Proposes Regulatory Framework for Automated Decisionmaking Technology, see https://cppa.ca.gov/announcements/2023/20231127.html.

Office of Mmgt. & Budget, *Memorandum for Heads of Executive Departments and Agencies*, THE WHITE HOUSE, M-24-10 (Mar. 28, 2024), https://www.whitehouse.gov/wp-content/uploads/2024/03/M-24-10-Advancing-Governance-Innovation-and-Risk-Management-for-Agency-Use-of-Artificial-Intelligence.pdf.

Cameron F. Kerry, *How privacy legislation can help address AI*, BROOKINGS (July 7, 2023), https://www.brookings.edu/articles/how-privacy-legislation-can-help-address-ai/.

Office of Management and Budget Issues New Requirements for Federal Agencies' Use of AI, PERKINS COIE https://www.perkinscoie.com/en/news-insights/office-of-management-and-budget-issues-new-requirements-for-federal-agencies-use-of-ai.html.

New York Privacy Act (Jan. 2023) https://nyassembly.gov/leg/?default_fld=&leg_video=&bn=S00365&term=2023&Summary=Y&Actions=Y&Text=Y.

For a survey of AI initiatives by the U.S. federal government, *see generally* United States Library of Congress, https://www.loc.gov/law/help/artificial-intelligence/americas.php#us.

John S. McCain National Defense Authorization Act for Fiscal Year 2019, Pub. L. 115-232, § 238, 132 Stat. 1658 (2018), https://www.congress.gov/115/bills/hr5515/BILLS-115hr5515enr.pdf.

The Office of Science and Technology Policy, Blueprint for an AI Bill of Rights: Making Automated Systems Work for the American People, THE WHITE HOUSE (Oct. 2022), https://bidenwhitehouse.archives.gov/ostp/ai-bill-of-rights/.

Executive Order: Removing Barriers to American Leadership in Artificial Intelligence, THE WHITE HOUSE (Jan. 23, 2025), https://www.whitehouse.gov/presidential-actions/2025/01/removing-barriers-to-american-leadership-in-artificial-intelligence/.

Initial Rescissions of Harmful Executive Orders and Acts, WHITE HOUSE (Jan. 20, 2025), https://www.whitehouse.gov/presidential-actions/2025/01/initial-rescissions-of-harmful-executive-orders-and-actions/.

Deepa Shivaram, *Trump has tossed a lot of Biden policies. But there's one AI measure he wants to keep*, NAT'L PUB. RADIO (Jan. 24, 2025), https://www.npr.org/2025/01/24/nx-s1-5269981/trump-biden-ai-executive-orders.

Trump Appoints Former PayPal Exec David Sacks as AI and Crypto Czar, REUTERS (Dec. 6, 2024 at 11:38 AM PST), https://www.reuters.com/world/us/trump-appoints-former-paypal-coo-david-sacks-ai-crypto-czar-2024-12-06/.

Fact Sheet: President Donald J. Trump Takes Action to Enhance America's AI Leadership, THE WHITE HOUSE (Jan. 23, 2025), https://www.whitehouse.gov/fact-sheets/2025/01/fact-sheet-president-donald-j-trump-takes-action-to-enhance-americas-ai-leadership/.

Chris Stokel-Walker, *Trump's Pick of David Sacks as AI and Crypto Czar Shows How Cozy his White House Will be With Silicon Valley*, FASTCOMPANY (Dec. 12, 2024), https://www.fastcompany.com/91246166/david-sacks-trump-ai-crypto-czar-explained.

Safia Kazi, *The Tangled Web of Executive Orders on AI*, ISACA (Feb. 4, 2025), https://www.isaca.org/resources/news-and-trends/industry-news/2025/the-tangled-web-of-executive-orders-on-ai.

Section 43201, *"Artificial Intelligence and information technology modernization initiative*, HOUSE.GOV (May 11, 2025), https://docs.house.gov/meetings/IF/IF00/20250513/118261/HMKP-119-IF00-20250513-SD003.pdf?utm_source=substack&utm_medium=email.

John Villasenor & Joshua Turner, *AI Policy Directors in the New Trump Administration*, BROOKINGS (Nov. 14, 2024), https://www.brookings.edu/articles/ai-policy-directions-in-the-new-trump-administration/.

Shatakratu Sahu & Amlan Mohanty, *What's Next for U.S. AI Policy*, CARNEGIE (Dec. 18, 2024), https://carnegieendowment.org/posts/2024/12/whats-next-for-us-ai-policy?lang=en.

Christiano Lima-Strong, *House Unveils AI 'Road Map' but Punts on Setting Priorities*, WASH. POST (Dec. 18, 2024), https://www.washingtonpost.com/politics/2024/12/18/house-unveils-ai-road-map-punts-setting-priorities/.

WHITE HOUSE, Winning the Race: America's AI Action Plan (July 2025), https://www.whitehouse.gov/wp-content/uploads/2025/07/Americas-AI-Action-Plan.pdf.

Bipartisan House Task Force Report on Artificial Intelligence, 118th Congress Task Force on Artificial Intelligence (Dec. 2024), https://www.speaker.gov/wp-content/uploads/2024/12/AI-Task-Force-Report-FINAL.pdf.

Chris Lehane, LINKEDIN, Jan. 30, 2025, https://www.linkedin.com/posts/chris-lehane-2562535_strengthening-americas-ai-leadership-with-activity-7290781762190815232-K8aF.

Adam Cancryn, *Biden Warns of Rising Democracy-Threatening 'Oligarcy' in Grim Farewell Speech*, POLITICO (Jan. 15, 2025 at 9:51 PM EST) https://www.politico.com/news/2025/01/15/biden-oligarchy-farewell-speech-00198565.

The Executive Order on Strengthening and Promoting Innovation in the Nation's Cybersecurity (Jan. 16, 2025), https://biden whitehouse.archives.gov/briefing-room/presidential-actions/2025/

01/16/executive-order-on-strengthening-and-promoting-innovation-in-the-nations-cybersecurity/.

Executive Order on Advancing United States Leadership in Artificial Intelligence Infrastructure (Jan. 14, 2025), https://bidenwhitehouse.archives.gov/briefing-room/presidential-actions/2025/01/14/executive-order-on-advancing-united-states-leadership-in-artificial-intelligence-infrastructure.

Ricki Lee, *US Tightens Grip on Chips with New Export Rules*, TECHINFORMED (Jan. 14, 2025), https://techinformed.com/us-tightens-grip-on-chips-with-new-export-rules/.

Law on Deepfakes—The Take It Down Act, https://www.whitehouse.gov/articles/2025/05/icymi-president-trump-signs-take-it-down-act-into-law/#:~:text=Rep.%20Roger%20Williams%3A%20S‰¤Today,shared%20without%20their%20consent%20removed.

Joe Mullih, *The TAKE IT DOWN Act: A Flawed Attempt to Protect Victims That Will Lead to Censorship*, ELECTRIC FRONTIER FOUND'N (Feb. 11, 2025), https://www.eff.org/deeplinks/2025/02/take-it-down-act-flawed-attempt-protect-victims-will-lead-censorship.

Chapter 6: AI Regulation in the European Union

The EU AI Act: https://artificialintelligenceact.eu/wp-content/uploads/2024/02/AIA-Trilogue-Coreper.pdf.

Reid Blackman & Ingrid Vasiuli-Feltes, *The EU's AI Act and How Companies Can Achieve Compliance*, HARV. BUS. REV. (Feb. 22, 2024), https://hbr.org/2024/02/the-eus-ai-act-and-how-companies-can-achieve-compliance.

Foo Yun Chee, *Amazon loses court fight against record $812 mln Luxembourg privacy fine*, REUTERS (Mar. 19 2025), https://www.reuters.com/technology/amazon-loses-court-fight-against-record-812-mln-luxembourg-privacy-fine-2025-03-19/.

European Commission, Antitrust: Commission fines Google €4.34 billion for illegal practices regarding Android mobile devices to strengthen dominance of Google's search engine, (July 17, 2018), https://ec.europa.eu/commission/presscorner/detail/en/ip_18_4581.

Safeguards

Artificial Intelligence Act: MEPs adopt landmark law, EUROP. PARL. NEWS (Mar. 13, 2024), https://www.europarl.europa.eu/news/en/press-room/20240308IPR19015/artificial-intelligence-act-meps-adopt-landmark-law#:~:text=Obligations%20for%20high"risk%20systems&text=Such%20systems%20mustässessänd,systems%20that äffect%20their%20rights.

High-level Summary: EU AI Act, High-level summary of the AI Act, (Feb. 27, 2024), https://artificialintelligenceact.eu/high-level-summary/.

Dan Milman & Alex Hern, *What will the EU's proposed act to regulate AI mean for consumers?*, THE GUARDIAN (Mar. 14, 2024), https://www.theguardian.com/technology/2024/mar/14/what-will-eu-proposed-regulation-ai-mean-consumers.

GPAI Systems

The European Union Artificial Intelligence *Act, Latest developments and key takeaways*, EY (July. 12, 2024), https://www.ey.com/content/dam/ey-unified-site/ey-com/en-gl/insights/public-policy/documents/ey-gl-eu-ai-act-07-2024.pdf.

Matt Hervey, *The EU AI Act and IP*, LEXOLOGY, https://www.lexology.com/library/detail.aspx?g=f08f23a7-306d-4afe-bc14-0878aec74b2c.

Axel Spies, Ron N. Dreben, Andrew J Gray IV, Meaghan H. Kent, Vishnu Shankar, & Mike Pierides, *EU AI ACT: How Far will EU Copyright Principles Extend*, MORGAN LEWIS (Feb. 12, 2024), https://www.morganlewis.com/pubs/2024/02/eu-ai-act-how-far-will-eu-copyright-principles-extend.

Technical Documentation

Lisa Peets, Marianna Drake, & Marty Hansen, EU AI Act: Key Takeaways from the Compromise Text, COVINGTON (Feb. 28, 2024), https://www.insideprivacy.com/artificial-intelligence/eu-ai-act-key-takeaways-from-the-compromise-text/.

Criminal Law

Melissa Heikkila, *Five things you need to know about the EU's new AI Act*, MIT TECH. REV. (Dec. 11, 2023), https://www.technologyreview.com/2023/12/11/1084942/five-things-you-need-to-know-about-the-eus-new-ai-act/.

High-Risk AI systems: EU AI Act: first regulation on artificial intelligence, EUROP. PARL. (Aug. 6, 2023), https://www.europarl.europa.eu/topics/en/article/20230601STO93804/eu-ai-act-first-regulation-on-artificial-intelligence.

A guide to high-risk AI systems under the EU AI Act, PINSENT MASONS (Feb. 13, 2024), https://www.pinsentmasons.com/out-law/guides/guide-to-high-risk-ai-systems-under-the-eu-ai-act.

High-level summary of the AI Act, EU Artificial Intelligence Act (Feb. 27, 2024), https://artificialintelligenceact.eu/high-level-summary/.

Official Journal of the European Union, *Regulation of the EU, G.D.P.R.*, (2016), https://eur-lex.europa.eu/legal-content/EN/TXT/PDF/?uri=CELEX:32016R0679.

European Commission for the Efficiency of Justice, *European Ethical Charter on the use of artificial intelligence (AI) in judicial systems and their environment*, (Dec. 3-4, 2018), https://rm.coe.int/ethical-charter-en-for-publication-4-december-2018/16808f699c.

Council of Europe, https://www.coe.int/en/web/cepej/justice-of-the-future-predictive-justice-and-artificial-intelligence.

European Union Agency for Fundamental Rights, Getting the Future Right: Artificial Intelligence and Fundamental Rights, Dec. 14, 2020, https://fra.europa.eu/en/publication/2020/artificial-intelligence-and-fundamental-rights.

Melissa Heikkiläarchive, *The AI Act is done. Here's what will (and won't) change*, MIT TECH. REV. (Mar. 9, 2024), https://www.technologyreview.com/2024/03/19/1089919/the-ai-act-is-done-heres-what-will-and-wont-change/.

Vance rails against "excessive" at Paris AI Summit, PBS NEWS (Feb. 11, 2025), https://www.pbs.org/newshour/politics/vance-rails-against-excessive-regulation-at-paris-ai-summit.

Chapter 7: AI Regulation in the People's Republic of China

China's Crackdown on Big Tech: The Role of Golden Shares, DATENNA, https://www.datenna.com/resources/chinas-crackdown-on-big-tech-the-role-of-golden-shares/ (last visited June 1, 2025).

Yaqiu Wang, *In China, the "Great Firewall" Is Changing a Generation*, POLITICO (Sept. 1, 2020), https://www.politico.com/news/magazine/2020/09/01/china-great-firewall-generation-405385.

Andrew Chatzky & James McBride, *China's Massive Belt and Road Initiative*, COUNCIL ON FOR. REL'NS (updated Feb. 2, 2023), https://www.cfr.org/backgrounder/chinas-massive-belt-and-road-initiative.

Maria Adele Carrai et al., *The Belt and Road Initiative and Global Governance: By Way of Introduction*, in THE BELT AND ROAD INITIATIVE AND GLOBAL GOVERNANCE 1, 2 (Maria Adele Carrai et al. eds., 2020).

"Yidai yilu" xingdong jihua ("一帶一路"行動計劃) [Action Plan on the Belt and Road Initiative], Zhengfu Wangluo (政府网) [GOV.CN] (Mar. 30, 2015), http://english.gov.cn/archive/publications/2015/03/30/content_281475080249035.htm.

Bill Drexel & Hannah Kelly, *Opinion: Behind China's Plans to Build AI for the World*, POLITICO (Nov. 30, 2023), https://www.politico.com/news/magazine/2023/11/30/china-global-ai-plans-00129160.

Cybersecurity Law of the People's Republic of China (promulgated by the Standing Comm. Nat'l People's Cong., Nov. 7, 2016, effective June 1, 2017).

Measures for Security Assessment of Outbound Data Transfers, CYBERSECURITY ADMINISTRATION OF CHINA, (July 7, 2022, effective Sept. 1, 2022), at Art. 5; Art. 6.

Samm Sacks & Manyi Kathy Li, *How Chinese Cybersecurity Standards Impact Doing Business In China*", CTR. FOR STRAT.& INT'L ST., (Aug. 2,

2018), https://www.csis.org/analysis/how-chinese-cybersecurity-standards-impact-doing-business-china.

China's Data Security Law: A new vision for the regulation of the digital economy, HOGAN LOVELLS (June 21, 2021), https://www.engage.hoganlovells.com/knowledgeservices/news/chinas-data-security-law-a-new-vision-for-the-regulation-of-a-digital-economy/ (last visited on Oct. 20, 2024).

Cyberspace Administration of China, Provisions on the Management of Algorithmic Recommendations in Internet Information Services, THE CENTRAL PEOPLE'S GOV'T OF CHINA (Dec. 31, 2021), https://www.chinalawtranslate.com/en/algorithms/.

Cybersecurity Administration of China, Internet Information Service Algorithmic Recommendation Management Provisions (TranRegulations on the Administration of Algorithmic Recommendations for Internet Information Services, CHINA LAW TRANSLATE (Jan. 4, 2022), https://www.chinalawtranslate.com/en/algorithms/.

China Reports First Arrest Over Fake News Generated by ChatGPT, REUTERS (May 10, 2023), https://www.reuters.com/technology/china-reports-first-arrest-over-fake-news-generated-by-chatgpt-2023-05-10/.

Sean Lyngaas, *Chinese Operatives Used AI-Generated Images in Social Media Disinformation Campaign*, Microsoft Says, CNN (Sept. 7, 2023), https://www.cnn.com/2023/09/07/politics/chinese-operatives-ai-images-social-media/index.html.

Translation: *Internet Information Service Algorithmic Recommendation Management Provisions*—Effective Mar. 1, 2022, DIGICHINA STANFORD UNIV. (Feb. 10, 2022), https://digichina.stanford.edu/work/translation-internet-information-service-algorithmic-recommendation-management-provisions-effective-march-1-2022/.

Benjamin Edelman & Jonathan Zittrain, *Internet Filtering in China*, RESEARCHGATE (2002), https://www.researchgate.net/publication/3419563_Internet_filtering_in_China.

Claire Fu & Daisuke Wakabayashi, *There Is No TikTok in China, but There Is Douyin. Here's What It Is*, N.Y. TIMES (Apr. 25, 2024), https://www.nytimes.com/2024/04/25/business/china-tiktok-douyin.html.

China Law Translate, PROVISIONS ON THE ADMINISTRATION OF DEEP SYNTHESIS OF INTERNET INFORMATION SERVICES (Jan. 10, 2023), https://www.chinalawtranslate.com/en/deep-synthesis/.

Klemens Katterbauer & Laurent Cleenewerck, *Artificial Intelligence and Its Impact on Healthcare Financing in China—A Legal Analysis*, 14 FIN. L. REV. (2024), http://www.ejournals.eu/FLR.

Feng-Kuang Chiang et al., *Exploring University Students' Perceptions of Generative AI in Education: Benefits, Risks, and Ethical Concerns*, SCI. REP. (2024), https://www.nature.com/articles/s41599-024-04168-x.

DigiChina, Translation: Internet Information Service Deep Synthesis Management Provisions (Draft for Comment, Jan. 2022), STANFORD UNIV. (2022), https://digichina.stanford.edu/work/translation-internet-information-service-deep-synthesis-management-provisions-draft-for-comment-jan-2022/.

BBC News '中文, 走近柬埔寨詐騙園的「殺豬盤」愛情陷阱', YOUTUBE (2024), https://www.youtube.com/watch?v=D_HrGegGc0E.

China Law Translate, Interim Measures for the Administration of Generative AI Services (July 10, 2023), https://www.chinalawtranslate.com/en/generative-ai-interim/.

Voice of America, *'Talk About Something Else': Chinese AI Chatbot Toes Party Line*, VOA NEWS (Aug. 9, 2023), https://www.voanews.com/a/talk-about-something-else-chinese-ai-chatbot-toes-party-line/7249469.html.

Office of the Central Cyberspace Affairs Commission, '世界互联网大会人工智能专业委员会成立', CHINA CYBERSPACE ADMINISTRATION (Nov. 20 2024), https://www.cac.gov.cn/2024-11/20/c_1733796047052950.htm.

Chinese AI Chatbot DeepSeek Censors Itself in Realtime, Users Report, THE GUARDIAN (Jan. 28, 2025), https://www.theguardian.com/technology/2025/jan/28/chinese-ai-chatbot-deepseek-censors-itself-in-realtime-users-report?utm_source=chatgpt.com.

The Death of Anonymity Online in China, MIT TECH. REV. (Dec. 22, 2023), https://www.technologyreview.com/2023/12/22/1085820/death-of-anonymity-online-china/?utm_source=chatgpt.com.

中国抗争者需要全球互联网·疫情中的审查 (2023年一月，第167期, Simplified Chinese), FREEDOM HOUSE, https://freedomhouse.org/zh-hans/report/zhongguomeitikuaibao/2023-1?utm_source=chatgpt.com#a3.

Emily S. Weinstein et al., *Beyond China's Black Box: AI, Talent & Innovation*, CTR. FOR A NEW AM. SEC. (July 10, 2023), https://www.cnas.org/publications/reports/beyond-chinas-black-box.

The Beijing Artificial Intelligence Principles, WIRED (May 28, 2019), https://www.wired.com/beyond-the-beyond/2019/06/beijing-artificial-intelligence-principles/.

Artificial Intelligence for Children Beijing Principles Released, FOR. POLICY (Sept. 15, 2020), https://foreignpolicynews.org/2020/09/15/artificial-intelligence-for-children-beijing-principles-released/.

Cyberspace Administration of China, Provisions on the Management of Algorithmic Recommendations in Internet Information Services, THE CENTRAL PEOPLE'S GOV'T OF CHINA (Jan. 4, 2022), https://www.cac.gov.cn/2022-01/04/c_1642894606364259.html.

China Reports First Arrest Over Fake News Generated by ChatGPT, REUTERS (May 10, 2023), https://www.reuters.com/technology/china-reports-first-arrest-over-fake-news-generated-by-chatgpt-2023-05-10/.

Cybersecurity Administration of China, Internet Information Service Algorithmic Recommendation Management Provisions (Translation), DIGICHINA (Stanford Univ., Feb. 10, 2022), https://digichina.stanford.edu/work/translation-internet-information-service-algorithmic-recommendation-management-provisions-effective-march-1-2022/.

Benjamin Edelman & Jonathan Zittrain, *Internet Filtering in China*, RESEARCHGATE (2002), https://www.researchgate.net/publication/3419563_Internet_filtering_in_China.

Klemens Katterbauer & Laurent Cleenewerck, *Artificial Intelligence and Its Impact on Healthcare Financing in China—A Legal Analysis*, 14 Fin. L. Rev. (2024), http://www.ejournals.eu/FLR.

Feng-Kuang Chiang et al., *Exploring University Students' Perceptions of Generative AI in Education: Benefits, Risks, and Ethical Concerns*, Sci. Rep. (2024), https://www.nature.com/articles/s41599-024-04168-x.

China's AI Ambitions: The Need for 'Ethics and Guidelines', Time (Aug. 24, 2023), https://time.com/7012765/zhuang-rongwen.

Kyle Chan, *In the Future, China Will Be Dominant. The U.S. Will Be Irrelevant*, N.Y. Times (May 19, 2025) https://www.nytimes.com/2025/05/19/opinion/china-us-trade-tariffs.html.

Dezan Shira & Associates, China's Ethical Review of Science and Technology: Draft Trial Measures, China Briefing (Jan. 30, 2024), https://www.china-briefing.com/news/china-ethical-review-of-science-and-technology-draft-trial-measures.

中国抗争者需要全球互联网，疫情中的审查 (2023年一月, 第167期), Freedom House, https://freedomhouse.org/zh-hans/report/zhongguomeitikuaibao/2023-1?utm_source=chatgpt.com#a3.

Matt Sheehan, *Tracing the Roots of China's AI Regulations*, Carnegie Endowment for International Peace (2024), https://carnegieendowment.org/research/2024/02/tracing-the-roots-of-chinas-ai-regulations?lang=en.

Matt Sheehan, *China's AI Regulations and How They Get Made*, Carnegie Endowment for International Peace (2023), https://carnegieendowment.org/2023/07/10/china-s-ai-regulations-and-how-they-get-made-pub-90117.

Matt Sheehan & Sharon Du, *What China's Algorithm Registry Reveals about AI Governance*, Carnegie Endowment for International Peace, (Dec. 9, 2022), https://carnegieendowment.org/posts/2022/12/what-chinas-algorithm-registry-reveals-about-ai-governance?lang=en.

Chapter 8: AI National Regulation Around the Globe

Australia

Australia's AI Ethics Principles, DEP'T OF INDUSTRY, SCI. & RESOURCES, GOV'T OF AUSTRALIA, https://www.industry.gov.au/publications/australias-artificial-intelligence-ethics-framework/australias-ai-ethics-principles (last visited Aug. 23, 2025).

Is AI regulated in Australia? What lawyers should know, THOMSON REUTERS (Dec. 20, 2023), https://insight.thomsonreuters.com.au/legal/posts/is-ai-regulated-in-australia-what-lawyers-should-know.

Brazil

Walter Pasquarelli, *Seizing the opportunity: The future of AI in Latin America*, ECONOMIST (May 22, 2022), https://impact.economist.com/new-globalisation/seizing-opportunity-future-ai-latin-america.

AI Initiatives in Brazil, OECD.AI, https://oecd.ai/en/dashboards/national/brazil (last visited Aug. 23, 2025).

Brazilian General Data Protection Law (L.G.P.D.), (Amended 2019), RENNÓ RENTEADO SAMPAIO https://iapp.org/media/pdf/resource_center/Brazilian_General_Data_Protection_Law.pdf (last visited Aug. 23, 2025).

Brazilian M.C.T.I., *The E.B.I.A.*, (2021), https://www.oecd.org/en/publications/access-to-public-research-data-toolkit_a12e8998-en/brazilian-strategy-for-artificial-intelligence_936c5793-en.html.

Brazilian Chamber of Deputies, *Brazilian Internet Framework*, (2016), https://bd-rest.camara.leg.br/server/api/core/bitstreams/50830ed2-cd53-4e77-b088-869e30e19dde/content.

Canada

The Artificial Intelligence and Data Act (AIDA)—Companion document, GOV'T OF CANADA, https://ised-isde.canada.ca/site/innovation-better-canada/en/artificial-intelligence-and-data-act-aida-companion-document (last visited Aug. 21, 2025).

Maya Madeiros & Jesse Beatson, *Bill C-27: Canada's first artificial intelligence legislation has arrived*, NORTON ROSE (June 23, 2022), https://www.nortonrosefulbright.com/en-ca/knowledge/publications/55b9a0bd/bill-c-27-canadas-first-artificial-intelligence-legislation-has-arrived.

Artificial Intelligence and Data Act, GOV'T OF CANADA, https://ised-isde.canada.ca/site/innovation-better-canada/en/artificial-intelligence-and-data-act (last visited Aug. 21, 2025).

Chile

Chilean AI regulation advances in congress with key committee vote, BN AMERICAS (May 15, 2025), https://www.bnamericas.com/en/news/chilean-ai-regulation-advances-in-congress-with-key-committee-vote.

France

OECD, *GAIIN: The Global AI Initiatives Indicator: AI Initiatives from France*, (2024), https://oecd.ai/en/dashboards/national/france (last visited Aug. 21, 2025).

National Strategy on AI/Stratégie nationale pour l'intelligence artificielle, AI, ORG. FOR ECON. COOPERAT'N & DEV'T, https://oecd.ai/en/dashboards/policy-initiatives/national-strategy-on-ai-5864 (last visited July 9, 2025).

AI: ensuring GDPR compliance, CNIL (Sep. 21, 2022), https://www.cnil.fr/en/ai-ensuring-gdpr-compliance.

France 2030, National Strategy for AI, https://digital-skills-jobs.europa.eu/en/actions/national-initiatives/national-strategies/france-national-strategy-ai (last visited May 30, 2025).

Germany

Germany AI Strategy Report, EUROP. COMM'N (Sept. 1, 2021), https://ai-watch.ec.europa.eu/countries/germany/germany-ai-strategy-report_en. See also National Strategie fur Kunstliche Intelligenz, https://www.ki-strategie-deutschland.de (last visited May. 30, 2025).

Artificial Intelligence Strategy of the German Federal Government, THE GERMAN FEDERAL GOV'T (Dec. 2022), https://www.ki-strategie-deutschland.de/files/downloads/Fortschreibung_KI-Strategie_engl.pdf.

India

Reporting for Artificial Intelligence (AI) and Machine Learning (ML) applications and systems offered and used by Mutual Funds, SECURITIES & EXCHANGE BD. OF INDIA, Circular No. SEBI/HO/IMD/DF5/CIR/P/2019/63, (May 9, 2019), https://www.sebi.gov.in/legal/circulars/may-2019/reporting-for-artificial-intelligence-ai-and-machine-learning-ml-applications-and-systems-offered-and-used-by-mutual-funds_42932.html.

Abhishek Dey & Melissa Cyrill, *India's Regulation of AI and Large Language Models*, INDIA BRIEFING (Mar. 27, 2024), https://www.india-briefing.com/news/india-regulation-of-ai-and-large-language-models-31680.html/.

Israel

Dan Or-Hof, *Proactive Caution: Israel's Approach to AI Regulation*, IAPP (Mar. 5, 2024), https://iapp.org/news/a/proactive-caution-israels-approach-to-ai-regulation.

Rivki Dvash, *Israel's New AI Policy: A Primer*, ISRAEL TECH POLICY INST. (Aug. 16, 2023), https://techpolicy.org.il/blog/israeli-court-ruling-border-controllers/.

Israel Ministry of Innovation, Science and Technology, Israel's Policy on Artificial Intelligence Regulation and Ethics (Dec. 2023), https://www.gov.il/en/pages/ai_2023.

Israel National AI Program Booklet, ISRAEL MINISTRY OF INNOVATION, SCIENCE, & TECHNOLOGY, (2024), https://innovationisrael.org.il/ai/wp-content/uploads/sites/4/2024/04/Israel-National-AI-Program-Booklet.pdf.

Israel Launches Second Phase of National AI Program with NIS 500 Million Investment in Research and Development Infrastructure, ISRAEL INNOVATION AUTHORITY (Sept. 17, 2024), https://innovation israel.org.il/en/press_release/second-phase-ai-program/.

Israel Publishes AI Regulatory Policy Document, LAW.CO.IL. (2024), https://www.law.co.il/en/news/2023/12/19/israel-publishes-ai-regulatory-policy-document/.

Oren Yunger & Dan Cahana, *From Cybersecurity to AI: How Israeli Companies Can Lead the Next Revolution*, CALCALISTECH (Mar. 20, 2025), https://www.calcalistech.com/ctechnews/article/r140ody h1g.

Japan

Hiroki Habuka, *New Government Policy Shows Japan Favors a Light Touch for AI Regulation*, CTR. FOR STRATEGIC & INT'L STUD. (Feb. 4, 2025), https://www.csis.org/analysis/new-government-policy-shows-japan-favors-light-touch-ai-regulation.

Christopher Pappas, *AI Implementation Challenges And How To Overcome Them*, ELEARNING INDUSTRY, 6 (Feb. 13, 2023), https://elearningindustry.com/ai-implementation-challenges-and-how-to-overcome-them.

Aditya Kumar, *Top 15 Challenges of Artificial Intelligence in 2025*, SIMPLILEARN (Feb. 17, 2025), https://www.simplilearn.com/challenges-of-artificial-intelligence-article.

朝日新聞デジタル, 再生医療規制見直し、２法案閣議決定 監視機関は見送り-政治, 朝日新聞社 (May 25, 2013), https://web.archive.org/web/20130525020520/http://www.asahi.com/politics/update/0524/TKY201305240029.html.

Financial Services Agency, Financial Instruments and Exchange Act (FIEA), FINANCIAL SERVICES AGENCY, https://www.fsa.go.jp/en/policy/fiel/index.html.

Will Knight, *Google's Gemini Robotics AI Model Reaches Into the Physical World*, WIRED (Mar. 12, 2025), https://www.wired.com/story/googles-gemini-robotics-ai-model-that-reaches-into-the-physical-world/.

Rohan Silva, *Biggest victim of Brexit is not UK but EU*, THE TIMES (Dec. 18, 2024), https://www.thetimes.com/comment/columnists/article/biggest-victim-of-brexit-is-not-uk-but-eu-mx8hj8t6t.

Katie Prescott, *Microsoft boss urges rethink of copyright laws for AI*, THE TIMES (Oct. 21, 2024), https://www.thetimes.com/business-money/companies/article/microsoft-ceo-copyright-laws-information-ai-pc9hh2c0p.

The Kingdom of Saudi Arabia

Global AI Ethics and Governance Observatory, *Saudi Arabia*, UNESCO, https://www.unesco.org/ethics-ai/en/saudiarabia (last visited Aug. 23, 2025).

Saudi Arabia, Digital Government Strategy 2023-2030, OECD.AI Policy Navigator (Aug. 14, 2025), https://oecd.ai/en/dashboards/policy-initiatives/digital-government-strategy-2023-2030-6950.

Singapore

National A.I. Strategy, AI for the Public Good, for Singapore and the World, SMART NATION SINGAPORE, (2024), https://www.smartnation.gov.sg/initiatives/national-ai-strategy.

Singapore proposes framework to foster trusted Generative AI development, INFOCOMM MEDIA DEVELOPMENT AUTHORITY, (Jan. 25, 2024), https://www.imda.gov.sg/resources/press-releases-factsheets-and-speeches/press-releases/2024/public-consult-model-ai-governance-framework-genai.

Singapore's Approach to AI Governance, SINGAPORE PERSONAL DATA PROTECTION COMM'N (Nov. 3, 2023), https://www.pdpc.gov.sg/help-and-resources/2020/01/model-ai-governance-framework.

SkillsFuture Mid-Career Enhanced Subsidy FAQ, GOV'T OF SINGAPORE, https://www.skillsfuture.gov.sg/enhancedsubsidy-faq (last visited Aug. 21, 2025).

South Korea

Kim Doo-sik, *AI's legal challenges in the country*, KOREA JOONGANG DAILY (Jan. 28, 2024), https://koreajoongangdaily.joins.com/news/2024-01-28/opinion/columns/AIs-legal-challenges-in-the-country/1968789.

Charmian Aw, *South Korea looks to Tighten Biometrics Laws Amid Generative AI*, NAT'L L. REV. (May 31, 2023), https://www.natlaw

review.com/article/south-korea-looks-to-tighten-biometrics-laws-amid-generative-ai.

Il Shin Lee, et al., *Year in review: Artificial Intelligence Law in South Korea*, LEXOLOGY https://www.lexology.com/library/detail.aspx?g=e30c96cb-8ec5-4ca9-b808-4b156e551877 (last visited Aug. 23, 2025).

The United Arab Emirates

Mark Sullivan, FAST COMPANY (Apr. 18, 2024), https://www.fastcompany.com/91108208/microsoft-riding-geopolitics-to-extend-its-ai-footprint.

UAE Strategy for Artificial Intelligence, United Arab Emirates, https://u.ae/en/about-the-uae/strategies-initiatives-and-awards/strategies-plans-and-visions/government-services-and-digital-transformation/uae-strategy-for-artificial-intelligence#:~:text=TheÜAE%20Strategy%20forÄrtificialÏntelligenceäims%20to,create%20new%20vital%20market%20with%20highëconomic%20value (last visited Aug. 23, 2025).

UAE National Strategy for Artificial Intelligence 2031, NAT'L PROGRAM FOR ARTIFICIAL INTELLIGENCE (2018), https://dig.watch/resource/the-uae-national-strategy-for-artificial-intelligence-2031.

Marissa Newman, et al., *Race for AI Supremacy in Middle East Is Measured in Data Centers*, BLOOMBERG (Apr. 11, 2024), https://www.bloomberg.com/news/articles/2024-04-11/race-for-ai-supremacy-in-middle-east-is-measured-in-data-centers.

Introducing TII's Falcon-H1 and Falcon Arabic, TECH. INNOVAT'N INST. https://falconllm.tii.ae.

The United Kingdom

Oliver Yaros & Ellen Hewpworth, *UK Government Publishes National Artificial Intelligence Strategy*, MEYER BROWN (Oct. 20, 2021), https://www.mayerbrown.com/en/perspectives-events/publications/2021/10/uk-government-publishes-national-artificial-intelligence-strategy.

Chapter 9: The Wise Counsel of Bar Association

United States-Based Bar Associations

ABA Comm. on Ethics & Prof'l Responsibility, Formal Op. 512 (2024), https://www.americanbar.org/content/dam/aba/administrative/professional_responsibility/ethics-opinions/aba-formal-opinion-512.pdf.

State Bar of Cal., Standing Comm. on Pro. Resp. & Conduct, Practical Guidance for the Use of Generative Artificial Intelligence in the Practice of Law (Nov. 16. 2023), https://www.calbar.ca.gov/Portals/0/documents/ethics/Generative-AI-Practical-Guidance.pdf.

Florida Bar Ethics Opinion 24-1 (Jan. 19, 2024), https://www.floridabar.org/etopinions/opinion-24-1/.

Joint Formal Opinion 2024-200 (June 2024). https://www.lawnext.com/wp-content/uploads/2024/06/Joint-Formal-Opinion-2024-200.pdf.

Illinois Supreme Court Policy on Artificial Intelligence (Jan. 1, 2025) https://www.illinoiscourts.gov/News/1485/Illinois-Supreme-Court-Announces-Policy-on-Artificial-Intelligence/news-detail/.

N.Y.C. Bar Ass'n, Report on Navigating Generative AI in Law Practice (2024), https://www.nycbar.org/wp-content/uploads/2024/08/20221329_GenerativeAILawPractice.pdf.

Navigating the 'seven Cs' of ethical use of AI by lawyers, Reuters (Dec. 20, 2024), https://www.reuters.com/legal/legalindustry/navigating-seven-cs-ethical-use-ai-by-lawyers-2024-12-20/.

New York State Bar Association Task Force on Artificial Intelligence, Report and Recommendation to the New York State Bar Association House of Delegates, (Apr. 6, 2024), https://fingfx.thomsonreuters.com/gfx/legaldocs/znpnkgbowvl/2024-April-Report-and-Recommendations-of-the-Task-Force-on-Artificial-Intelligence.pdf.

Guide to Getting Started with AI, LegalFuel (Jan. 7, 2025), https://www.legalfuel.com/guide-to-getting-started-with-ai/.

Pa. Bar Ass'n Comm. on Legal Ethics & Pro. Resp. & Phila. Bar Ass'n Prof'l Guidance Comm., Joint Formal Op. 2024-200, id. at 7 (2024).

Texas Bar Professional Ethics Committee Opinion 2024-6 (Nov. 19, 2024), https://www.texasbar.com/AM/pec/vendor/drafts/PO_2024_6.pdf.

D.C. Bar Ethics Opinion 388 (2024), https://www.dcbar.org/for-lawyers/legal-ethics/ethics-opinions-210-present/ethics-opinion-388.

Other Countries' Bar Associations

Int'l Bar Ass'n, THE FUTURE IS NOW: ARTIFICIAL INTELLIGENCE AND THE LEGAL PROFESSION (2024), https://www.ibanet.org/document?id=The-future-is-now-artificial-intelligence-legal-profession.

Int'l Bar Ass'n Alternative & New Law Business Structures Comm., GUIDELINES AND REGULATIONS TO PROVIDE INSIGHTS ON PUBLIC POLICIES TO ENSURE AI'S BENEFICIAL USE AS A PROFESSIONAL TOOL, at 9, 132 (2024).

European Union

The General Data Protection Regulation, EU Regulation No. 2016/679, 2016 O.J. (L 119), https://gdpr-info.eu/ (the GDPR).

Difference between EU and China: https://iapp.org/news/a/preparing-for-compliance-key-differences-between-eu-chinese-ai-regulations.

European Commission, EUROPEAN APPROACH TO ARTIFICIAL INTELLIGENCE, SHAPING EUROPE'S DIGITAL FUTURE, https://digital-strategy.ec.europa.eu/en/policies/european-approach-artificial-intelligence (last visited Feb. 23, 2025).

Tim Gaudszun & Jeffrey Shin, AI Watch: Global Regulatory Tracker—European Union, WHITE & CASE LLP (Feb. 27, 2025), https://www.whitecase.com/insight-our-thinking/ai-watch-global-regulatory-tracker-european-union.

Council of Bars & Law Societies of Eur., CCBE Considerations on the Legal Aspects of Artificial Intelligence (2020), https://www.ccbe.eu/fileadmin/speciality_distribution/public/documents/IT_LAW/IT

L_Guides_recommendations/EN_ITL_20200220_CCBE-considerations-on-the-Legal-Aspects-of-AI.pdf.

Peter Homoki et al., CCBE Guide on the Use of Artificial Intelligence-Based Tools by Lawyers and Law Firms in the EU, COUNCIL OF BARS AND LAW SOCIETIES OF EUROPE & EUROPEAN LAWYERS FOUND. (2022), https://www.ccbe.eu/fileadmin/speciality_distribution/public/documents/IT_LAW/ITL_Reports_studies/EN_ITL_20220331_Guide-AI4L.pdf.

Council of Bars & Law Societies of Eur., CCBE STATEMENT ON THE USE OF AI IN THE JUSTICE SYSTEM AND LAW ENFORCEMENT (May 25, 2023), https://www.ccbe.eu/fileadmin/speciality_distribution/public/documents/Statements/2023/EN_ITL_20230525_CCBE-Statement-on-the-use-of-AI-in-the-justice-system-and-law-enforcement.pdf.

Council of Bars & Law Societies of Eur., POSITION PAPER ON THE PROPOSAL FOR A REGULATION LAYING DOWN HARMONISED RULES ON ARTIFICIAL INTELLIGENCE (Artificial Intelligence Act) (Oct. 8, 2021), https://www.ccbe.eu/fileadmin/speciality_distribution/public/documents/IT_LAW/ITL_Position_papers/EN_ITL_20211008_CCBE-position-paper-on-the-AIA.pdf.

Argentina

Agency for Access to Public Information (AAIP), GOV'T OF ARGENTINA, https://www.argentina.gob.ar/aaip (last visited Mar. 13, 2025).

Diego Fernandez, Recommendations for Reliable Artificial Intelligence, International Network of Privacy Law professionals (Sep. 18, 2023), https://inplp.com/latest-news/article/recommendations-for-reliable-artificial-intelligence/.

Guide for Public and Private Entities on Transparency and Personal Data Protection for Responsible Artificial Intelligence, BAKER MCKENZIE INSIGHT PLUS (Sept. 30, 2024), https://insightplus.bakermckenzie.com/bm/data-technology/argentina-the-dpa-published-the-guide-for-public-and-private-entities-on-transparency-and-personal-data-protection-for-responsible-artificial-intelligence.

Valentina Martínez, *Regulating Artificial Intelligence in Argentina*, WSC LEGAL, https://wsclegal.com/regulating-artificial-intelligence-in-argentina/ (last visited Mar. 13, 2025).

Milagros Denise Tallarico, *Argentina Approves Protocol for the Use of Generative Artificial Intelligence in the Judiciary*, WORLD L. GROUP (Nov. 19, 2024), https://www.theworldlawgroup.com/membership/news/news-argentina-approves-protocol-for-the-use-of-generative-artificial-intelligence-in-the-judiciary-1.

Milagros Denise Tallarico, *Argentina: Artificial Intelligence in Justice: 2024 Advances and 2025 Challenges*, WORLD L. GROUP (Dec. 16, 2024), https://www.theworldlawgroup.com/membership/news/news-argentina-artificial-intelligence-in-justice-2024-advances-and-2025-challenges.

Federico Ast, *Prometea: Artificial Intelligence in the Judicial System of Argentina*, ASET (June 6, 2020), https://medium.com/astec/prometea-artificial-intelligence-in-the-judicial-system-of-argentina-4dfbde079c40.

Australia

Supreme Court New South Wales, Practice Note SC Gen 23—Use of Generative Artificial Intelligence (Jan. 28, 2025).

Victorian Law Reform Commission, Artificial Intelligence in Victoria's Courts and Tribunals: Consultation Paper (Oct. 17, 2024), https://www.lawreform.vic.gov.au/publication/artificial-intelligence-in-victorias-courts-and-tribunals-consultation-paper/.

Daniel Heywood & Stephanie Loccisano, Integrating AI Into NSW Expert Reports: A Cautious and Conservative Approach, ALVAREZ & MARSAL (Jan. 30, 2025), https://www.alvarezandmarsal.com/insights/integrating-ai-nsw-expert-reports-cautious-and-conservative-approach#:~:text=Practice%20Note%20SC%20Gen%2023,in%20the%20New%20South%20Wales.

Australia Government Department of Industry, Science & Resources, Proposal for Introducing Mandatory Guardrails for AI in High-Risk Settings (Sept. 2024).

Queensland Law Society, Australian Solicitors' Conduct Rules 2023, rr. 3-10 (Sept. 27, 2024).

IBA Alternative & New Law Business Structures Comm., GUIDELINES AND REGULATIONS TO PROVIDE INSIGHTS ON PUBLIC POLICIES TO ENSURE AI'S BENEFICIAL USE AS A PROFESSIONAL TOOL, at 148 (2024).

Brazil

Eduardo Villa Coimbra Campos, *Artificial Intelligence, the Brazilian Judiciary, and some Conundrums*, SCIENCE PO CHAIR DIGITAL, GOVERNANCE & SOVEREIGNTY (Mar. 3, 2023), https://www.sciencespo.fr/public/chaire-numerique/en/2023/03/03/article-artificial-intelligence-the-brazilian-judiciary-and-some-conundrums/.

Montgomery & Associados, Regulation of the Legal Profession in Brazil: OVERVIEW, MONTGOMERY & ASSOC. (Jan. 13, 2023), https://montgomery.adv.br/en/regulation-of-the-legal-profession-in-brazil-overview/.

OAB Approves Recommendations for the Use of Artificial Intelligence in Legal Practice, THE LEGAL 500 (Feb. 5, 2025), https://www.legal500.com/developments/press-releases/oab-approves-recommendations-for-the-use-of-artificial-intelligence-in-legal-practice/.

Brazil AI Act, Artificial Intelligence Act, https://artificialintelligenceact.com/brazil-ai-act/ (last visited Mar. 12, 2025).

General Data Protection Law (LGPD), Law No. 13.709 of August 14, 2018, PRESIDENCY OF THE REPUBLIC OF BRAZIL, https://www.planalto.gov.br/ccivil_03/_ato2015-2018/2018/lei/L13709compilado.htm (last visited Mar. 12, 2025).

Canada

Federation of Law Societies of Canada, MODEL CODE OF PROFESSIONAL CONDUCT (Apr. 2024), https://flsc.ca/wp-content/uploads/2024/11/2024-Model-Code-of-Professional-Conduct.pdf.

Treasury Board of Canada Secretariat, GUIDE ON THE USE OF GENERATIVE ARTIFICIAL INTELLIGENCE, (Oct. 15, 2024), https://www.canada.ca/en/government/system/digital-government/digital-government-innovations/responsible-use-ai/guide-use-generative-ai.html.

Tara Raissi, *New AI Guidelines Are Only a Starting Point for Canadian Legal Professionals*, CANADIAN LAWYER (July 5, 2024), https://www.canadianlawyermag.com/news/opinion/new-ai-guidelines-are-only-a-starting-point-for-canadian-legal-professionals/387183.

Law Society of British Columbia, Guidance on Professional Responsibility and Generative AI, CANADIAN BAR ASSOCIATION, ETHICS OF ARTIFICIAL INTELLIGENCE FOR THE LEGAL PRACTITIONER (Oct. 2023), https://www.cba.org/Publications-Resources/Practice-Tools/Ethics-of-Artificial-Intelligence-for-the-Legal-Pr.

Pablo A. Palazzi, Mercedes Elaskar, Caterina D. Macek & Ariana Urba, Artificial Intelligence 2024 Comparisons, CHAMBERS & PARTNERS (2024), https://allende.com/en/technology/artificial-intelligence/chambers-global-guide-artificial-intelligence-2024-07-01-2024/.

Federal Court of Canada, Notice to the Parties and the Profession: The Use of Artificial Intelligence in Court Proceedings, at 3 (May 7, 2024).

Chile

Chile Launches National AI Policy and Introduces AI Bill Following UNESCO's Recommendations, UNESCO, (May. 4, 2024) (last updated Oct. 10, 2024), https://www.unesco.org/en/articles/chile-launches-national-ai-policy-and-introduces-ai-bill-following-unescos-recommendations-0.

Macerena Gatica, *Chile stares EU: a bill of law to regulate AI*, INT'L NETWORK OF PRIVACY LAW PROFESSIONALS (May 16, 2024), https://inplp.com/latest-news/article/chile-stares-eu-a-bill-of-law-to-regulate-ai/.

Mónica Humeres et al., *Cooling Down AI Regulation Controversies: Three Closure Processes*, SAGE JOURNALS (2025), https://doi.org/10.1177/20539517241311067.

Artificial Intelligence Policy in Chile, CETYS—Center for Technology and Society, https://cetys.lat/wp-content/uploads/2021/09/chile-Eng.pdf (last visited Mar. 13 2025).

Int'l Bar Ass'n Alternative & New Law Business Structures Comm., Guidelines and Regulations to Provide Insights on Public Policies to Ensure AI's Beneficial Use as a Professional Tool, 105 (2024).

Code of Professional Ethics, Chilean Bar Association, https://colegioabogados.cl/el-colegio/codigo-de-etica-profesional/ (last visited Mar. 13, 2025).

China (People's Republic of China)

China's Personal Information Protection Law (PIPL), Bloomberg Law (Apr. 12, 2022), https://pro.bloomberglaw.com/insights/privacy/china-personal-information-protection-law-pipl-faqs/.

Yi Wu, How to Interpret China's First Effort to Regulate Generative AI Measures, China Briefing (July 27, 2023), https://www.china-briefing.com/news/how-to-interpret-chinas-first-effort-to-regulate-generative-ai-measures/.

The Global Federation for AI Law Education Establishes in Guangzhou, SCNU NEWS CTR. (Sept. 3, 2024), https://english.scnu.edu.cn/a/20240903/1229.html.

China: New Interim Measures to Regulate Generative AI, Baker McKenzie (Aug.15, 2023), https://insightplus.bakermckenzie.com/bm/data-technology/china-new-interim-measures-to-regulate-generative-ai_2.

France

Alain Duflot, Artificial *Intelligence in the French Law of 2024*, 5 LEGAL ISSUES IN THE DIGITAL AGE, at 43 (2024).

Germany

Bundesrechtsanwaltskammer (BRAK), A Digital Justice System—Demands and Proposals of the German Legal Profession, Position No. 60 (Nov. 2021).

Japan

Japan Fed'n of Bar Ass'ns, Basic Rules on the Duties of Practicing Attorneys (2021), https://www.nichibenren.or.jp/library/en/about/data/Basic_Rules_Practicing.pdf.

Int'l Bar Ass'n Alternative & New Law Business Structures Comm., Guidelines and Regulations to Provide Insights on Public Policies to Ensure Artificial Intelligence's Beneficial Use as a Professional Tool, at 187 (2024).

Attorney Act, Act No. 205 of 1949 (Japan), https://www.japaneselawtranslation.go.jp/en/laws/view/3636/en (last visited Mar. 7, 2025).

New Zealand

Lawyers and Conveyancers Act (Lawyers: Conduct and Client Care) Rules 2008, SR 2008/214r (N.Z.) (as reprinted July 1, 2021) available at https://www.legislation.govt.nz/regulation/public/2008/0214/latest/whole.html.

New Zealand Law Society Te Kāhui Ture o Aotearoa, Generative AI Guidance for Lawyers (2024), https://www.lawsociety.org.nz/professional-practice/rules-and-maintaining-professional-standards/generative-ai-guidance-for-lawyers/.

Singapore

Lim Chong Kin & Cheryl Seah, *Law and Practice in Artificial Intelligence 2025*, CHAMBERS & PARTNERS (May 22, 2025), https://practiceguides.chambers.com/practice-guides/artificial-intelligence-2025/singapore.

International Bar Association Alternative & New Law Business Structures Comm., GUIDELINES AND REGULATIONS TO PROVIDE INSIGHTS ON PUBLIC POLICIES TO ENSURE AI'S BENEFICIAL USE AS A PROFESSIONAL TOOL, 256 (2024).

Guide on the Adoption of LegalTech for Law Practices, THE LAW SOCIETY OF SINGAPORE (Oct. 16, 2023), https://www.pdpc.gov.sg/-/media/Files/PDPC/PDF-Files/Resource-for-Organisation/AI/SGModelAIGovFramework2.pdf.

Ethical AI for Lawyers in Singapore: Key Responsibilities, THOMSON REUTERS LEGAL INSIGHT (June 23, 2024), https://insight.thomsonreuters.com/sea/legal/posts/ethical-ai-for-lawyers-in-singapore-key-responsibilities.

South Korea

Attorney-At-Law Act (S. Kor.), https://elaw.klri.re.kr/eng_mobile/viewer.do?hseq=56111&type=part&key=7 (last visited Mar. 7, 2025).

The Korean Bar Association's Code of Ethics for Attorneys, (translated by Wonji Kerper & Changmin Lee), 29 WASH. INT'L L.J. 649 (2020), https://digitalcommons.law.uw.edu/wilj/vol29/iss3/10/.

National Strategy for Artificial Intelligence, MINISTRY OF SCIENCE AND ICT, REPUBLIC OF KOREA, (2019), https://wp.oecd.ai/app/uploads/2021/12/Korea_National_Strategy_for_Artificial_Intelligence_2019.pdf (last visited Mar. 7, 2025).

The United Arab Emirates

AI in UAE: The Legal Blueprint That's Reshaping Tech Compliance, LEXOLOGY (Feb. 14, 2025), https://www.lexology.com/library/detail.aspx?g=372eb31c-08f4-4a17-b62c-d8f173c1edc0 (last visited Mar. 7, 2025).

OECD AI Policy Observatory, United Arab Emirates Country Dashboard, ORG. FOR ECON. COOPERAT'N & DEV'T, https://oecd.ai/en/dashboards/national/united-arab-emirates (last visited Sep. 21, 2025).

Digital Dubai, Dubai Artificial Intelligence Principles & Ethics, https://www.digitaldubai.ae/docs/default-source/ai-principles-resources/ai-ethics.pdf (last visited Sep. 21, 2025).

Digital Dubai, AI System Ethics Self-Assessment Tool, https://www.digitaldubai.ae/self-assessment (last visited Sep. 21, 2025).

Sandeep Bhalothia & Aman Grag, *AI, Machine Learning & Big Data Laws and Regulations 2024—UAE*, GLOBAL LEGAL INSIGHTS (2024), https://www.globallegalinsights.com/practice-areas/ai-machine-learning-and-big-data-laws-and-regulations/uae/.

AI Ethics: Principles & Guidelines, MINISTER OF STATE FOR ARTIFICIAL INTELLIGENCE, DIGITAL ECONOMY & REMOTE WORK APPLICATIONS (Dec 2022) https://ai.gov.ae/wp-content/uploads/2023/03/MOCAI-AI-Ethics-EN-1.pdf.

Smart Dubai, AI Ethics: Principles & Guidelines, SMART DUBAI (2018), https://www.digitaldubai.ae/docs/default-source/ai-principles-resources/ai-ethics.pdf.

United Arab Emirates, NATIONAL STRATEGY FOR ARTIFICIAL INTELLIGENCE 2031 (2017), https://u.ae/en/about-the-uae/strategies-initiatives-and-awards/strategies-plans-and-visions/government-services-and-digital-transformation/uae-strategy-for-artificial-intelligence (last visited Mar. 4, 2025).

The United Kingdom

The Law Society of England and Wales, Artificial Intelligence (AI) Strategy (Sept. 16, 2024), https://www.lawsociety.org.uk/topics/ai-and-lawtech/artificial-intelligence-ai-strategy.

Solicitors Regulation Authority, SRA Code of Conduct for Solicitors, RELs and RFLs (Nov. 25, 2019), https://www.sra.org.uk/solicitors/standards-regulations/code-conduct-solicitors/.

The Law Society of England and Wales, ANNUAL REPORT & BUSINESS REV. 2022/23, https://www.lawsociety.org.uk/about-us/business-review-and-annual-report (last visited Mar. 18, 2025).

The Law Society of England and Wales, GENERATIVE AI: THE ESSENTIALS (Aug. 2024), https://www.lawsociety.org.uk/topics/ai-and-lawtech/generative-ai-the-essentials.

Uruguay

Code of Ethics, URUGUAYAN BAR ASSOCIATION, https://www.cau.org.uy/codigo-de-etica/ (last visited Mar. 13, 2025).

Kate Lida, Ethical AI for the Public Sector, in Spotlight Series: Uruguay, OXFORD INSIGHTS (May 30, 2023), https://oxfordinsights.com/insights/spotlight-series-uruguay/.

Model Artificial Intelligence Governance Framework (Second Edition), INFOCOMM MEDIA DEVELOPMENT AUTHORITY & PERSONAL DATA PROTECTION COMMISSION (Jan. 21, 2020).

Artificial Intelligence, INFOCOMM MEDIA DEVELOPMENT AUTHORITY (IMDA), https://www.imda.gov.sg/about-imda/emerging-technologies-and-research/artificial-intelligence (last visited Mar. 13, 2025).

Latin America

Andrés Mosqueira & Shaanty Emmanuel Rubio Gonzalez, *Foster innovation or mitigate risk? AI regulation in Latin America*, WHITE & CASE (Nov. 18, 2024), https://www.whitecase.com/insight-our-thinking/latin-america-focus-2024-ai-regulation.

Chapter 10: A Call to Action

Jan Hatzius et al., *The Potentially Large Effects of Artificial Intelligence on Economic Growth (Briggs/Kodnani)*, GOLDMAN SACHS: ECON. RESE. (Mar. 26, 2023, at 9:05 PM EDT), https://www.gspublishing.com/content/research/en/reports/2023/03/27/d64e052b-0f6e-45d7-967b-d7be35fabd16.pdf.

Eduardo Porter, *AI could help ending the dominance of the credentialed classes*, WASH. POST (Mar. 19, 2024), https://www.washingtonpost.com/opinions/2024/03/19/artificial-intelligence-workers-regulation-musk/.

Mauro Cazzaniga, Florence Jaumotte, Longji Li, Giovanni Melina, Augustus J. Panton, Carlos Pizzinelli, Emma J. Rockall, & Marina Mendes Tavares, *Gen-AI: Artificial Intelligence and the Future of Work*, INT'L MONET. FUND (Jan. 14, 2025), https://www.imf.org/en/Publications/Staff-Discussion-Notes/Issues/2024/01/14/Gen-AI-Artificial-Intelligence-and-the-Future-of-Work-542379?cid=bl-com-SDNEA2024001.

Kyle Wiggers, *Asking chatbots for short answer can increase hallucinations, study finds*, TECHCRUNCH (May 8, 2025), https://techcrunch.com/2025/05/08/asking-chatbots-for-short-answers-can-increase-hallucinations-study-finds/.

APPENDIX B

The AIM-AI Governance Framework

We lay out the broad brushstrokes of our AIM-AI Governance Framework in Chapter 10 of this *Short and Happy Guide*. Here we provide an overview of the framework and its sub-components.

The AIM-AI framework classifies AI applications into four governance zones, each with specific regulatory sub-components that define oversight mechanisms, liability models, and enforcement strategies, as summarized below. Governments can use this as a starting point to develop a national AI governance framework (or enhance existing AI governance models by using AIM-AI principles).

AIM-AI Governance Zones and Policy Implementation

1. SAFE-AI (Socially Accountable and Fair AI for Everyone)

Regulatory Strategy: Light-touch regulation (fast-track approvals, industry self-regulation, voluntary certification).

Sub-components:

FAST-AI (Facilitated AI Standards & Testing) → Regulatory fast lanes for AI in education, healthcare, accessibility, and climate solutions.

ETHIC-AI (Ethical Trust & Industry Compliance for AI) → AI safety guidelines developed through public-private partnerships.

CERT-AI (Certification & Evaluation for Responsible Technology) → National AI Certification Programs for developers meeting ethical and safety standards.

2. *FAULT-AI (Fairness, Accountability, and Liability for Trustworthy AI)*

Regulatory Strategy: Risk-mitigating regulation (bias audits, explainability mandates, redress mechanisms).

Sub-components:

CHECK-AI (Compliance & Human Evaluation for Clear Knowledge in AI) → Algorithmic fairness and bias audits for AI in hiring, finance, law enforcement, and healthcare.

GUARD-AI (Governance, User Rights & Data Accountability in AI) → AI liability laws ensuring that AI failures hold developers and deployers accountable.

EXPLAIN-AI (Explainability & Algorithmic Interpretability Norms) → Mandatory explainability standards for AI in consumer-facing applications.

3. *ABUSE-AI (Artificial Intelligence for Breaches, Unlawful Surveillance and Exploitation)*

Regulatory Strategy: Strict prohibitions and legal enforcement (AI bans, cybersecurity laws, criminal penalties).

Sub-components:

BAN-AI (Blacklisting AI for National Security) → National AI blacklists prohibiting AI-driven deepfake misinformation, cyber fraud, and AI-enabled cyberattacks.

SHIELD-AI (Security & Harmful Interference Elimination through Legal Deterrence) → Strict penalties for AI misuse in fraud, disinformation, and election interference.

BLOCK-AI (Border-Level Oversight & Control of Key AI Technologies) → AI export control laws to restrict AI models from reaching adversarial nation-states.

4. *REBEL-AI (Regulated Ethical and Balanced Enforcement for Legitimate AI Activism)*

Regulatory Strategy: Case-by-case governance (whistleblower protections, human rights reviews, ethical AI oversight).

Sub-components:

SHIELD-AI (Ethical Variant) (Safeguarding Human Integrity & Ethical Liberties in AI) → Whistleblower protections for AI-driven investigative journalism.

REVIEW-AI (Rights Evaluation & Verification of Ethical Whistleblowing in AI) → Legal panels to review AI whistleblowing cases and ensure journalists are not unfairly prosecuted.

LIBERTY-AI (Legal Inclusion of Balanced Ethics & Rights for Tech-based Yields in AI) → Human rights oversight for AI-driven dissent and activism.

The sub-components of AIM-AI ensure targeted, risk-aware regulations for different AI applications. They encourage AI-driven innovation in SAFE-AI applications while removing unnecessary regulatory barriers. By mandating accountability in FAULT-AI applications bias, unfair decisions, and unintended harm may be prevented. Moreover, strict national security safeguards against ABUSE-AI, protecting democracy and digital safety need to be implemented. By providing legal oversight for REBEL-AI, we can ensure that AI is not misused for authoritarian control or censorship.

When used as a blueprint for governance, AIM-AI can deliver multiple benefits to different stakeholders. For governments, a structured policy toolkit can be instituted to support AI-driven economic growth without compromising ethics or security. Businesses also gain as developers when there is a clear compliance roadmap for AI projects, ensuring fair regulation without stifling innovation (the latter being a major concern for AI entrepreneurs). For international organizations, there is much to be gained here too: A universal AI governance framework adaptable to different legal, cultural, and economic contexts is good for everyone - corporation and citizen alike.

Index

References are to Pages